The Urgency of a New Dawn
Prison Thoughts and Reflections

Nfor N. Nfor

Langaa Research & Publishing CIG
Mankon, Bamenda

Publisher:
Langaa RPCIG
Langaa Research & Publishing Common Initiative Group
P.O. Box 902 Mankon
Bamenda
North West Region
Cameroon
Langaagrp@gmail.com
www.langaa-rpcig.net

Distributed in and outside N. America by African Books Collective
orders@africanbookscollective.com
www.africanbookscollective.com

ISBN: 9956-763-73-X

© Nfor N. Nfor 2016

All rights reserved.
No part of this book may be reproduced or transmitted in any form or by any means, mechanical or electronic, including photocopying and recording, or be stored in any information storage or retrieval system, without written permission from the publisher

Dedication

Dedicated to my wife, Mary Nan NFOR and the children, for the enormous sacrifices they have had to make, their immeasurable understanding, and the pains they have had to endure due to my total commitment to the struggle for the restoration of the statehood of our Fatherland, British Southern Cameroons. With Almighty God, from above, protecting me, they have been the source of inspiration and the rock of the energy that kept me moving forward without blinking. Without their unflinching support, steadfast love and care, I would not have been able to do even the little. No one but God alone can reward them.

And to all freedom fighters of our land, who in pains and sacrifice and with iron determination to contribute to global peace and universal human dignity and equality, have seen their emancipation from political, cultural and economic subjugation and slavery as a first step and in that wise have remained faithful to the cause in defence of TRUTH, LEGALITY, DEMOCRACY and JUSTICE. To those who have died, they died for a noble cause, for a better humanity: they will forever be remembered in honour, for victory is theirs.

Table of Contents

Acknowledgements..vii
Preface...xi

Part I: Sign Posts..1
Chapter One When the Gods Spoke......................................3
Chapter Two: Conquering the Fear Syndrome....................15

**Part II: Consequences of Annexation
and Colonial Occupation**..33
Chapter Three: The Development Of
Underdevelopment..35
Chapter Four: Constitutionalisation of Annexation
and Alien Rule..61
Chapter Five: The Two Cameroons and the
Bakassi Peninsula Conflict: What Is at Stake?....................95

Part III: In Defence of Identity..127
Chapter Six: Recurrent Fractured Foundation...................129
Chapter Seven: For National Renascence..........................161
Chapter Eight: The Winning Spirit.....................................179

Annextures...211
*Annex (I): Boundary Treaty Between The
British Southern Cameroons And French
Cameroun*..211
*Annex (II): U.N. General Assembly 4th
Committee Vote On Independence Of
Southern Cameroons*..217
*Annex (III): U.N. General Assembly Vote
On Resolution 1608 Of April 21, 1961*..............................223

Bibliography..227

Acknowledgements

My special thanks go to my numerous detention and prison companions, be it in Buea, where I was first arrested and detained for this noble cause, Mamfe, Menji, Mbort-Nkambe, Kumbo, Bamenda, Mutengene, among others, for their remarkable support, love and measure of dedication to the struggle. This, like fuel, lit, strengthened and sustained the unyielding quest for freedom and justice in me to see and build bridges across artificial barriers for national emancipation and restoration. This made it possible for me to see and appreciate how hungry our people have been for freedom, justice and independence, which they have, for many years, lost due to treachery and the Yaoundé propaganda machine of deceit, falsehood and excessive use of force, trademark of an expansionist colonial regime, to instil perpetual fear in the annexed and colonised.

The coloniser, who is always standing on the wrong side of history, and like an embankment built of sand and mud against a ferocious torrent of human progress, has never won a war against a determined people to have the change they most need. However, like armed robbers, the coloniser is always defeated and in his own traps.

My gratitude also goes to the Southern Cameroonian patriots of Bamenda and beyond who, in love and kindness, did their best to support us. Their love and sacrifices gave us the stamina to withstand the overbearing nature of the coloniser. You assured us that those of us behind bars were carrying the people's cross. By your acts, prayers and support you assured us that this is a people's cause and that we are together, and in solidarity, we will triumph and rebuild our Fatherland for the good of all.

As difficult as it is to name all those who helped in one way or the other, on behalf of the many, I am grateful to I. M. Sona, *alias* 'International Chief', and Pa Stephen Ndi, for their time spared to read and make valid contributions to the manuscript. I equally appreciate the many Pastors and Christians who visited us, preached, prayed and encouraged us, and the many Christians and Muslims who, due to circumstances, could not reach us but prayed day and night for God to protect us and set us free from the hands of the Yaoundé colonial regime.

The role of women in supporting us while in solitary confinement, wherever we were in the national territory, has always been exceptional. To them all, I forever remain grateful. An exceptional debt of gratitude must be paid to the wives of the detainees, family members and friends, the many SCNC activists who toiled day and night for our welfare.

Finally, I am exceptionally grateful and thankful to my wife, Mrs Mary Nan Nfor, and our children for their steadfast love and immeasurable understanding and devotion to the cause of freedom for our people.

I owe my gratitude to Mrs Josephine Fru Tumabang and Divine Yuyun, who under stress of my persistent detentions patiently put my scattered writings in readable manuscript.

We are all challenged to irrevocably rise and work for a better world and greater humanity, living, sharing and working for a just and peaceful world. We must stand and work for enduring peace based on justice through dialogue and not peace obtained at great cost and odds on the mass graves of women, innocent children as victims of wars and mass starvation, and the slaying of valiant men and youths in wars that could have been avoided. Man, by nature, does not crave for war. Even the dictator or colonialist who uses weapons to murder others in cold blood will not willingly acquiesce to be eliminated by another.

The true nature of the human spirit and the history of humankind teach us that enduring peace can never be maintained by the piling of weapons of mass destruction, either by the superpowers or even by each sovereign nation. On the contrary, this is not only an illusion; weapons threaten even the limited peace we know.

The pilling of weapons of mass destruction can never provide the political salvation which Man needs. It will be attained by Man's total commitment to the golden rule: 'Do unto others what you want done to you.' I believe it is in this light that US President Bill Clinton in an address to the UN on September 21, 1999, declared,

"We believe we can be secured through the force of argument and not through the force of arms."

For a better future for our children, I salute all the valiant Southern Cameroonians at home and abroad, who have come to the firm conviction and hold as an article of faith that, to be a master of your own destiny you must, at all cost, reject foreign domination and alien rule. This is not only an inalienable and inherent right of any people; it is the surest anchor and guarantor for the preservation of their future and that of their descendants.

NFOR, N. NFOR

Preface

The movement for independence in British Southern Cameroons, like in all colonial Africa, gained greater momentum after World War II. In British Southern Cameroons, the establishment of a government in Buea in 1954 demonstrated this and from thence, Southern Cameroons became a separate region electing its own representatives to the Federal Legislature in Lagos and no longer to the Eastern Regional House in Enugu. With constitutional evolution, a House of Chiefs was added in 1957, giving birth to a bicameral legislative system like that of the United Kingdom, where you have the House of Lords and House of Commons.

Constitutional and parliamentary democracy functioned effectively in Southern Cameroons, and with the full embrace of multiparty and free, transparent and open elections, there was smooth transfer of power from the CPNC of Dr E.M.L. Endeley to the KNDP of J.N. Foncha in 1959. In 1960, a new Constitution was adopted for the Southern Cameroons, which, as other dependent territories, was expected to lead the territory to independence. But by a twist of events, instead of this Constitution leading to this specific UN Trust Territory to sovereign independence through international colonial conspiracy, the UN imposed a plebiscite, prescribing and limiting the territory to independence by joining' any of its two large neighbours, namely, Nigeria, to the west, and la République du Cameroun, to the east. This was in total violation of the spirit and letter of both Article 76(b) of the UN Charter, the Trusteeship Agreement and UN (GA) Resolution 1514 of 1960 and against the will and legitimate aspirations of the people. By this act, the UN postponed perfect decolonisation in Southern Cameroons as Southern Cameroonians were made to surrender an ultimate decision on their political future to the imperialists to do as pleased.

The consequences of this have proven to be far devastating to the inhabitants than can ever be imagined. The lesson we are forced to learn here is that a colonial power can gang up and against the legitimate will of the colonised and transfer its estate the colony to another, far more insidious but overtly shielded because it is cloaked under the black man's rule. This, in reality, is black colonialism, or neo-apartheid. This is how Southern Cameroonians are deceived: they are independent but their nation, annexed and reduced to two provinces of la République du Cameroun, has ceased to exist. They are told that they are a free people, but they are disenfranchised and live daily under the reign of terror of the '*gendarmes*'. Groaning under the yoke of foreign domination and alien rule, and as the footstool of la République du Cameroun, Southern Cameroonians live in the paradox of poverty in the midst of abundance, and with their feet and hands in chains and shackles in this third millennium certified with the ascendancy of fundamental human rights and freedoms.

This has created a conflict of phenomenal dimension that challenges peace and stability in West Africa when not handled with care to the satisfaction of the victims. Conflict is natural in all societies, and people who love themselves and their society must devise strategies about how to solve such conflict and prevent it from escalating. Nja'ah maintains: "Only artificial states or nations may not accept the existence of conflict" (2001:p.iv). The act of 1961 was a balloon submerged under water but which, respecting natural law with a redemptive message, must come afloat. For global peace, justice and democracy, we make haste to call on humankind committed to human freedom and dignity not to stand by and watch but to step forward and support the victims of the treachery of 1961, to avoid the conflict from escalating into a bloody war provoked by the colonial power determined to keep its colony against the legitimate will of the people.

Challenging Southern Cameroonians of this age, to my mind, is what must be done to right the wrongs of yesterday. This is the task of the moment, which cannot be postponed until the next generation. It is incumbent upon each generation to solve the problems it creates or encounters as a pre-condition to bequeathing a rich legacy to the future generation. It is by this positive action that this generation will be remembered and praised, and not cursed. Kwame Nkrumah in his book, *I Speak of Freedom*, declares:

"There is a tide in the affairs of every people when the moment strikes for political action ... We must act now. Tomorrow may be too late and the opportunity will have passed..." (1973, p.xii).

For Southern Cameroonians to rise in solidarity to the challenge of the moment, they must search within their souls and find answers to these questions: Who are we? What legacy are we bequeathing to our children? Who are the legitimate owners of the Southern Cameroons land? Why are Southern Cameroonians regressing morally, spiritually and materially as compared to citizens of la République du Cameroun? Why is it that Southern Cameroonians do not enjoy the inalienable rights which they inherited? Why has Southern Cameroons - a shining example of plural democracy in colonial Africa - as a political and legal entity in international law, disappeared from the map of Africa and the world? Why it is that even the most talented Southern Cameroonian is only fit to be an assistant or at best to occupy a sinecure post under la République du Cameroun?

The answers are not far to seek. Southern Cameroons has been annexed and is under colonial occupation. Transformed into a farm and the gold mine of the annexationist regime, it is being exploited and plundered for the exclusive good of la République du Cameroun. To turn things inside out for good, each Southern Cameroonian must, as a Spartan, be patriotic and shun greed, corruption, even the corruption of the mind, and treachery. National interest must rise and stand supremely above individual interest and gains. La République du Cameroun has taught us an unforgettable lesson: how, with crumbs, it uses some spineless Southern Cameroonians who fall prey to their offers against the supreme will or national interest of Southern Cameroons and the legitimate aspirations of Southern Cameroonians. Nevertheless, after getting what they want and alienating the individual from his people, the wasted Southern Cameroonian is dumped like used toilet roll. These repeated experiences should compel us to understand the true character of the occupier of our land and inspire us to go all out in defence of collective identity and national restoration.

The freedom of our people can only be a permanent reality with the restoration of the statehood and sovereign independence of British Southern Cameroons. To this end, there are no two ways and no half measures. La République du Cameroun must be ousted and the political kingdom recaptured and controlled by Southern Cameroonians. The exercise of full sovereignty over the entire territory of British Southern Cameroons by Southern Cameroonians is not only legitimate and legal; it is the road map to their freedom, development, and is the condition for peace based on justice in the West African sub-region.

Can we learn a lesson from this anecdote? There lived three young men who so dearly loved their father. Their father, unlike biblical Jacob who loved Joseph more than any of his other eleven children, loved his three children equally. Unfortunately, this father became sick and died. These young lads, boiling with fury, could not bear the devastating weight of the loss of their father. They could not imagine a future without their kind, cheerful, caring and loving father. The only way out for them was to seek revenge, see 'Death', the killer of their father, and murder it in cold blood.

They set out, with zeal, to find out where Death lives. After a painstaking inquiry and long search, they contacted an old woman, who, after patiently and sympathetically listening to them, directed them into the evil dark forest. With unyielding determination, they took their weapons and set out. After days of search in the dark forest visited by no living being, they saw a pit deep down into the earth.

Believing this awful pit to be the abode of this monster, death, they set out to explore it. They soon found some pieces of silver and gold and their attention was diverted. Hoping to find more treasure, they explored on. Soon they became very tired and hungry and decided to send the youngest home to bring food for all of them. On his return with food, an evil thought came into him.

He ate to his full satisfaction and put poison in the remaining food so that once his two brothers ate and died in the evil forest, where there would be no trace of his act, the gathered treasure and property left by their father will all be his.

In the forest, self-interest and greed possessed the two elder brothers. Between themselves, they agreed to murder their youngest brother on his arrival so that all the silver and gold and the property left by their father belonged only to the two of them.

As soon as the youngest lad arrived, the two wasted no time; they jumped onto him and murdered him. Satisfied with a job well done, they sat down to eat their meal. They both died.

These young lads set out for a noble cause, namely, to murder Death and save humanity from this monster. However, they were tempted and they took their eyes off the noble ultimate goal, namely, saving Man from this monster, Death, and making him immortal. Treachery and greed took them to their graves. Painfully, they never accomplished their mission. Why? Greed and self-seeking interest for momentary things that glitter took all of them early to their graves!

To help Southern Cameroonians, as a people, make the right and hard choice, which is between FREEDOM and DIGNITY for all, on the one hand, and perpetual servitude with few picking the crumbs under la République du Cameroun on the other, I have brought them face to face with reality by removing the scales from their eyes. I claim not to have done all and the best. If I have succeeded in opening your eyes to recognise the reality, namely, that Southern Cameroons is a distinct nation not an integral part of la République du Cameroun, and that in this subjugated status even our descendants shall know no freedom, justice and prosperity. If with my prayers this unites us to rise for our freedom and can inspire you to do more, then the patriotic spirit that challenged and guided me to commune with you is richly rewarded.

British Southern Cameroons is the ordained and legitimate heritage of Southern Cameroonians. The restoration of its statehood and independence is non-negotiable. Southern Cameroonians of this generation, men and women, the intellectuals and the unschooled, the old and the young, men and women, irrespective of ethnic origin, religious background, must see their contribution to the liberation of Southern Cameroons from annexation as a divine mission and historic duty. This is service to humanity, for the glory of the Most High. This is a mission of honour you must execute proudly and with distinction. Without doubt, not everyone, in the history of a nation, is ever so opportune. You have nothing to lose by being on the liberation train but the chains around your neck and shackles on your feet. Surely, you have FREEDOM, DIGNITY AND HONOUR to gain by being on the side of TRUTH, LEGALITY and the legitimate strive for JUSTICE, HUMAN FREEDOM, DIGNITY and GLOBAL PEACE.

NFOR, N. NFOR
Bamenda

Part I

Sign Posts

Chapter One

When the Gods Spoke

In traditional Africa, as in all similar settings, Man predicts by reading natural phenomenon, and the interpretation of omens receives top priority. This is not primitive science. It is above all, belief in a Supreme Being, omnipresent, omnipotent and omniscient. My people, the Wimbum, call Him '*Nyu Ngong*', meaning god of the world who is above all other gods. To the African this Supreme Being is not confined in some particular place. He is present with his people at all times and everywhere. This Supreme Being at will sometimes manifests Himself in His creation. This is part of the mystery about Him, the invisible being. Man is never at any time separated from his creator, who is always loving and caring. The African exhibits his sense of the fear of the Lord or reverence of this Supreme Being in all his interactions with nature and fellow men for in all these there is the god-nature.

Walking to a friend's house or to the market place, the conscience is tickled to go soul-searching when one hits his foot. Is it the right or the wrong foot? Or should an animal, such as a cat, a squirrel, or a chameleon cross the road or should some kind of bird sing from above in the woods, a divine explanation is sketched. With the elders, this is most often based on studies and observations, and such knowledge is passed down from generation to generation.

But when the gods of Southern Cameroons spoke in 1961, using national symbol and objects of technological development, the elders were absent and the political elite awfully failed to read the handwriting on the wall. Concerned about the welfare of future generations, the gods had to speak again in 2001 by rejecting the sacrilegious anti-people act of the Fons of Ngoketunjia (Division) County.

In 1961, two spectacular things happened upon the departure of British authorities from British Southern Cameroons.

When the Union Jack was being lowered so that the Green, Red and Yellow with two Gold Stars be flown, the Union Jack, instead of floating down gently and being respectfully folded, as is always the case, the flag dropped down in one sad, angry heap.

The second embarrassing phenomenon was the failure of the CM 1 to function immediately after J.O. Field was seen off. The CM 1, an Austin Princess, was the State Car used by the Commissioner, J.O. Field who, as representative of H. M. The Queen was the Head of State of British Southern Cameroons. The Prime Minister J.N. Foncha, as Head of Government, used the CM 2.

After seeing off J.O. Field, Mr Foncha, as the final political head, took his back seat in the CM 1 with the obvious intention of handing his old CM 2 to the Deputy Prime Minister. But as the driver took his seat behind the steering wheel of the Austin Princess with the joy of driving his boss to the Prime Minister's Lodge, the engine refused to work. Both the driver, who could not explain what suddenly went wrong, and the anxious onlookers were drenched in cold sweat with feverish embarrassment. That the car got back to the Prime Minister's Lodge with Mr Foncha seated inside, it was thanks to the determination of the energetic and dynamic young people who pushed the Austin Princess from the Clerks' Quarters, Buea, up the windy road and into the Scholes. It went in and never came out again.

Forty years after, another embarrassment occurred, this time in the northern part of the British Southern Cameroons.

In an effort to please their master in Yaoundé, the Fons of Ngoketunjia County met in Ndop to denounce the Southern Cameroons National Council (SCNC), or what in the language of their master, they call the 'secessionists'. After closed door deliberations, under the supervision of the Prefects and the repressive forces, they came out for a traditional public denunciation and condemnation. Wood ash was brought and put in the centre. The Fons took their positions, with Fon Yakum Ntaw as the spokesman in front. So that the watchful masters should hear and report to Yaoundé how faithfully the Fons were working, he had to speak in a foreign language, which the gods of the land do not understand. But the time-honoured oath of fidelity, the gods, being the authors thereof, knew and understood its impact on the people and the land very well.

He spoke against the SCNC calling it an evil that brought disaster, leprosy, smallpox, war, misery, mass suffering to Cameroonians who are living in peace, happiness, unity and prosperity under the good government of His Excellency President Paul Biya. He lauded President Paul Biya, describing him as a god-sent leader, a man of peace, the saviour of Cameroon.

He then scooped up wood ash in his right hand, as did every other Fon, ready for the final act of chasing away evil from the land.

"When evil comes, what do we do?" asked Fon Yakum Ntaw enthusiastically.

"We chase it away," yelled back the crowd, keeping up with traditional practice.

Fon Yakum Ntaw asked the question three times and the crowd answered three times. According to tradition inherited from our forefathers, on the third answer, all unanimously blew the wood ash into the air, thus driving away the evil. Keeping up with traditional practice and belief, so it was done.

But incredibly, instead of the wood ash blowing evil away from the actors, a mighty wind, as a hurricane, blew the wood ash into the faces and eyes of the performers who had to individually dodge it in style, to avoid being blinded by it. In addition to the wood ash, there was also the heavy sandy dust blown into the air by the heavy wind that came up so suddenly. It was great pity seeing our Fons, used to majestic steps in huge colourful regalia, here forced to run, dive for cover and dodge a terrible wind laden with dust and wood ash.

Someone, not of our cultural background will, with the wave of the hand, dismiss this as meaningless. This will be too hasty a conclusion made. For those unfamiliar with our traditions and culture, I shall make some brief statements on the unique position the Fon occupies in our society.

Once an individual prince ascends to the ancestral throne, he is put aside for a unique, lofty role. As an embodiment of the will and aspirations of his people, he is their mouth piece. He exhibits and defends no personal interest, ambition and individual will power. He does not even acquire personal property. When he speaks, it is the people that have spoken. He is described as having a thousand eyes because the people are his eyes. He is the embodiment of the customs and traditions of the people. He is both a political, cultural and spiritual leader, and acts on collective moral authority. He is highly honoured and venerated. No longer an individual, his designations range from 'Father of the People' and 'The Lion', among others. He is even praised as the 'sun that shines on all humans and makes the crops to ripen for harvest'. Above him is only one being, the invisible Nyu Ngong, the Supreme Being, the God of the world and of all humanity.

Sitting on the ancestral throne, holding and drinking from the ancestral cup and putting on the ancestral regalia, he is the link between the departed (the living-dead) and the living. 'The TRUTH and nothing but the TRUTH' is his watchword, and his mission is to seek justice, good health, population increase and prosperity for his people. Seen and held as a source of goodness, he is presumed to be infallible. Upon their enthroning, the Kingmakers, on behalf of all the people, make the oath to never to betray him. He can neither be betrayed by his subjects nor is he expected to get involved in evil against his people and the land. He represents his people in front of the gods of the land, and reveals the will of the gods to his people. In his delicate role as the balance of forces, he must not misrepresent the one to the other.

The palace he occupies is regarded as the centre of the world, and it belongs to the people. It is the people's sanctuary. It is the centre of all social, cultural, economic, religious and political activities and ceremonies. Whenever there is a ceremony in the palace, it is the people's affair and never the Fon's. The Fon, on his own, does not make decisions or legislate; he executes the will of the people as adopted by various institutions.

The palace plays one unique role. It does not discriminate as to who comes in. It is a sanctuary for all. Every one is the child of the Fon, and the Fon is the father of all humanity. Thus the Wimbum address the Ta Nfor or Fon as *'Tarmangong'*, a limitless and indiscriminate title implying his role as the guardian of all humanity. Even in time of war, if an enemy being pursued for capture or to be killed were to succeed in reaching palace ground or falling in front of or at the feet of the Fon, as often said, he is automatically a free man. Held in high esteem as one next to the gods, the Fon is not limited by his human body. Having been raised in the conscience of the living to a semi-god, he is claimed to not fall ill. And if he is no more, before the official proclamation of his death, it is said in usual low tunes that 'the sun has set' or that 'fire has quenched in the land'. The Fon does not die; he 'disappears' or 'is lost' and 'found'. The throne is never vacant. The throne is the symbol of authority, not the individual. He who is on the throne can be seen as the embodiment of the will of the people, the custodian of the culture of the people and the defender of their identity and legitimate aspirations, honouring their will. He lives and reigns forever, for the throne and the people live forever.

This is the social, cultural, religious and political complex environment within which, the one set aside as Fon, rules and reigns. The high respect he enjoys is thanks to the faith the people have in him, for he incarnates and defends the people's will and aspiration. The *'Ngumba, Kwifon'* or *'Nwarung'*, as the different ethnic communities of the Grassland variously know this powerful all male secret society, can dethrone him, but he has no powers to disband or dissolve this all-male powerful institution. The Fon rules within a complex democratic culture with entrenched emphases on the effective separation of powers. Outwardly, the Fon is seen to wield overwhelming powers, but in actual fact and reality, the system in force guards against the concentration of much power in one man or one institution. In fact, the cry is rife that, under Yaoundé autocratic foreign rule, most Fons have become dictators on the ancestral throne, this in itself being rebellion against the time-honoured system of governance. In conclusion, therefore, the Fon is only a leader among equals and must remain loyal to the institutions of the land and abide to the cultural norms of the land and remain accountable to the gods and the people.

But here, the Fons of Ngoketunjia, like all natural rulers of occupied British Southern Cameroons, reduced to mere auxiliaries of the administration of the Yaoundé annexationist regime and acting as such, pretended to speak to the gods of the land on behalf of their abandoned people. In their sacrilegious act they instead rebelled against the gods, ancestors or the living-dead, as they misrepresented their people and the reality on the ground. The gods of the land are not dead. They cannot be fooled or bribed with silver and gold. The gods of Bambalang, Bafanji, Balikumbat, Bamali, Bamunka, Bangolan, Baba I, Babungo, Babessi, just to name a few of the thirteen villages that make Ngoketunjia County, know fully well that their people, in general and on average, are today poorer, disempowered, fragmented and far more miserable than they were under the British Southern Cameroons Government in Buea. They have lost their honour and sense of dignity as they have been disempowered under the Yaoundé annexationist regime.

Indeed there was really something fundamentally wrong here. Fons, in their unique roles, do not make an oath, no matter the circumstance. It is the people who make the oath under the Fon's watchful eyes and authority. In the case of a traditional oath, such as the one under examination here, a highly respectable sub-chief or high priest, not the Fon, conducts it. On the other hand the rule of the Fon, either for political or religious rights and matters, is limited within the territory under his jurisdiction: it never goes beyond this space. But here, everything was turned upside down in the typical style of la République. Maybe the auxiliary roles they now play to the benefit of their mentor in Yaoundé has made them blind to who they are in reality. If not, how could Fon Yakum Ntaw of Bambalang have been leading in fulfilment of such a politico-religious role in Ndop, the territory of Bamunka, with the Bamunka Fon there to take instructions?

But the truth is that the Fons were seeking to please Yaoundé. Were they coerced to do the impossible? The truth cannot be hidden from the gods. The gods have heard the cries of the people, as their land has been rendered barren by the construction of the Bamendjin Dam to increase the volume of water for the Edea Dam in la République du Cameroun to provide electricity for the master. The gods have seen how with the draining of the water to increase the volume of the water of the Edea Dam, food production has dropped both in quantity and quality, thus making the farmers poorer. The gods, as well as Fon Yakum Ntaw, know that though the cost of damages was evaluated at more than CFA francs 3 billion and the proconsuls conservatively approved only CFA francs 679,096,765, like compensations approved for the land claimed for the abandoned Bamenda Airport, nothing has been paid to the victims. Yes, the gods and the population of Ngoketunjia County know that the educated youth has become a burden rather than an asset to their parents and communities for they cannot be employed. The gods have come to know that to weaken the solidarity of the people, the annexationist regime has imposed the policy of divide and rule. Because of that, the people distrust each other, and inter-village quarrels and bloody clashes have become rampant, thus giving the omnipotent prefect and the gun-toting *gendarmes*, free licence for exploitation and even the power of life and death over the people. The gods bitterly lament as their earthly representatives, the Fons, now auxiliaries of the government administration, have become appendages of the evil Yaoundé regime and are no more the true representatives of the gods to the people and vice versa.

Can Fon Yakum Ntaw of Bambalang accept to give up the throne and surrender Bambalang to become a section of Bangolan or Bamunka? Can he accept that Bambalang be reduced to a section of Bamoum in la République du Cameroun, so that the Sultan of the Bamoum appoints one of his princes as head of Bambalang? Will the Bambalang people accept to become subjects of the Sultan of Bamoum, even if Fon Yakum Ntaw were to surrender the Bambalang throne?

No people vote for their extinction or willingly surrender to servitude. If animals fight against extinction, how much more do human beings that are rational and are created in the image of God! God on seeing that what he created was perfect, commanded Man to multiply, replenish the earth and dominate the world and not to be dominated by another. He who subjects himself to foreign domination and alien rule violates God's first command.

So, for whom were the Fons speaking? Were they acting in the interest of Mr Paul Biya and la République or the people? Who were they representing? Were they speaking the truth when claiming that, by mobilising Southern Cameroonians to celebrate the 40th Anniversary of their confiscated Independence (1961-2001), the SCNC was preaching evil? Were the Fons telling the truth when claiming that the SCNC wants British Southern Cameroons to secede from la République du Cameroun? Was British Southern Cameroons part of French Cameroun that attained independence on January 1, 1960? Under international law the boundaries of a territory become permanent and immutable from the moment the territory attains independence. French Cameroun attained independence on January 1, 1960, and joined UN membership in September 1960 as la République du Cameroun. With termination of trusteeship, British Southern Cameroons attained its own independence on October 1, 1961 inheriting the territory of British Southern Cameroons as defined by treaties. The so-called federation between la République du Cameroun and British Southern Cameroons was to take place one year and nine months after French Cameroun had attained independence. But this UN-envisioned federal union of two states equal in status never came into being, for the UNGA Resolution 1608 of April 21, 1961 was never implemented, and so, no union between British Southern Cameroons and la République du Cameroun was formed in conformity with Article 102 of the UN Charter. No legal instrument binds the two distinct nations as one nation.

Judging from Fon Yakum Ntaw's background as a security officer, who rose to a distinguished rank and with his training in law, everyone in their right mind will expect him to know and defend the truth, insisting that truth should, like the rays of the bright sunshine sparkle for all to see. To those who are determined, for self-interest, to substitute truth with falsehood and light with darkness, may I ask when the Union Jack was lowered on that eventful day of October 1, 1961, which flag went up? Was it the flag of the Federal Republic of Cameroon or the flag of la République du Cameroun? What did the two Gold Stars on the Flag represent? If the two Gold Stars represented the two states that formed the loose federation, which were the two states? When did the peoples of the two states decide that one of the two Gold Stars should be removed? Why? What is the implication of the unilateral removal of one of the two Gold Stars and the change of the name from Federal Republic of Cameroon to la République du Cameroun, which is the name French Cameroun got at independence? Why did President Ahidjo, in 1972, by decree, abolish the Southern Cameroons Government in Buea, and reduced this distinct nation to two provinces of his country, la République du Cameroun, ruled by his proconsuls?

The first two omens discussed above took place in Buea, in Fako County, the seat of political power. These acts were centred on symbols of sovereignty of modern nation states. The Union Jack that symbolised British authority in British Southern Cameroons suffered such embarrassment because the gods of the land were angry with the British who, after introducing democratic principles and practices which the people cherished, turned around and imposed the plebiscite with two obnoxious questions and independence by joining. By this act, they (British) betrayed the will and legitimate aspirations of Southern Cameroonians as well as violated Article 76(b) of the UN Charter, the Trusteeship Agreement and UN General Assembly Resolution 1514 of 1960, regarding the right to unconditional independence for all territories under foreign rule. British Southern Cameroons, like then-Tanganyika, was a self-governing Trust Territory under United Kingdom Administration. So far, British Southern Cameroons stands to be the only dependent territory (UN Trust) that attained self-government in 1954, and to date, is not yet independent. All other such territories have long gained sovereign independence in conformity with UN Charter and resolutions in force.

As Ambassador Clement J. Zabloiski of the U.S. had said on the floor of the UN – and so argued G.M Thomson (MP) in the British House of Commons - the UN-prescribed federation of two states of EQUAL STATUS was going to be a political disaster for the British Southern Cameroons. In 1961 in Buea, the gods of the land sounded the warning and gave the sign, affirming in 2001, that the reality that Southern Cameroonians had become a stateless people having passed from a less harsh system of colonial rule to annexation and colonial occupation, where the use of brute force has become the order of the day. Effective decolonisation in Southern Cameroons was thus postponed. This is the historic mission that has been taken up again, this time, by the Southern Cameroons National Council (SCNC), in its nonviolent struggle for the freedom, right to self-determination, justice and independence of British Southern Cameroons, and the development and prosperity of all Southern Cameroonians.

In 2001, the centre of action for the 40th Anniversary Commemoration of the confiscation of British Southern Cameroons independence was in Bamenda. The gods demonstrated their disaffection by instantly rejecting the treacherous action of the Fons who, now, as auxiliaries of the annexationist regime, have lost touch with reality and cannot therefore claim to speak for the suffering people without wavering.

Oh, gone are the good days of Fon Achirimbi, Fon Mbinglo I, Ta Nfor Tarndap and Chief Nyenti, among others, who spoke for, and uncompromisingly defended their people.

Truth is sacred for it is of God. It is the light of the world and the foundation of justice and enduring peace and sustainable development. As light, which gives hope and forces darkness to retreat in shame, TRUTH does the same to falsehood and lies which misinform and keep people in chains, ignorance and mass suffering.

The liberation train is on, with or without you. It is moving because the SCNC is speaking and defending the TRUTH. Wise counsel beckons you to jump on the train now, before it is too late. If, in 1961, our people had not yet tasted the bitter pills of annexation and colonial occupation and assimilation and had not experienced Fon Achirimbi's fire (under French Cameroun), the next forty years left shattered hopes and painful scars and bitter memories in each Southern Cameroonian family. Once in the pit you have one and one option only, namely: How to get out? When the gods spoke in 1961, the message was not understood; it had to be repeated in 2001. This time around, the traditional rulers were ridiculed for they failed to defend the truth in the interest of the people they are ordained to represent. When the gods speak, it is because they have heard the cries and seen the suffering of the afflicted people. But the gods need honest, faithful, visionary and selfless human beings to lead the people out of bondage. The gods stand with the faithful and selfless leaders who inspire people to achieve their freedom, dignity and collective self-worth, and not with self-seeking traitors.

The Creator created all men free and equal. He gave each people a homeland and inheritance. He created men in His own image to dominate and rule the world, and by the Creator's inspired wisdom, men, everywhere, were to be their own masters and were never to be dominated by men themselves, and each people was to be master of their inheritance and never be subjected to and dominated by people of another land. That is why the Israelites were set free from Egypt, and so will Southern Cameroonians from the brutal annexation and neo-apartheid of la République du Cameroun.

As Bambalang and Bamoun existed in 1961 and still exist today, there can be no justification to convince any sane man as to why British Southern Cameroons, which existed in 1959 as the equal of French Cameroun, has had to disappear so that la République du Cameroun, successor state French Cameroun, should become stronger, mightier and greater. Of course, this had been at the expense of the Southern Cameroonian people. British Southern Cameroons is the heritage of Southern Cameroonians, and Southern Cameroonians can only be freemen and women in a free and independent British Southern Cameroons. The annexation and occupation of British Southern Cameroons by la République du Cameroun has brought misery and underdevelopment to Southern Cameroonians. The restoration of the statehood and sovereign independence of British Southern Cameroons will restore Southern

Cameroonians to their freedom and dignity.

But one thing, indeed an absolute thing, must be made clear. Southern Cameroonians must look inward and re-discover themselves. They must be the true architects of the urgent positive change they most need. By their collective effort, they must be makers of their progressive history. Southern Cameroonians, like all other peoples under subjugation, must agree with Martin Luther King Jr. who declares: "Change does not roll on the wheels of inevitability, but comes through continuous struggle. Therefore, we must straighten our backs and work for our freedom. A man can't ride you unless your back is bent." Change, we must admit, is the most enduring of all human affairs, and to concretely move from a lower level to a higher level worthy of our being, obstacles that kept us in chains must be overcome.

Chapter Two

Conquering the Fear Syndrome

The Chambers Universal Learners Dictionary defines fear as "a feeling of great worry or anxiety caused by the knowledge of danger." Fear overwhelms one when he envisions potential danger. Even if this feeling is based on some experience, the truth is that its effect is to hold back the individual from falling into similar circumstances. Fear, therefore, is about what can happen, much more than about what is happening or about the past. Fear is natural, and like pain, every living being has suffered it or is bound to experience it in one way or the other.

Fear is an emotional response when one is in danger or when one senses danger. Fear forces the victim to shrink inside for self-preservation, to create boundaries to protect the self, to distrust and to doubt those around as well as the environment. The Wikipedia Encyclopaedia defines fear as "a protective emotion, which signals danger and helps a person to prepare for and cope with it. Fear includes physical, mental, and behavioural reactions." Fear leads one to anticipate harm and plan on how to avoid it or generate the willpower to fight back in self-defence.

According to Buddhism there are two kinds of fears: healthy and unhealthy. Healthy fear is positive and leads one to act rationally towards prevention. If a smoker, on learning that cigarette smoking causes lung cancer, were to stop smoking to save himself and others, this is positive or healthy fear. Healthy fear leads to sound judgment and positive action. Healthy fear leads us to take stock of our situation and make plans on how to overcome issues.

But when one fears spiders, insects, snakes, getting old, death, sickness, darkness and thunder, among others, such a person is expressing unhealthy fear. One is then disturbed and worried over things or situations which cannot be changed, controlled or avoided. This serves no purpose, instead compels the individual to lead an unhappy and uneventful life. The Creator sent each one on Earth to live a happy life and to so live is to face life and make it meaningful, is to radiate confidence, is to lead a proactive life; it is to be an agent of positive change in your community. To be an agent of positive change is to be responsible and sensitive to human conditions, is to care and feel for others and never to subject yourself to be controlled by circumstances.

The Bible also talks of two kinds of fear (NKJV, Psalm 111:10). These are the beneficial type of fear, which should be encouraged, and the detrimental type of fear, which should be avoided, and to be self-fulfilling, every effort should be made to overcome this negative fear. Firstly we are told that the fear of the Lord is the beginning of wisdom. Fear of the Lord does not mean we should be afraid and run away, but that, for His greatness and power, we should honour and reverence the Lord. This brings blessings and benefits and leads to good understanding.

The Bible refers to detrimental fear as the "spirit of fear": "For God has not given us a spirit of fear, but of power and of love and of a sound mind" (NKJV, 2 Timothy 1:7). God could not have created man in His likeness and given Man a sound mind to rule the world, and at same time imposed in Man the spirit of fear and timidity. The spirit of fear is contrary to the will of God for Man, and it is not for the good of Man. Once you understand God's purpose for you on Earth, and you have perfect love for God and you trust Him, you have no cause fearing to stand for truth and justice, for by this, you are doing God's will for Man.

Fear which paralyses man is evil for it raises tyrants into demi gods and makes injustice prevail.

The famous Catholic Newspaper, L'Éffort du Cameroun, in its Editorial of January 1968, states:

> Fear is a bad thing. It empties man of all he is and all he has. It inhibits intelligence, annihilates the will, and chases away what he has that makes him man – **FREEDOM.** What was once man now becomes a robot, an automation with conditioned reflexes. The reasoning animal becomes an animal *tout court,*

even less than a normal animal because in a man subjected to fear, the only instinct is that of self-preservation; and, *as his intelligence hardly still functions, the actions which this man undertakes just to preserve his life can sometimes achieve the opposite result.* (Emphasis mine).

What we get from this definition is that without freedom, Man, created in God's image, loses his natural being, his integrity, his true character, his will power to be the master whom he was created to be. This makes him fall prey to and be used for the glory of another being and not the Supreme Being, the creator of the universe. According to divine will for Man, each human being was created free and equal, none created master over another, and none created a slave of another: none created rich and none created poor. Man created in God's image is destined to be ruler over God's creation and never to be dominated by another man. In conclusion, therefore, a slave who surrenders to his slave master and accepts his debased status as God-given, and submits in perpetuity is as guilty before God as the slave master who, in violation of God's law imposes his will on another and ill-treats the slave for his personal pleasure. In rising against injustice in society and crimes against humanity, Man is using his freedom to defend God's will for Man.

Freedom here, according to God's will, must be understood in defending the truth, doing what is right and defending goodness and justice at all times anywhere and everywhere. Here is God's purpose for giving Man freedom. Freedom is to be used for general good for humankind and for the glory of the Lord.

Like every natural phenomenon, fear is both negative and positive.

Negatively, fear is an enemy of Man. It is an invisible being, a creation of the mind which can make a man, even an oppressor, urinate and excrete in his pants. Fear does not exist outside Man. It is primarily an enemy from within. When the *gendarmes* through torture, intimidation, instil fear in you, what they succeed in doing is to magnify the fear in you and make it assume an overwhelming nature thus depersonalising you in the presence of a *gendarme* in future. Conscious of this fact, the *gendarmes* hold that "The Fear of the *Gendarme* is the beginning of wisdom." With this embedded in the victim the mere presence of a *gendarme* or even the sight of a red beret strikes terror from within.

Fear inhibits Man's inherent potentials. It retards human progress through imaginary impossibilities. It destroys the fabrics that hold society together. As fear dominates, peace and social justice retreat, giving room to chaos, indiscipline and injustice. Fear builds distrust and creates foes, where they do not necessarily exist. Sycophants, looking for cheap favours, exploit this weakness in dictators and present their critics who speak out in the interest of the masses who defend the truth as the dictator's enemies or enemies of the system. Under Yaoundé's dictatorship, men and women of conscience and conviction who speak and defend the truth are called subversive elements.

The most negative aspect of fear is when people subjected to slavery, colonisation or annexation, as is the case with Southern Cameroonians, become accomplices and by adopting a culture of silence, accept their dehumanisation as God-given. Some, not ready to work for change, seeking self-preservation, get contented with finger-pointing and accusing others for being responsible, forgetting that by doing nothing to put an end to the evil, they are worse than those they are accusing. Conforming to the imposed policy of divide and rule, they doubting their ability to, in solidarity, right the wrongs of yesterday, each reclines into his shelf and becomes self-seeking for self-survival. By this, they become traitors of their inherent collective identity and their descendants. To adopt a culture of silence is to disobey God's will for Man and a people. Indeed, to remain silent in the phase of injustice is to betray God's ordained will for Man and each people. Each people are unique and to each people, God made a special investment and through their contribution, there is the blooming of human civilisation.

God created Man to live in happiness and this explains why He provided Man's needs and gave him intelligence to discern between good and evil and, a will to act against evil so that justice and goodness may reign to create the necessary condition for human excellence, peace and prosperity. To adopt a culture of silence in the phase of sustained gross injustice is the height of treachery and complicity. Lamenting over gross injustice in society, Martin Luther King Jr, standing with the oppressed against the oppressor points his accusing finger at the so-called good people who refuse to raise a finger. He states: "The ultimate tragedy is not the oppression and cruelty by the bad people but the silence over that by the good people."

An African great theologian and crusader for human freedom, Archbishop Desmond Tutu, crying against injustice and likewise condemning those who keep their lips sealed, said: "If you are neutral in situations of injustice, you have chosen the side of the oppressor. If an elephant has its foot on the tail of a mouse and you say you are neutral, the mouse will not appreciate your neutrality."

Put succinctly, in a liberation struggle, be it in South Africa, Angola, Algeria, East Timor or British Southern Cameroons, there is nothing in the law of nature which permits the adoption of neutrality with regard to oppression. There are only two sides to reality: FOR or AGAINST, with the oppressed fighting for justice or with the oppressor perpetrating gross injustice, human inequality, promoting impunities and human suffering while the elect in society live on the sweat of the oppressed masses. To fail to raise a finger against injustice is to vote with the oppressor and promote human calamity and societal decadence. To keep sealed lips for the fear of offending the oppressor and losing your post or saving your own life is to legitimise the reign of evil and challenge the will of God for Man and each people and their heritage.

In society where foreign domination has been imposed, decision, courage and action are cardinal to change things around and create condition for progressive history. In such historical challenging moments when decision must be made and action taken, heroes are not those who patiently stood by waiting for the music of chance, they are not those who being undecided sat on the fence or got lost in the crowd, it is those who stand out on the edge inspiring and giving courage and hope to the masses thus, charging humanity in them and making them agents of positive action for their freedom and dignity.

The knowledge of good and evil is to enhance Man's capacity to conquer the evil of falsehood, injustice and enthrone the goodness of truth and justice. The conquest and the ability to subdue or attain mastery of the natural environment are not as important in the furtherance of human excellence and civilisation as is the conquest of social injustice in human society. Without justice in society, advancement in science and technology is turned inward and exploited to serve the self, and thus becomes the instruments of the destruction of Man by his own kind. Not only that, even religion which is to draw Man closer to his creator becomes a divisive force and a societal deadly virus when used negatively.

The essence or the *raison d'être* of government in society is to cater for and guarantee social harmony and the ultimate good of human welfare and happiness. When falsehood replaces truth and injustice replaces justice meant to serve, defend and protect Man, it becomes an instrument of his destruction. Dictators and tyrants hide behind the army and security apparatus because they have alienated themselves from the masses by their anti-people policies, intolerance of dissent and systematic resort to repressive measures to stay in power. Trusting no one, not even the numerous repressive institutions they have created and those kept in charge, dictators spend a large chunk of the national budget on arms and building spy networks for self-survival. This jeopardises the provision of social amenities, health delivery and, improvement in education, industrialisation to create opportunities for employment for the youths and the general improvement of the living standards of the masses.

Contrary to this, there is positive fear. Positive fear is empowering and creative. It imbues in us a creative force, which urges us to act positively and do something to avoid a bad situation from happening or from becoming chronic. Positive fear is concerned with creating an enabling environment for a better humanity. Believing in human dignity, positive fear leads people to draw inspiration from history, to act according to the will of God and build a system which pre-empts the rise of tyrants as leaders or, when evil is identified, proper action is taken to stop it from spreading.

When in 1961, with the planned departure of the British troops from British Southern Cameroons, *gendarmes*, police and soldiers of la République du Cameroun arrived with their over bearing aggressive attitude and some Southern Cameroonians warned about the imminent consequences of an army of occupation, these patriots were expressing positive fear. When in 1972 some campaigned against Ahidjo's imposed referendum and were arrested and banished into the BMMs, they were expressing positive fear for they foresaw the consequences of the programmed referendum on the freedom and dignity of Southern Cameroonians and the identity of British Southern Cameroons as a distinct state from la République du Cameroun, which under the UN Charter and international law should, as of right enjoy sovereign independence.

(a) Other acts of the political leaders of la République du Cameroun that were genuine indicators for the birth of positive fear are:

(b) Ahidjo's proclamation of a Federal Constitution on September 1, 1961 with himself as the Federal President when such a constitution had never been debated by the Southern Cameroons Parliament.

(c) Ahidjo's boasting at his UC Congress in Ebolowa, July 1962 that no new constitution was adopted at Foumban in July 17-21, 1961 but that he amended la République du Cameroun's Constitution of February 1960 to dub it the Constitution of the Federal Republic of Cameroon.

(d) The nationalisation of the British Southern Cameroons Police and seizure of the famous Police Band.

(e) The abolition of the British Southern Cameroons Mobile Wing, and the closure of the training centre in Jakiri.

(f) The takeover and transfer of the Produce Marketing Board to Douala and the confiscation of the more than 78 billion Frs. CFA stabilisation fund belonging to British Southern Cameroons coffee, cocoa and banana farmers.

(g) The takeover and transfer of Cameroon Bank, the Government Printing Press to Yaoundé and closure of other financial institutions and development agencies such as the Ntem Palm Oil Plantation, Development Agency, Santa Coffee Estate, PowerCam - Electricity Corporation, Wum Area Development Authority (WADA) etc.

(h) Closure of air, sea and river ports – Tiko International Airport, Besong Abang, Bali, Weh, Victoria natural deep sea port, Tiko sea port, Mamfe River port, thus concentrating all maritime and air transport in la République du Cameroun.

(i) Closure of transportation infrastructure – (Southern) Cameroons Air Transport (CAT), the abandonment of the Bamenda Ring Road, the Kumba – Mamfe – Bamenda Road thus forcing transportation of goods and persons between the south and north of Southern Cameroons only through la République du Cameroun which has good roads.

(j) The imposition of one party dictatorship in 1966, abolition of Westminster parliamentary democracy in 1972 and balkanisation of British Southern Cameroons into two provinces of la République du Cameroun territory and ruled by francophone proconsuls.

Early action to counter the debilitating consequences of these annexationist policies of the Yaoundé regime would have long saved British Southern Cameroonians from the slavery in which they today find themselves.

Positive fear becomes creative force when people act in solidarity and concert in defence of their collective identity and personality. Survival in decency is natural to, and it is Man's greatest desire without which he loses his humanity and dignity which is found complete within the defence of group interest and inherent identity.

We must understand that every colonial regime operates on divide and rule policy because individually we are very weak. In small groups we are exploited, remain vulnerable and the enemy plays one group against the other. But standing as a people, conscious of and defending our collective interest, we are strong and invulnerable. Meaningful and solid sense of identity is derived from enduring collective identity.

Since 1961 Southern Cameroonians have been expressing positive fear of the Yaoundé authoritarian regime but have failed to transform it into a creative force for their collective survival in dignity. Even before the plebiscite it was a well-known fact that the Yaoundé regime was inherently immoral and insensitive to the feelings of those it ruled. To allay the fears of Southern Cameroonians when efforts to cancel the plebiscite were rudely frustrated by the powers that had the knife and the yam, the KNDP government had to assure Southern Cameroonians that the union was to be a loose federation and Southern Cameroonians were going to continue enjoying their 'English way of life' and freedom as the state of British Southern Cameroons was going to remain under the same system of government with its legal, political, administrative, and educational systems unchanged. There were to be no radical changes, Southern Cameroonians, majority of who were illiterate, were assured. But the reverse today is the case. To restore Southern Cameroonians to their God-given dignity, positive fear must be transformed into creative force.

Why? It is a well-known fact that once a political system is built on immorality, such a system is out to destroy humanity. Morality and politics are inseparable in the evolution of good governance. We cannot have politics devoid of ethical values and expect to have good governance. Politics is about human affairs and interests in an organised society. Man is a gregarious being and he excels in a state of discipline, free enterprise, respect, honesty, tolerance, hard work and reward for excellence, healthy competition and collaboration with other human beings. When freedom abounds, there is cross fertilisation of ideas as people freely debate and discuss issues and seek solutions to problems that confront society. This is the concrete foundation of human progress.

Morality and ethics, on the other hand, concern human behaviour, the human spirit, complementarities, mutual interaction and inter-relationships. Politics comes in to ensure that, since men differ in talents and abilities, societies or human communities of the nation are differentially endowed, there must be adopted an acceptable way of doing things so that the weak are not deprived of their rights to good life and dignity and are not exploited by the strong and that from the national cake, all have a fair share. Since politics is about Man in society, and with politics, society should be structurally organised for maximum benefit to Man, it is thus conclusive that the foundation of effective human authority over his kind must be rooted in morality and time-honoured and tested values. Where and when a political system is bankrupt of this, it is anti-people, it is a dictatorial system. In such a system those at the helm of state affairs do not fear God. But when those who fear the Lord are in authority, when those in authority are those who respect and defend human freedom, equality and dignity, and love humanity, the people live in peace, happiness and enjoy prosperity (Prov. 29:2) for those who lead enjoy the consent of the ruled and are responsible and sensitive to the aspirations of the people. For the people to live in happiness, they must be ruled in justice and according to the will and fear of God.

The right of Southern Cameroonians to transform positive fear into a creative force for their collective survival in dignity is strengthened by the fact that before 1961 they lived under a people-centred and a people-serving-oriented political system. But made to lose what they had by the Yaoundé authoritarian regime is like forcing a child to eat a bitter substance after having eaten honey. It is like taking a fish out of water and expecting it to survive in the desert and multiply its kind. Any further tolerance of annexation or postponement of liberation is giving room to the Yaoundé regime to destroy British Southern Cameroons to a state of disrepair or irreparability.

Southern Cameroonians must resist the urge to give in to negative fear in order to build a heroic history. Society is not sustained by cowards nor is progressive history charted by those who fear to raise a finger and a voice in defence of justice and human freedom. Negative fear never makes achievers. Fear is a wet blanket. It inhibits great talents. Achievers and great men are those who overcome the urge to fear, who discipline great appetite and the lust for money, materialism, power for its own sake, and pleasure in order to stand for ideals and power at the service of Man for the glory of the Creator. Memories of the Great Walk-out of British Southern Cameroons MPs from the Eastern Regional House, Enugu, and the Federal House, Lagos, in 1953 after declaring "Benevolent Neutrality" in Nigerian politics should inspire Southern Cameroonians of this age. This patriotic act caused constitutional and political changes leading to the establishment of the British Southern Cameroons Government in Buea in 1954 in conformity with its special status as a UN Trust Territory. This is what positive fear that generates positive action yields for a people. To become achievers we must tame fear, indeed, we must conquer and banish fear and direct our energies, talents towards the lifting of British Southern Cameroons from the pit of annexation, colonial occupation and underdevelopment and placing it on the path of progressive history.

The more than forty years of our being under the Yaoundé tyrannical rule that has left us with terrible scars must make us hate to the core any system that is undemocratic, insensitive, irresponsible and intransigent to the feelings and will of the people. An undemocratic government is anti-people. Those given the opportunity to govern must be the faithful and loyal managers of the common good, transparent and accountable to the people in whom sovereignty resides. Leaders must be stewards and not lords and bosses. Those given the opportunity to lead must firstly be exemplary good followers. Remember none is born to rule but by demonstrated good character and demonstrated ability to defend the common interest and legitimate aspirations such are given the chance by the people to lead and must remain sensitive and accountable to the people. The relationship between those who govern and the governed should be that of partnership where dialogue and consultation are a right and a duty. Never again should so much power be concentrated in one man and in the centre under the lame argument of building a strong and united nation. We need strong democratic institutions that empower the people and direct human affairs and those who serve in those institutions must be humble, disciplined, responsible, accountable, trustworthy and submit to the rule of law.

It is not an individual endowed with overwhelming power that makes a nation strong and great. It is the people with total faith in the political system they have created offering great opportunities for economic development and prosperity, giving each citizen hope, faith in and a sense of belonging that makes a nation strong, great and promising. It is the collective will of the people that makes a nation strong and united not decrees and bullets. The strength of a nation is not determined by its size but its potential dynamism and capacity to forge ahead and respond effectively and efficiently to its challenges. Unity does not mean uniformity and conformity. The state of Israel is strong and defends its own but it is smaller in size than present day Northern Zone, that is to say, British Southern Cameroons is about three times the size of the nation of Israel.

The strength of national unity in an African nation state lies in its diversity and the capacity of the leaders to articulate policies that channel such diversity for national culture. National unity in an African nation-state must of absolute necessity imply identification and marshalling of diverse ethical and cultural works of value, heroic acts of the different peoples and their histories into one fine whole that mirrors all but one people. Modern African states are a conglomeration of different sovereign states and kingdoms of yesterday. To see diversity as contradictions and seek unity through assimilation is to destroy the flowering of unity and beauty in diversity. But to accept the reality that the forest must be made up of a multitude of different kinds of trees of varied ages and sizes is to create the condition for a dynamic and progressive nation. That is, unity in diversity. Unity does not mean uniformity and conformity. We talk of unity because we know there are parts that make the whole what it is and what it is supposed to be; held and bound together in trust for the common good.

To transform positive fear into a creative force for national liberation and reconstruction, the masses must be given political education and armed with the truth about their place in history and their nation. They must be educated to understand the circumstances under which they find themselves. Sound education must be seen as the tool for one's development. Quite often than not the colonised and annexed, like slaves, are fed with lies, falsehood, debasing images and half-truths about themselves and made to look outward or up to an external force for solution to their problems. This imposes a dependence complex, which delays fulfilment. It is a deliberate policy of the regime to distance the masses from ideas that transform human condition through their positive efforts. Truth and falsehood are like light and darkness; as light forces darkness to retreat so does truth to falsehood. Fear abounds where falsehood has taken sway. Arming the masses with the truth and convincing them of a glorious future once the imposed evil is overcome is the empowerment of the masses. It is like giving a valiant soldier the necessary weapons for self-defence and the attack on the enemy. The masses must be convinced that they collectively possess the capacity to transform their condition for good, that they should be masters of their destiny and not the underdogs of others.

In the new Southern Cameroons, that is British Southern Cameroons restored on a firm foundation of constitutional democracy to give good hope and a heritage to our children, the wrong notion forced down our consciences by the Yaoundé regime that peace is the absence of war, and patriotism is demonstrated through superfluous motions of support through chorusing praise songs, through applauding and saying "yes" when inwardly we know that a shouting "NO!" is the right answer, just to please the powers that be, must be buried and forgotten. The all hail the King singsong that the Yaoundé political monster provided us with peace, good governance and development has been an illusion. They sang the infamous songs to divert our attention from the raging war – the tormenting psychological war, the war of the polarisation of the society into the have and have-nots, the masters and servants, the rulers and the ruled, lords and the subjugated consequent upon colonial heritage and language blocs. This tacitly opened the gates for brutal repression of the annexed, the merciless plunder of the natural resources, the destruction of our cultural heritage, legalised corruption, looting from the national coffers and organised capital flight by the holy cows of the state. Our most endowed nation provided excess cash for the elect to play about with and loot while our people languished in mass poverty. While this was cushioned at the top the masses suffered from disenfranchisement and de-empowerment to the point that the will of the masses did not matter in the continuance of the tyrant in power, he only needed to feather the nests of the army generals, supreme court judges and instruct the governors and divisional officers in the field to claim victory in any election in his name for their self and clique preservation. This, he called *'démocratie avancée'*. After all, *'l'impossible n'est pas Camerounais'*, and *'Cameroun c'est le Cameroun'* ('Nothing is impossible in Cameroun', and 'Cameroun is Cameroun'), the hand clappers and the gullible are proudly told. And for the preservation of the interest of the ruling ethnic oligarchy and the hangers-on who pick the crumbs, more strings of superfluous motions of support are ignited.

No. The nasty and painful experiences under a system inherently evil that has dehumanised Southern Cameroonians and liquidated our state must empower and endow Southern Cameroonians with wisdom and an unyielding spirit of patriotism to, in Africa, become the apostles and champions of democracy, respect for fundamental human rights and freedom, the rule of law, the right of every citizen to equal opportunity and a decent life. Our nation, the Southern Cameroons, must be restored to democracy and good governance to be the shining example of international co-operation with an open door policy for mutual benefits, firstly with its neighbours and secondly, with all other nations of Africa and the world. We must love to be loved. And we must respect others to be respected. We must dutifully and prayerfully ensure that our nation is ruled by humble, responsible and God-fearing leaders who, in the transparent pursuit of justice, our people will enjoy genuine peace, enduring stability and sustainable development and progress. This is the ultimate goal of conquering fear through the transformation of positive fear into a creative force for the good of all our people and nation.

To conquer fear imposed by the reign of terror from Yaoundé, Southern Cameroons national consciousness must become a force governing and directing the life of every Southern Cameroonian either in British Southern Cameroons or elsewhere. National consciousness, it must be understood, is the motive force of the spirit of nationalism. Southern Cameroonians must firstly know who they are and be proud of who they are. They must be proud of and love their nation and be ready to defend it. By being ready to defend, it is to believe in the right of Southern Cameroons to exist as a nation equal to la République du Cameroun and other nations of the world. It should be made clear here that without the equal right of British Southern Cameroons to exist as a nation, a Southern Cameroonian ceases to enjoy his full rights and dignity as a free citizen. The triumph of British Southern Cameroons nationalism must lead to the right of Southern Cameroonians controlling their economic, cultural, and political life. Southern Cameroons nationalism is the logical manifestation of the inalienable right of Southern Cameroonians to assert themselves as the legitimate owners and rulers of the entire territory of the Southern Cameroons. It imposes on Southern Cameroonians the urgency of first seeking the political kingdom, for one cannot logically talk of his nationalism and patriotism when his country is annexed, colonised, occupied and under foreign domination. Indeed, one cannot claim to be free when his homeland is under foreign military occupation and alien rule. The imposition of the reign of terror, it should be recalled, has been consequent upon annexation and subjection of Southern Cameroonians to black colonialism, in a word, neo-apartheid, which the world has failed to appreciate its devastating effect. The owners of the land, I mean Southern Cameroonians, must be the rulers of their inheritance as ordained by the Creator from the beginning of time. It was firm conviction based on natural law expatiated upon by international law that led James Fintan Lalor, an Irish nationalist and patriot, to declare:

> The Principle I state, and mean to stand upon, is that: the

entire ownership of Ireland, (**Southern Cameroons**) up to the sun and down to the centre, is vested of right in the people of Ireland; (**Southern Cameroons**) and they and none but they, are the land owners and law-makers of this land; *that all laws are null and void not made by them, and all titles to land invalid not conferred or confirmed by them; and full right of ownership may and ought to be asserted by any and all means which God has put in the power of man. In other, if not plainer words, I hold and maintain that the entire soil of a country belongs of right to the entire people of that country, and is the rightful property, no of any one class, but of the nation at large, in full effective possession, to let to whom they will, on whatever tenures, terms, rents, services, and conditions they will; one condition, however, being unavoidable and essential, the condition that the tenant shall bear full, true, and undivided fealty and allegiance to the nation, and the laws of the nation whose lands he holds, and shall own no allegiance whatsoever to any other prince, power, or people, or any obligation of obedience or respect to their will, orders, or laws.* I hold, further and firmly believe that the enjoyment by the people of this right or first ownership of the soil is essential to the vigour and vitality of all other rights, to their validity, efficacy, and value; to their secure possession and sage exercise. For let no people deceive themselves, or be deceived by the words and colours and phrases and forms of a mock freedom, by constitutions, and charters, and articles, and franchise. These things are paper and parchment, waste and worthless. Let laws and constitutions say what they will, this fact will be stronger than all laws, and prevail against them – the fact that those who own your lands will make your laws, and command your liberties and your lives. But this is tyranny in its widest scope and worst shape; slavery of body and soul, from the cradle to the coffin – slavery with all its horror (Quoted in ABBIA, Special Issue, May 1982, pp. 18 – 19). (Emphasis mine)

British Southern Cameroons nationalism, which must imply the collective will of the people for national rebirth is the struggle to recapture lost political power, territorial integrity, sovereignty and honour. British Southern Cameroons nationalism is the collective spirit and force of the people to oust black colonialism, indeed neo apartheid of la République du Cameroun which has reduced Southern Cameroonians to beggars and slaves on their own land, which has deprived Southern Cameroonians of their God-given land and its natural wealth, which has enslaved their bodies, souls and intellects. And we must remember that he, who controls your land and your ancestral shrines, does not only make you landless, he makes you his footstool, his eternal slave through his imposed laws. In this status, servitude will be the heritage you will bequeath to your descendants.

In the people's struggle for freedom, justice and independence there is nothing as positive neutrality or sitting on the fence. You are either with the patriots against the enemy or you are firmly with the enemy against the patriots. Southern Cameroons nationalism of today is aimed at recapturing political power as the first step to national reconstruction after decades of annexation, colonial occupation, and imposition of brutal alien rule, pillage and neglect. In this there is no fence for fence sitters. Anybody who is not on board the SCNC train is with the enemy wasting time to build an embankment with sand against a furious tide, namely, national self-determination which is an unstoppable phenomenon in human history. Falsehood has never defeated truth and injustice against a people has never overcome the will of the people to regain their rights and justice. The handwriting on the wall is clear for the LEGITIMATE WILL of the people must triumph. Southern Cameroons will be FREE with or without you; but you are safer on the SCNC train singing the victorious song.

British Southern Cameroons was part of colonial Africa and along other dependent territories fought against colonialism and imperialism. Anti-colonialist struggle in British Southern Cameroons adopted the non-violent approach. The SCNC, having learnt from the errors of yesterday, is taking firm footsteps of non-violence with new vigour, a clear agenda and ultimate non-negotiable goal, namely, sovereign independence. This uncompromisingly requires that la République du Cameroun under international obligation withdraws to its boundary inherited at independence. Furthermore, it requires that la République du Cameroun must be pressured to renounce its claim over British Southern Cameroons and recognise British Southern Cameroons inherent right to exist as a sovereign nation. This will enable independent British Southern Cameroons to; in solidarity with other independent nations of Africa build a strong democratic and united Africa. Africa cannot uncompromisingly fight against white colonial rule, white minority rule and apartheid only to turn round and condone annexation, black colonial rule and neo-apartheid by an African nation. The evil inherent in imperialism, colonialism, foreign domination and alien rule should not be seen in colour and racism: whatever its form and manifestation, it is an evil threatening world peace and humanity and must be fought by all and destroyed.

United Africa we crave for should be made up of sovereign democratic nations and free people committed to working for African renaissance with a strong and influential voice in world affairs. A strong and united Africa can only be built by sovereign nations of Africa founded on constitutional democracy with enabling institutions in which the citizens are ruled by leaders democratically elected from among the people concerned and through the necessary checks and balance, the leaders remain accountable, responsible and sensitive to the will of the people. In freedom, the rule of law and peace based on justice and economic independence, each African nation, exercising sovereign independence, will effectively contribute to a united Africa with an influential voice in world affairs. Only a free people think positively, act constructively and make lasting impact on human history.

Part II

Consequences of Annexation and Colonial Occupation

Chapter Three

The Development of Underdevelopment

British Southern Cameroons has politically, economically, culturally, morally and spiritually been destroyed and rendered bankrupt. It has lost its inherent nature, beauty and harmony. Like a house in ruins, it is today in urgent need of reconstruction on a solid foundation. This reconstruction must of absolute necessity go with restructuring and transformation to meet the legitimate aspirations of its citizens, the demands of the new age after gross injustice under brutal black colonial rule, in brief, neo-apartheid.

In constructing a house much thought, labour, resources and time is invested to obtain the type of house that will render service to the immediate owner, the future children, friends, guests and more. My people, the Wimbum say that, 'a house is never full'. That is to say you can never deny others access into the house on grounds that it is full and cannot receive more people. Sincerely speaking, the deep meaning is that a house is never built for the owner alone; it is built for people and the number is never predetermined. This received wisdom has its deep roots in the nature of Man.

To the Wimbum, the human is a community man and a gregarious being. He belongs to the community or society and not the other way around. Belonging to the community, it is incumbent upon each member not to be a liability but to be a genuine asset indeed, an agent of positive change. The Wimbum believe in the dynamism of Man; Man as a gregarious being, a visionary who is always striving for the best which is attainable through sacrifice and hard work in conjunction with other members of the family, friends and the society at large. In this line of thought, the worth of a man is measured by their character, output and contribution towards the enhancement of the community spirit and society to which they belong in general.

In the construction of a house, time is spent in selecting the right material, labour is harnessed, finance is assembled, serious thought is given to the project and it is then designed. If in building a house this much is demanded, it is therefore conclusive that in building a nation, nationals are bound to invest far more for the nation state so as to accord the individual and the national human community the international personality they deserve. As in the construction of a house, serious thought is given to guaranteeing a solid foundation using material such as bamboo, stone, steel and concrete, nation-building must be engineered with the right mixture of the political, economic and cultural will and legitimate aspirations of the people. This is to say the people of the nation in question must be the true architects of the nation they deserve.

But when there is distortion and disorientation, and when foreign influence dominates, a lacking foundation is bound to be laid. It is common knowledge that once the foundation of a house is poorly laid, the house will automatically collapse. This is why no house is built on sand or on clay, for it can never endure wind or rain.

The first step to laying a solid foundation for the British Southern Cameroons nation was taken concretely in 1953 with the declaration of "Benevolent Neutrality" in Nigerian politics. This was followed by the holding of the Mamfe Conference, May 22-24, 1953 that brought together the people's representatives from all over the national territory. Out of this conference came a memorandum that uncompromisingly demanded for separate political status for the UN Trust Territory of British Southern Cameroons under United Kingdom administration. This was legitimate political action which patriots put forward at the right time for a legal and legitimate solution in the supreme interest of the Southern Cameroonian people.

One significant thing is clear here and needs to be emphasised: the people individually and collectively sacrificed and suffered in order to defend their rights and secure a better future for their descendants. In suffering, they identified with one another and understood that in unity they will triumph as a people and on that count, they turned to London to remind the UK Government that British Southern Cameroons, though administered as part of Nigeria for the convenience of the Administering Authority, was not an integral part of the British colony of Nigeria. But, that British Southern Cameroons was a UN Trust Territory, separate and distinct under international law, it could never become an integral part of Nigeria. In defence of their status as a UN Trust Territory protected by the UN Charter and the Trusteeship Agreement, and defending their inalienable right to self-determination, they demanded to form a separate government. This gave birth to the establishment of the Southern Cameroons Government in Buea, and on October 26, 1954, the House of Assembly was inaugurated by Brigadier E. J. Gibbons, the Commissioner, who, as the representative of H.M, the Queen was the President of the House and the Executive Council while Dr E.M.L. Endeley was the Leader of Government Business or Premier.

The political, economic and cultural transformation, which came with the birth of a new status and power of decision making, was dramatic and self-evident. It gave birth to self-esteem, self-confidence and a new image visible and respected both nationally and internationally. It was from 1954 that Dr Endeley, as Head of Government of Southern Cameroons, started appearing in Lagos, London and at the UN Headquarters in New York to speak on behalf of his people, the Southern Cameroonians. The new status also gave rise to economic and cultural development as the new climate of democracy. Freedom of assembly, freedom of movement, exchange of ideas, educational development, improvement in health care and communication facilitated the free flow of services and goods even to parts of the country that were inaccessible before 1954. Since then, national consciousness and patriotism grew, and Southern Cameroonians, though still working under foreign rule, began shaping their destiny.

The Southern Cameroons legislative institution was, three years later, enhanced with the creation of the House of Chiefs, which like the British House of Lords, served as the Upper House and complemented the making of laws for the emerging British Southern Cameroons nation state. The creation of the House of Chiefs was in recognition of the powers and influence which the Southern Cameroons natural rulers wielded in their respective areas of jurisdiction, but it was also an enactment of the historic fact that Southern Cameroons was an amalgamation of separate autonomous states and, though small, held cultural values, laws and traditions worth preserving, protecting and modernising for the building of a modern British Southern Cameroons state. Judged rightly, it was found politically and culturally expedient that this transformation could best be attained if those serving as the custodians and executors of the inherent African cultural values, norms and laws – indeed what kept the mini nations strong and vibrant – were effectively involved in the building of the modern British Southern Cameroons nation-state.

The ease with which democracy found fertile soil in British Southern Cameroons was a clear indication that the Southern Cameroons heterogeneous societies were governed by a dynamic and open culture that is receptive to new ideas and values. Such a culture is one equally endowed with rich ideas and values to contribute or export to other communities for the blooming of human civilisation. The evidence of the triumph of democracy, tolerance and respect for the will of the people as expressed through the ballot box, and respect for the rule of law was demonstrated when in 1959, Premier Endeley of the CPNC narrowly lost in a general election and as a true democrat conceded defeat and peacefully handed over powers to J.N. Foncha of the KNDP. This was at a time when transfer of power from the ruling party to an opposition party in respect of the will of the majority was not popular in the African continent. Democracy was still at its embryonic stage, for although the colonial powers faithfully practised it in Europe to maintain their colonies, the idea of the ballot box which expresses majority rule against colonial rule was unimaginable in Europe's acquired overseas territories. To block such a thing from happening, the whites in South Africa, for example, ruled through apartheid for about a hundred years which reduced the majority of blacks — the right owners of the land — to serfdom with no right of decision regarding how South Africa was governed until, change came about at great cost with the overthrow of apartheid regime in the 1990s. While the colonial powers theoretically preached democracy, they controlled the colonies and trust territories under the pretext of guiding the leaders to avoid taking wrong steps or falling into communist hands. They set the standards, created the rules, determined the time frame, and all these to protect their interests. They were the gods of the democracy they preached.

Although democracy flourished, and in 1960, a new Constitution was adopted with the hope of leading the Trust Territory to independence, imperial manipulation imposed unwholesome conditions for decolonisation in British Southern Cameroons. To sustain imperial interest, political pluralism was exploited to impose a plebiscite with two questions that postponed genuine decolonisation. It is indeed incredible that a people who embraced democracy, the rule of law, political pluralism and freely conducted open and transparent elections, came to forfeit their democratic and legitimate right to exercise full sovereignty over their national territory at the end of trusteeship (colonial) rule upon imperial manipulation. Decolonisation, in conformity with Article 76(b) of the UN Charter, the Trusteeship Agreement and UN General Assembly Resolution 1514 XV of December 1960, was to automatically grant sovereign independence to the British Southern Cameroons. But, in violation of all these, Southern Cameroons was to attain the ultimate goal of decolonisation through independence by joining any of its two neighbours, namely, Nigeria to the west, or la République du Cameroun, to the east. For more than four decades, British Southern Cameroons had a lot in common with Nigeria, while from 1916 to 1961, British Southern Cameroons and le Cameroun Français were as different as day and night. As two distinct Trust territories of the UN under two colonial powers with contrasting colonial philosophies, the two Cameroons could not even communicate in a common language: the one was a stranger to the other. This is how the poor foundation for the building of the

Southern Cameroons nation state came to be laid, for it was externally conceived, designed, financed, controlled and executed with Southern Cameroonians being led as lamb to slaughter. This imposition to serve foreign interests was a coup against the legitimate will and inalienable rights of the Southern Cameroonian people. Through international colonial conspiracy, some colonial powers manipulated the UN to violate its own Charter. In this enterprise of the preservation of foreign interest, which inevitably promised future political disaster, British Southern Cameroons was a guinea pig.

Annexation as an Instrument for the Development of Underdevelopment

For a genuine understanding of this topic, it is of prime importance that the key concepts are defined. These are development, underdevelopment, and the development of underdevelopment.

(a) Development:

Development is a multifaceted and multidimensional process of improvement of human condition in society. Central to development is the strife for positive change in human condition and total way of life, and since Man lives in society, the development of a given society cannot be externally imposed and directed. To be sustainable and transforming, it must grow from within. The people of any given society must be the creators of their own culture, one that is forward looking and that fashions the instruments and conditions for positive change. Development is therefore by Man, of Man and for Man. The focal point and prime mover or agent of development is Man himself, conscious, creative, imaginative, responsible, sensitive and freely interacting in society and the natural environment.

Commenting on development, Walter Rodney, states: "At the individual level, it implies increased skill and capacity, greater freedom, creativity, self-discipline, responsibility and material well-being."² Since Man is a social animal, we cannot talk or evaluate human development outside of society. We cannot talk of the developed Man or personality in a backward society. We cannot talk of a developed society under colonial rule, when the destiny of the people and their land is in the hands of foreigners and under foreign laws. It is equally self-evident that no inhabitant of a conquered, annexed, occupied or colonised society can talk of enjoying freedom. Man's ingenuity and creative powers are at their optimum in an open, dynamic and liberal society in which the people are their own masters. While freedom of association, expression and thought create the conditions for development, development in turn enhances human freedom. This therefore leads us to the conclusion that Man's freedom and development are a true measure of, and are inseparably tied with, the state of affairs in society.

Man, from all of recorded history, has always dutifully made the effort to master the natural environment as a means of improving his physical, material, intellectual and spiritual wellbeing. He does this consciously in the exercise of his freedom. In this quest and enterprise, Man lives socially, and each society comes into interaction with other neighbouring societies. Interactions between societies and human communities sometimes yield positive as well as negative results. This happens because the supreme interest of any people is centred on securing, preserving, defending and promoting their inalienable right to exercise their freedom and to exist as a distinct people preserving their cultural heritage and territory. These are the true measure of their distinct identity in their external environment. Development is therefore not only concerned with the mastery of natural hazards as a means of improving material well-being and social life, but it is more importantly concerned with self-guarding the independence of the people against real and/or imagined enemies. Once the freedom of a people can easily be infringed upon, their continuous right to development is halted, as they now become labourers for their new masters. This is the consequence of negative contact or contact with powerful aggressors and expansionists.

Development is both quantitative and qualitative, and inherent in each culture is the capacity for advancement for a better life and living condition, which enhance the dignity of Man. Development is native to all peoples and cultures. The need to fashion tools, right from the early Man, was consequent upon his desire to master his environment, to attain increased productivity and reduce the exertion of his physical energy in his quest for quantitative and qualitative products to enable him lead a meaningful life. This was based on the human's understanding that survival was closely linked to his capacity to produce both for self-sustenance and for exchange. "Every people", declares Walter Rodney, "have shown the capacity for independently increasing their ability to live a more satisfactory life, through exploiting the resources of nature. Every continent independently participated in the early epochs of the extension of the human's control over his environment – which means in effect that every continent can point to a period of economic development."[3]

The ultimate purpose of development and the true measure of development is the development of the human. Adebayo Adedeji defines development as "the realisation and unfolding of (the human's) creative potential through improvement, not only in his material conditions of living which enable him to fulfil his physiological needs, but also through the satisfaction of his psychic needs." In other words, development is a process by which the human's overall personality is enhanced. And development for society means the "development of the collective personality of society. Development thus defined is a multivariate quantitative and qualitative change and may not be immediately measurable cardinally."[4]

(b) Underdevelopment:

After seeing what development is and how it is brought about, it is important we understand what underdevelopment is.

It will be erroneous to hastily conclude that underdevelopment simply means the absence or the opposite of development, because development as defined above is native to all peoples and cultures of all ages. The human's greatest desire is to not only survive and perpetuate his kind; it is to survive decently and bequeath a rich legacy to his descendants. Every age in every culture wants to leave a mark in the sands of history for those that follow and humankind in general.

Nevertheless, we see that the human's legitimate ambition to be self-fulfilling is not only challenged by natural hazards, it is equally challenged by the greed of other humans. When a society comes into contact with another which has a different core culture and an aggressive worldview, the greedy and powerful is inclined to reduce the weak or small to its footstool, and for this rival culture to perpetuate its superior interest, it imposes domination and exploitation on the weak for its aggrandisement. When this takes place, the domineering power exploits the dominated. Underdevelopment is used here in comparative terms, comparing the levels of development between two or more societies based on the nature of the relationship that brought the two contrasting societies closer and has held them together. If such a relationship is positive and is sustained by mutual respect and co-dependence, each will reap the good fruits of the relationship. But, if it is based on domination, and is sustained by exploitation and oppression of the one by the other, it will result into development for the domineering power or the powerful and underdevelopment for the victim of the negative relationship that manifests in the domination and exploitation of the weak by the powerful state.

Nothing better than the history of the slave trade explains and illustrates the origin of the theory of underdevelopment, and how this exploiter-exploited relationship helped to advance the faster development of Europe and North America while accounting for the deterioration and stagnation of the African and Latin American continents in particular. Colins Leys holds: "The starting point of underdevelopment theory is the period in which any given region of today's third world began to be progressively incorporated into a permanent relationship with the expanding capitalist economy. Sometimes the initial relationship was largely one with simple plunder and extortion though generally represented as trade (as in the case of the slave trade). But even where the trade rested on exchange the evidence is that it was conducted on very unequal terms, mainly because it was backed up by superior force on the side of the capitalist trader. The profits formed part of the original or primitive accumulation of capital in Europe, which was necessary before capitalist accumulation based on wage labour could occur."[5]

The staggering reality of this relationship between plunder and the plundered is that the former, really a greedy expansionist power, reaps avariciously from where he did not sow, and above all, invests nothing of the surplus profits in the territory being exploited or plundered. The term 'surplus profits' is used here purposely because either during the slave trade or colonial period, what the imperialist plundered out of Africa far outweighed any kind of effort or labour invested on their part except for their coming as plunderers. In this relationship, the intensity of the plunder is determined by the inability of the peripheral territory to successfully challenge the metropolitan power. To succeed even with little effort, the metropolitan power imposes the policy of divide and rule and corrupts the elite which it uses as lackeys and appoints as errand boys and agents of repression to nip in the bud any dissent. At the collapse of slave trade to sustain the plunder in the third world, Europe partitioned Africa into spheres of influence or as their colonial possessions. This was not because Africa was 'no man's land' but it was to enable them to perpetuate the accumulation of surplus capital while sinking Africa into degradation and stagnation. Walter Rodney maintains that "underdevelopment with which the world is now preoccupied is a product of capitalist, imperialist and colonialist exploitation. African and Asian societies were developing independently until they were taken over directly or indirectly by the capitalist powers. When that happened, exploitation increased and the export of surplus ensured depriving the societies of the benefit of their natural resources and labour."[6]

Colonialism, which imposed direct political control and foreign laws, came with new emphasis aimed at sustaining the exploitative relationship in order to maximise the profit margin in favour of the colonising power. While this empowered the coloniser, the colonised was de-empowered as much as they were disenfranchised, dispossessed, subjugated and fragmented. With stationed repressive forces and policy of divide and rule, the people were rendered incapable of defending their rights to dignity, a better life and rightful place within the world community.

Colonial African political economies were generally mercantilist, with emphasis on the export of primary commodities and importation of finished products from the metropolis. This accounts for double exploitation, for while the raw commodities were carried away for free, the manufactured goods were paid for at a cut throat price. In pushing forth this dependence into a permanent feature of the relationship, the building of new industrial capacities was never countenanced. At the same time their policy was implemented to kill indigenous industrial and manufacturing capacities. The development of an African entrepreneurial and petit bourgeois class was hardly encouraged and, in any case, colonial economic policies were in their design and effect antagonistic to the emergence of such a class.[7] This colonial policy was necessary to sustain the in-built mechanism of the exploiter and the exploited relationship of dependence. This is well documented by Walter Rodney in his famous book *How Europe Underdeveloped Africa*.

Here, the intensification of exploitation, as will be explained further, was facilitated by direct political control of the colonial territories. As it is explained in this book, he who controls your land makes your laws and directs your everyday life for his leisure and convenience, and colonialism deprived Africans of their freedom and political power over their inheritance. While the primitive slave trade concerned itself with the African human commodity as presented at the coast, colonialism completely took over all of Africa and imposed a new relationship of exploitation far more intense, vicious and direct. The colonial political grip on Africa had to be cushioned by economic strangulation. The incontrovertible conclusion here, therefore, is that underdevelopment in Africa in general and any African nation in particular, is neither predicated on the absence of human skill and necessary raw materials nor is it consequent upon its peculiar internal evolution that is slow and is uniquely anti-development, but it is the resultant effect of the exploitative relationship brought about and imposed by slave trade followed by European imperialism and colonialism which is sustained till date through neo-colonialism.

(c) Development of underdevelopment:

The development of underdevelopment is used here purposely to explain how the annexation and colonial occupation of British Southern Cameroons by la République du Cameroun has diabolically ruined Southern Cameroons and its people far more than Southern Cameroons' relationship with the United Kingdom between 1858 and 1886 as a Christian colony, then from the partition of Africa as part of German Kamerun from 1884 to 1914, and again with the United Kingdom following the defeat of Germany in WW1 from 1916 to 1961. Above, we have seen development as native to all peoples and cultures, and as a multivariate process of positive change for the total wellbeing of the human and society, which the free man is the prime mover and beneficiary of. On the other hand, underdevelopment is seen as a relationship in which a powerful state transforms a weak and/or small state into a pond whose natural resources the imperial state plunders recklessly for its development, and which subjects the people of the colonised state into abject misery and stagnation.

The theory of the development of underdevelopment, as applied by la République du Cameroun, paints an uglier picture than this. In the development of underdevelopment, la République du Cameroun has not only been concerned with the plunder of the natural resources of British Southern Cameroons; it started with economic vandalism. The development of underdevelopment here was occasioned by the systematic and diabolic annihilation of existing financial institutions, economic infrastructure, economic survey records and maps, with the sole purpose of erasing the history and distinct identity of British Southern Cameroons. Until the evil hand of history linked it with la République du Cameroun, the two states existed independent of each other. With the hidden agenda of annexing the British Southern Cameroons, obliterating the international boundary between the two, balkanising the former UN Trust Territory, and reducing it into two provinces of la République du Cameroun territory, it would have been a futile exercise to abolish political institutions while maintaining financial institutions and viable economic infrastructures created by a state that has been annexed, recolonised and occupied. The existence of such institutions, built on the culture of democracy to defend and promote human freedom and dignity, would have been an anathema, not only because Southern Cameroons was reduced to two provinces of la République du Cameroun, but more importantly, because such institutions would have served as a counter force to annexation, colonial occupation and assimilation. The memories of a Southern Cameroons state that once existed would be kept alive by these non-abolished financial and economic institutions. Reasons for destruction are not far to seek. Such nostalgic memories would kindle the flames of Southern Cameroons nationalism, which would challenge the right of la République du Cameroun to exercise full sovereignty over Southern Cameroons as an indistinct integral part of la République du Cameroun.

By destroying or abandoning the abolishment of existing financial and economic infrastructures such as the Victoria natural deep sea port, Tiko sea port, Mamfe river port, Tiko international airport, Besong Abang, Bali and Weh inland airports, Cameroon Air Transport (CAT), Victoria, Kumba-Mamfe-Bamenda Road, Kumba-Mbonge-Ekondo-Titi and Bamenda Ring Road networks, the PowerCam Electricity Corporation, Santa Coffee Estate, Kimbe Game Reserve, Ntem Palm Estate, the Development Agency; by nationalising such financial institutions such as the Government Printing Press in Buea, CamBank and the Produce Marketing Board; and by transferring their headquarters to Yaoundé and Douala respectively in la République du Cameroun, Southern Cameroons was reduced to a mere economic appendage or liability which could not survive on its own. From the Produce Marketing Board alone, some CFA francs 78 billion saved over the years as stabilisation fund to sustain high production of cocoa, coffee and bananas by the co-operative farmers, were confiscated by the Yaoundé regime and used for the development of la République du Cameroun. Thus, the development of underdevelopment was aimed at reducing the territory of Southern Cameroons to its knees, and its citizens – now subjects of la République du Cameroun upon annexation and occupation – as beggars in their own land who, without anything to be proud of and to hold unto, must subserviently look up to Yaoundé for survival.

The immediate consequences of the closures and transfers of these financial and economic institutions were the layoffs of Southern Cameroonians who had faithfully been working for their state, some of whom started before 1961, and through these services supported their families. Added to this, are other services and small businesses that depended on the main corporations to flourish, but unfortunately were arbitrarily closed. As a consequence of this, many were rendered poor and unemployed. Poverty – so long as it makes the victim constrained and powerless – is violence against the dignity of the human. If poverty reduces human freedom and dignity, then state imposed conditions that cause mass poverty as seen here, are violence in the most extreme form, occasioning a sort of silent genocide. Here, the annexationist Yaoundé regime deliberately applied policies targeting Southern Cameroonians so as to push them into perpetual poverty, subservience and dependence, thus slavishly submissive.

Annexation and black colonisation of British Southern Cameroons by la République du Cameroun would have been difficult without making the former intrinsically dependent on the latter. For this, the roots of separate existence had to be erased to lay the foundation for perpetual dependence on Yaoundé. The capital of British Southern Cameroons, Buea, which was the equal of Yaoundé, was reduced to one of the ten provincial capitals of la République du Cameroun, ruled by a Francophone proconsul.

The foundation of the UN-sponsored federal union was

designed to give undue advantage to la République du Cameroun. Though British Southern Cameroons was deceived with the empty words of being a component of the two-state federation with la République du Cameroun, the UN's failure to implement Resolution 1608 of April 21, 1961 indisputably accorded to independent la République du Cameroun, which had political, military, judiciary and economic power, an undue advantage. With a hidden agenda, la République du Cameroun moved fast to annex and extend its sovereignty over British Southern Cameroons, while the UN failed to implement its envisioned federal union of two states of EQUAL STATUS in its two former Trust territories, only watching with a legendary culture of silence. Understanding its founding mission of promoting democracy, the rule of law and maintaining world peace based on justice and international co-operation amongst all nations – large and small – this act betrayed the trust and confidence that the British Southern Cameroonians had in the UN and the international system in general.

Sustaining the Development of Underdevelopment:

After destroying the political institutions, for example, state parliament, government, political parties, that could mobilise resistance and defend the identity of British Southern Cameroons, the Yaoundé regime was determined to maintain its gains. On the question of representation under the one party system, it was the political bureau that decided on who goes to parliament: the duty of Southern Cameroonians – who had grown under healthy competition of political party ideologies and programmes, single-member constituencies, parliamentary democracy and the power of the ballot box – was reduced to that of confirming the list of deputies presented by the political bureau presided over by Ahidjo, who was advised by French experts. Southern Cameroonians who had grown used to single-member constituencies were brought into a list system in which the division, as an administrative unit under the heavy hand of the President's appointee, became a constituency. With the imposition of the one-party state, it was conclusive that freedom of assembly, movement, expression and opinion was buried in British Southern Cameroons. This gave room to the blossoming of the dictatorial rule of the President who was also the chairman of the imposed one-party. In this system, the Member of Parliament (MP) is said to represent the entire nation and not the area from which they come. MPs are answerable to their boss, the Chairman of the Party and President of the Republic, by whose grace and mercy they got their candidatures endorsed on the list by the Chairman of the state party for the disenfranchised and oppressed masses.

The imposition of one-party oligarchy in 1966 effectively brought British Southern Cameroons – which was a shining example of democracy – the rule of law and freedom in colonial Africa to its dark age. The consequences of this singular act for a people, for whom democracy had become national culture and a way of national life, can only be compared with dumping a live fish on to the hot sands of the Sahara desert and expecting it to survive and multiply. Southern Cameroonians, unable to bear this tyrannical yoke and determined to transform the political culture of la République du Cameroun by sacrificing life and property, fought hard and reintroduced multipartism in 1990. This has not even changed the mind-set of the Yaoundé regime. This only confirms the truism that light and darkness or justice and injustice can never co-habit in one room, let alone be bed fellows.

Under the Yaoundé dispensation, both the parliament and the judiciary are mere extensions of the executive arm of the government, and by coercion civil servants must belong to the ruling party even in this age of legalised multi-party dispensation. Since the President is the head of government, parliamentarians only debate bills, and even those in the military must support and guarantee, during elections, that the President's party wins an absolute majority. It should be pointed out that election results are known ahead of election day as it is the 'holy cows' of the ruling party that decide how many seats should be allocated or set aside for opposition political parties. By this dictatorial system, the opposition parties do not help in shaping policies. The leading opposition party is not seen as an alternative government either. It is instead seen as an enemy which should be destroyed or at least, through corruption, bribery and election rigging, rendered meaningless and ineffective, and maintained in limbo as a performance of multi-party democracy.

To talk of Southern Cameroonians represented in government is to miss the point. Although Southern Cameroonians by an unwritten law are barred from occupying any of the powerful ministries or strategic parastatals, even the most faithful to the regime are not trusted; they are appointed only as assistants, vices or occupy sinecure posts. In the Ministry of Mines and Power, the managing directors of the public corporations under the Ministry, such as SONARA and SNH, which deal with petroleum products, the top posts are the exclusive preserve of the Francophone few who are answerable only to the President. Thus, upon the entrance of any Southern Cameroonian into government, their survival in and the role they play is predicated on their worshipping the President and glorifying the assimilationist policy. Southern Cameroonians in government do not represent nor do they speak for and defend British Southern Cameroons' interests. Those who qualify to be appointed are those who are in favour of the Yaoundé establishment, indeed the traitors, and those who are against the Southern Cameroonian people. Self-centred to the core, they are like dead fish that can only swim with the current. Greed has sapped away the humanness in them. They cannot defend their own, their Southern Cameroonianness. Their skill at producing fake motions of support for the ethically bankrupt Francophone system is legendary.

To build a crop of dependent elite, the Anglo-Saxon educational system that prepared citizens for self-esteem, national consciousness, patriotism, self-reliant development and commitment to the defence of the common good, has been watered down in favour of the Francophone system. Firstly, as the absolute majority of higher educational and prestigious institutions are located in la République du Cameroun territory, the few Southern Cameroonians offered admission face an uphill task as

80% of the lectures are in French. Secondly, the few Southern Cameroonians admitted are confronted not only by a strange social environment, but more so by a rigid administrative system and strange educational programme that calls for serious adjustment and hard work to succeed. Thirdly, the socio-cultural environment is rooted in French culture. In the early days, administrative staff was all Francophone, the majority of whom were French citizens. These problems notwithstanding, the Yaoundé authorities did not care much and till this day, little or nothing is being done to satisfy the legitimate aspirations of Southern Cameroonians. Consequent upon the unwritten policy, that which is rigorously being implemented is the policy of assimilation.

Higher professional schools are located only in la République du Cameroun territory and competitive exams based on Francophone syllabi are set in French, and whenever effort is made to translate, it is poorly done, to the disadvantage of the Southern Cameroonian candidates. Although the Higher Teachers College (ENS, French acronym), has an annex in Bambili-Bamenda, after more than 30 years of existence, it is still housed in old dilapidated colonial buildings, and everything is controlled from Yaoundé. Most competitive exams into the prestigious professional schools are written only in Yaoundé or Douala, and Southern Cameroonians are discriminated against as they are generally classified as the enemies of the regime. With linguistic problems, even the few lucky ones have to make extra effort to pass the exams while many get frustrated and abandon their studies or leave to study abroad. Their success at some of the most respected universities abroad brings them no advantage upon return. If employed, they face the hazard of equivalence and are generally placed under Francophone supervisors who lack the experience, technical know-how and academic attainment of the Southern Cameroonian. The message is clear: an annexed has no rights, but if subservient and worshipfully loyal, they may be rewarded with a sinecure post and may be accorded the mercy to pick up the crumbs.

The policy of sustaining the development of underdevelopment becomes markedly measurable in the economic domain. Firstly, the bourgeois misleading tactics of measuring economic development by looking at per capita income or Gross Domestic Product is a capitalist way of covering reality. If 5% of the population owns 75% of the national income, leaving only 25% for the remaining 95% of the citizens, how does the use of income per capita help us understand the state of affairs with the majority living in squalor? How does the fact that the billionaire feeds his dog either with chicken, goat, or cow meat and rice and when it is sick he invites the veterinary to administer the necessary drugs, help us understand the condition of the widow whose husband was killed by the repressive forces and the two-year old son is dying of malaria or cholera but cannot be taken to hospital for lack of funds? Legendary abundance for the few and misery and squalor for the many cannot be a measure of development. The poor have no freedom. They are weak and powerless. They lead meaningless, short and violent lives. Poverty should be understood as the evidence of constraint. It is a "remarkable fact that economic unfreedom, in the form of extreme poverty, can make a person a helpless prey in the violation of other kinds of freedom."[8]

Examining the birth of the development of underdevelopment or economic vandalism in Southern Cameroons as from 1972, some financial institutions and economic infrastructures have been enumerated above. It is worth noting that these were not closed down because they were unviable and could not be rehabilitated, but this was deliberately done to bring Southern Cameroons under the crushing axe of la République du Cameroun to justify annexation in the eyes of the apologists. To drive home the point that these were viable economic ventures, it is important we examine the assets of the Produce Marketing Board in Victoria at the time of closure and transfer to Douala.

Office
1. (Victoria) Limbe Branch Main Office 400.000.000 CFA francs
2. Office de Conditionnement 100.000.000
3. Bota Stores Office 40.000.000

TOTAL 540.000.000

Residential Building
1. Chief of Branch's House 120.000.000 CFA francs
2. Assistant Chief of Branch's House 50.000.000
3. Junior Service Quarters 180.000.000
4. Residential House No.1 40.000.000
5. Residential House No.2 40.000.000

TOTAL 430.000.000

Stores
1. Giant Mills store – (Bonadikombo) 250.000.000 CFA francs
2. Bota Main Stores 350.000.000
3. Bota Mill Store 100.000.000

TOTAL 700.000.000

Milles
1. New Mills at Bonadikombo 162.000.000 CFA francs
2. Old Mill at Bota 50.000.000

TOTAL 212.000.000

Land
1. Land at West Coast 10.000.000 CFA francs
2. Land at One Mile Limbe 8.000.000

TOTAL 18.000.000

Source: Albert W. Mukong (ed). The Case for the Southern Cameroons, CAMFECO, (USA), 1990, p134.

Added to these huge assets, was the stabilisation fund discussed above and the skilled and experienced Southern Cameroonian manpower led off following annexation and colonial occupation.

It is also worth pointing out that at the time of transferring to and concentrating maritime trade in Douala it was far cheaper to export goods from the Victoria sea port than from the Douala sea port. As stated in the petition by the Fako parliamentarians to the Minister of Trade and Industrial Development, the cost of exporting one tonne of produce from Victoria was 62,283 frs against 75,679 frs at the Douala port, giving a difference of 13,391 frs per tonne. This does not however include the cost of transporting the goods from Southern Cameroons to Douala, the high cost of storage, the corruption and bureaucratic bottlenecks that Southern Cameroonians came to encounter and other overhead costs.[9] This petition of the Fako Members of Parliament yielded no fruit. The action taken was in conformity with Yaoundé's hidden agenda to annex the Southern Cameroons, render it economically subservient and foreclose the emergence of a Southern Cameroons indigenous bourgeoisie.

After closing and transferring the economic and financial institutions enumerated above, it became necessary to ensure that no new ones were set up, and if inevitable, once set up, should be kept in the hands of Francophone managers and staff, and controlled from la République du Cameroun. Southern Cameroons, its natural resources notwithstanding, is barren of industries. While SONARA, the oil company, may have its headquarters in Limbe (Victoria), it is an empty shell to deceive the Southern Cameroonian people and the international community. Victoria, which should have been a developed town, has until today nothing to show for being an 'Oil City'. Even the natives of Victoria have benefitted nothing as the entire management is in the hands of Francophone, and royalty is paid but to the Douala city council in la République du Cameroun. Though black gold is from the Southern Cameroons soil, petrol is imported into Southern Cameroons as it has no depot of any kind. As it is with oil, so is it with other minerals which are exploited openly or clandestinely by those who control the economy of the land.

Timber, another great source of foreign exchange, is one more interesting case that cannot escape attention here. The French-based multi-national logging companies are headquartered in Sangmalima, South Province, la République du Cameroun. These companies harvest timber in Meme, Mamfe, in the South West Province of Southern Cameroons, and on the logs is stamped Sangmalima. Consequently, royalty is paid to Sangmalima councils while nothing comes to the councils and to the people of Meme and Mamfe in Southern Cameroons. This means that the councils and populations affected are deprived even of the crumbs that fall from the master's table as stipulated by the law while their environment is being recklessly destroyed.

What should be understood here is that although la République du Cameroun embarked on the exploitation of Southern Cameroons since the birth of the loose federation in 1961, annexation gave the Yaoundé regime total political power over and control of the territory. This facilitated economic pillage and unbridled exploitation of the natural resources of the territory. Until 1972, the Federated State Government in Buea stood like an unwanted wall. But with annexation consequent upon dissolution of the federation, and abolition of the State Government in Buea, presidential decrees and ministerial orders dismantled the dismantleable and moved the moveable at the pleasure of the Francophone political power elite and the bourgeoisie who enjoyed total political patronage from the boss in France and the installed political agents in Yaoundé.

As European imperialism worked toward the discouragement of the emergence of African bourgeoisie or middle class, it has been the zeal of the Yaoundé establishment to make sure that the Francophones enjoy absolute monopoly and have an overriding cumulative advantage in all domains – the right to rule exclusively, to dominate numerically and control the commanding positions in the military, judiciary, civil service, business class, and academia, amongst others. This is necessary to strengthen the exploiter-exploited relationship, reducing the latter to abject misery and subservience. This explains the total denial of Southern Cameroonians' equal right to occupy some political posts that wield great influence and power and those strategic state public corporations that control great wealth, for example, SONARA, SNI and SNH, amongst others. It also makes explicit the concentration of higher institutions and professional schools in Yaoundé and Douala, la République du Cameroun, where the Francophone structure has been implemented. The total absence of industries in Southern Cameroons is a deliberate policy in consonance with the policy of assimilation, unbridled exploitation of and reduction of the territory into a cheap source of raw materials and labour.

With annexation, Southern Cameroons has become a peripheral territory of the French Province of la République du Cameroun. To foreclose the emergence of an indigenous bourgeoisie that may in future pose a threat to unbridled exploitation or that may team up with an emerging politically-conscious and nationalistic elite, and to fight back and liberate the Southern Cameroons, a new economic policy has been imposed in Southern Cameroons, every change being radical, too abrupt and allowing no room for debate and transition. In consequence of the assimilation policy, no change has ever been to protect the interests of Southern Cameroons.

At unification, the Produce Marketing Board, the Development Agency, CamBank, the Electricity Corporation and Santa Coffee Estate were viable economic ventures. Added to these were foreign and indigenous enterprises and companies such as UAC, John Holt, Nanga, Kilo, Neba Automobiles and Atabong, amongst others. With the closure of Victoria and Tiko ports and Tiko airport, and the transfer of the Produce Marketing Board from Victoria to Douala, foreign companies unable to meet with the new regulations, the Francophone rigidly-centralised bureaucracy and unbridled corruption folded. The closure of the ports and airport was bound to be economically catastrophic, for one business feeds the other. Despite their early start and proven competence, indigenous Southern Cameroons companies have found it hard to survive and compete favourably with their Francophone counterparts due to incomprehensible bureaucratic bottlenecks that fuel corruption, transforming it into the culture of the polity. These, coupled with heavy taxes on capital, many Southern Cameroonian businesses have deliberately been made to crumble.

With the transfer of the Produce Marketing Board and the confiscation of the huge stabilisation fund – an act designed to bring down the vibrant co-operative system – the emerging large scale farmers and the produce buyers that supported the small scale cocoa, coffee, banana and rubber growers declined.

In a young economy, easy access to information, loans from banks, government patronage and award of contracts are crucial to building up a strong bargaining base. Southern Cameroonians have been barred or grossly disadvantaged with regard to these. In the struggle to survive, some Southern Cameroonians believed that by totally embracing the Francophone culture and moving their business to la République du Cameroun territory, they could survive and progress; some individuals thought that through marriage they would be accepted as equals or be accorded a sense of belonging; others went all out to betray and deny their roots as Southern Cameroonians by changing their names in order to survive. Unfortunately whenever the chips were on the table, they discovered that they had been used cheaply to betray their own kind. Many have gone down in ignominy because, at the end, they were spurned away after having been used against their people.

Endnotes

1. Nfor, N. Nfor, The Southern Cameroons: The Truth of the Matter, Bamenda 2003, Annex 1, pp. 58-64.
2. Walter Rodney; How Europe Underdeveloped Africa, 141 Colder Shaw Road London W13, 1986, p.9
3. Ibid, p.11
4. Adebayo Adedeji, Towards a Dynamic African Economy; Selected Speeches and Lectures, 1975 – 1986, Franck Cass, 1989, p.97-8.
5. Colins Leys, Underdevelopment in Kenya: The Political Economy of neo-colonialism, University of California Press,

Berkeley and Los Angeles, 1975, p.8-9.

6. Walter Rodney, Op. Cit p. 22.

7. Tunyi Olagunju, Adele Jinadu & Sam Oyovbaire, Transition to Democracy in Nigeria, 1985 – 1993, Ibadan, 1993, pp1-2.

8. Amartya Sen, Development as Freedom, Oxford University Press, Oxford, 1999, p.8

9. Ndongko, W. A. Planning for Economic Development in a Federal State: The Case of Cameroon, 1960-1971, Weltforum Verlag, Munchen, 1975, p.144.

10. Ibid, p.133.

11. Fourth-Five Year Development Plan 1976-1981, Yaoundé, pp. 293-355. Nfor N. Nfor; Cameroon Reunification: Costs and Problems of National Integration, (MSC Thesis, ABU Zaria, 1980, unpublished) Table 18, p.184.

12. Albert W. Mukong (Ed), The case For The Southern Cameroons, CAMFECO, (USA), 1990, P.135

Chapter Four

Constitutionalisation of Annexation and Alien Rule

Theatre Operation: Conforming Colonial Treaties

The Yaoundé expansionist state – having disregarded the principle of international jurisprudence of *uti possidetis juris*[1] and the critical date[2] with impunity on one hand, and the AU Constitutive Act, Article 4(b) on the other hand – has designed a constitutional framework to seal the annexation and colonial occupation of Southern Cameroons, and in perpetuity imposes foreign domination and alien rule on the subjugated. With adequate falsification and distortion of the history of the two distinct Cameroons, the British Southern Cameroons question is presented to the international community as a minority issue, thus making it a trivial internal matter of the jurisdiction of Yaoundé. Post-World War I Versailles Peace Treaty and Anglo-French treaties that forever buried German Kamerun notwithstanding, Yaoundé advances the flimsy argument that Cameroon was one under German colonial rule.[3] The question which these agents of annexation avoid answering is: How did German Kamerun become French Cameroun to attain independence from France? To sustain the colonisation and occupation of the British Southern Cameroons and push on the minority thesis, la République du Cameroun has reduced the former to a tribe equated with any of the tribes within its inherited borders.

Our task in this chapter is to expose how the United Nations failed or how imperfect decolonisation in British Southern Cameroons facilitated annexation, colonisation and occupation, and how, to deceive and mislead the democratic world, la République du Cameroun has, as it is characteristic of a colonial power, imposed its Napoleonic/Gaullist Constitution and rule on this former UN Trust Territory administered by the UK for over four decades. The issue here is not whether it is a good constitution that could usher in good governance or not; the issue is about which instrument of international law grants la République du Cameroun political and legal sovereign rights over British Southern Cameroons.

Asked in another way, after attainment of independence on January 1, 1960, by what instrument of international law did la République du Cameroun's international boundary shift from the east of the Mungo River westward to include all of British Southern Cameroons, thus making la République du Cameroun share international maritime boundary with Nigeria?

Before we get into examining the constitutionalisation of annexation and alien rule, it is instructive to understand that the so-called federal union of two states equal in status of 1961-1972 was an illusion. As can be deduced from la République du Cameroun's hidden agenda that has been executed with impunity and characteristic expertise of the devil, the Federal Republic of 1961-1972 was a transitional period used by Yaoundé to placate British Southern Cameroons and deceive the democratic world that the United Nations envisaged the federal union of two states equal in status between British Southern Cameroons, and la République du Cameroun was implemented according to the expressed will of the people.

The failure of the United Nations to implement its Resolution 1608 of April 21, 1961— the only definitive action that would have given birth to the Federal Union, if the negotiations went to the satisfaction of the two founding partners, namely, British Southern Cameroons, and la République du Cameroun — meant that no Federal Union was formed. The United Nations' vault face action declared the result of the plebiscite null and void, for it was only a forerunner and never in itself an instrument for a Federal Union of two former UN Trust territories.

It must be stated, without mincing words, that the UN, by abandoning mid-stream what it set out to accomplish — namely, independence by joining its two former trust territories — made it possible for la République du Cameroun to walk in like a wolf through the back door and impose its will on defenceless British

Southern Cameroons. This was achieved without the UN and the United Kingdom raising a finger as Administering Authority, and la République du Cameroun embarked on building its desired bilingual French Cameroun state through intrigues, corruption, fraud and the barrel of the gun.

Determined to sustain annexation and make it a right of la République du Cameroun, the Yaoundé expansionist regime has, as it suits its whims and caprices, adopted a constitutional framework aimed at erasing the lingering memories of the British Southern Cameroons state. After destroying all British Southern Cameroonian institutions of statehood, and balkanising the territory into two provinces of la République du Cameroun ruled by its appointed proconsuls who owe no allegiance to the people, decentralisation in the 1996 constitution is presented as cold water to quench the inferno rising against annexation and foreign domination in British Southern Cameroonians.

As declared in the Ahidjo-amended Constitution, the Federal Republic of Cameroon was "formed as from 1st October 1961, of the Territory of the Republic of Cameroon, henceforth called East Cameroon, and the Territory of the Southern Cameroons henceforth called West Cameroon."[4] Each of the partners in the UN-envisaged Federal Union was to come in with its distinct territory, legal, political, administrative, educational system and cultural values as inherited at independence from their respective colonial masters. From 1961 to 1972, while West Cameroon (Southern Cameroons) maintained parliamentary system, bicameral parliament, the rule of law, multi-party democracy, human and press freedom, for example, East Cameroon (la République du Cameroun) functioned under a rigid centralised system. La République du Cameroun was a one-party state. With opposition effectively decapitated by the repressive regime aided by French troops, the remnants were either underground, on exile, or in the numerous torture chambers. It was against this background that British Southern Cameroons, enjoying constitutional democracy, went into a non-implemented UN-sponsored Federal Union, indeed a co-habitation with a feudal state.

Such a falsely conceived union, from day one, looked like a stage set for a dialogue between a hungry lion, anxious for a meal, and a healthy lamb anxious for a better future. The UN-envisaged Federal Union between British Southern Cameroons and la République du Cameroun was a union of incompatibles and its dismal failure was imminent. But we know that any union between distinct peoples and nation states is a free association of equals in which none gives away its inherent identity, its territory, people, its cultural values, history and inherent right to exist. Above all, for such a union to be legal, it must conform to international norms and principles, and partners do not forfeit their right to exist through withdrawal if not satisfied with the union or mutual dissolution of the union by the founding partners when deemed beneficial to so do.

The 1996 Constitution:

Since 1961, Yaoundé has imposed three constitutions on British Southern Cameroons. While the Constitutions of 1961 and 1972 were crafted to superficially placate Southern Cameroonians and the world with a semblance of 'union', the philosophy that informed its drafting and the practical execution of governmental policies left no one in doubt as to the fact that the mission of Yaoundé was to wipe out the identity of British Southern Cameroons. The success of Yaoundé's repressive policies encouraged the expansionist regime to conceive a legal instrument that will seal the fate of British Southern Cameroons – which has been reduced to being an integral part of la République du Cameroun. And to fight against the clamour for self-determination and the restoration of the statehood and sovereign independence of British Southern Cameroons, Southern Cameroonians are in the 1996 Constitution placated with decentralisation.

To mislead and placate gullible Southern Cameroonians co-opted into the Government of la République du Cameroun, the Constitution talks loosely of decentralisation, which is presented here to counter the British Southern Cameroons legitimate cry for freedom and justice. The purpose of decentralisation is to give legal meaning to the political slogan of 'Cameroon is one and indivisible', and to make real the annexation, colonial occupation of British Southern Cameroons and assimilation of British Southern Cameroonians. This is to make concrete Pierre Mesmer's conclusion that the Foumban Talks were for the annexation of British Southern Cameroons to create a bilingual Francophone African country. This will equally justify the presentation of Southern Cameroonians called Anglophones as one of the tribes of la République du Cameroun, thus their agitation becomes a minority issue and subject of the state's domestic laws. To better understand the analysis of the 1996 Constitution below, it is necessary that we understand what decentralisation is.

Briefly speaking, decentralisation is a concept that is used to demonstrate how power and authority are organised and implemented in a nation. In a unitary state, in which the units, whatever may be the term used for, are subordinate to the central government, these subordinate units exercise delegated powers. Awa maintains that "…the term decentralisation implies the existence of a primary centre in a political system and there are units which are clearly subordinated to this centre. That is the central government possesses inherent authority, but devolves some power on the units as a means of facilitating the administration of the country. A decentralised government is, strictly speaking, a unitary government."[6] The pertinent point to be understood is that the central government uses its discretion to devolve power to the units when it wants, and can at any time curtail or withdraw the powers so devolved. The units, and those appointed, exercise delegated powers at the pleasure of the boss to whom they owe all allegiance. Those in authority in the units are not elected by the inhabitants nor are they accountable to those they rule; it is their loyalty to the boss at the centre that qualifies them for appointment. Such a system is highly corrupt and undemocratic, and underdevelopment is its hallmark for the leaders are insensitive to the legitimate aspirations of the people they rule.

Decentralisation, as applied here, is called into play to counter the British Southern Cameroons struggle for peaceful separation, freedom, justice and independence which Yaoundé found difficult to nip in the bud. It is a euphemism for annexation and a comforting deception for colonisation and alien rule. Those who see decentralisation as a panacea to Southern Cameroons legitimate struggle and inalienable right to national self-determination may want to ask the following questions: Why did Yaoundé abolish the non-implemented UN-envisioned Federal Union only to turn round and impose another Constitution proposing decentralisation and creation of Regions? Which territory is being decentralised? How did British Southern Cameroons, a distinct state from la République du Cameroun, become part of the latter that falls under the legal instrument of decentralisation? And, in whose interest is this political and legal agenda?

To answer these questions amongst others, we have to turn to the '*Constitution de la République du Cameroun*' or the Constitution of the Republic of Cameroon.

However, before attempting to find answers to these questions, it is instructive to review, albeit briefly, the debate and agitation in the early 1990s about a democratic constitution that should genuinely reflect the aspirations of the two peoples and two nations. The debate for a new Constitution was forced upon the dictatorial establishment by the struggle for the reintroduction of multiparty democracy, the rule of law, human freedom and freedom of the press, good governance, and justice for all the peoples by British Southern Cameroonians suffocating under the CPDM autocracy. The lack of these values, guaranteeing the good health of the state, gave birth to many other vices, and the two Cameroons forcefully held, was choking under the firm grip and the misrule of an ethnic oligarchy namely, the Beti clan.

During the debates, Southern Cameroonian leaders including J. N. Foncha, S. T. Muna, Cardinal C. Tumi, Rev. Awasum, and leaders of legalised political parties such as Mola Njoh Litumbe and Ni John Fru Ndi, whose party, the Social Democratic Front (SDF) was the largest, all opted for a federal system. At the Tripartite Talks of November 1991, J. N. Foncha, the Southern Cameroons political leader whose party, the Kamerun National Democratic Party (KNDP), won the vote for negotiated Federal Union of the two Cameroons – British Southern Cameroons and la République du Cameroun – insisted on return to the UN sponsored two states federation of equal status. This position was largely supported by British Southern Cameroonians. Advocates of federalism were not just Southern Cameroonians. Some Francophone, especially the older generation of politicians turned business magnet such as Soppo Priso and Prince Manga Bell, strongly supported Foncha's position. To block such an anti-status quo debate, President Paul Biya closed the Tripartite Talks and used his presidential prerogatives to create a Technical Committee with his kinsman, Joseph Owona as Chairman, to draft a new Constitution. In the Technical Committee of eleven, the four Southern Cameroonians, Barrister Sam Ekontang Elad, Benjamine Itoe, Dr Simon Munzu, and Dr Carlson Anyangwe from different political parties, including the CPDM, strongly advocated the restoration of the 1961 federal system, albeit with necessary modifications. Since their anti-status quo position could not be entertained, they walked out, and this necessitated the holding of the Buea All-Anglophone Conference (AAC) of April 1993 to consult the people and enable Southern Cameroonians to adopt a common position in defence of their identity, legitimate aspirations and destiny. The Buea conference was attended by more than 5000 people from all walks of life. The outcome, in addition to the Buea Declaration, was a draft of the Federal Constitution translated into French to be easily understood by the Francophone leaders and people. Copies were sent to President Paul Biya and Professor Joseph Owona, the head of the Technical Committee. None paid attention to the cherished position of Southern Cameroonians; they were, as ever before, simply ignored with impunity that ended the appeal by the people for meaningful dialogue for harmonious co-existence.

In January 1996 President Paul Biya, like his predecessor Ahidjo, under the pretext of amending the 1972 Constitution, imposed an entirely new one. As it will be seen in the analyses, the *'raison d'être'* was/is the constitutionalisation of annexation, foreign domination and alien rule of British Southern Cameroons. It should be pointed out that the withdrawal of Southern Cameroonian representatives from the Biya convened constitutional talks in Yaoundé meant nothing. In no way did it prevent the expansionist regime from imposing another undemocratic constitution on the Southern Cameroonian people. Like the 1961 and 1972 Constitutions, the 1996 is yet another one crafted without the participation of Southern Cameroonians and imposed on the people and nation annexed and subjugated to alien rule. What must be understood here about the Southern Cameroonian people is that no matter the depth of the cup of endurance, it must overflow when the time is up or when the right moment comes. On the other hand, green bananas put in a fridge will not complain of the extreme coldness; the bananas will still get ripe and turn yellow when the time comes.

Before we examine the 1996 Constitution in greater detail, it is of prime importance that we turn to the annexation law of 1st September 1961, termed the Federal Constitution. The annexation law dubbed the Constitution of the Federal Republic of Cameroon – was proclaimed and imposed on British Southern Cameroons on 1st September 1961, one month to termination of trusteeship, on 1st October 1961. This was the Constitution of la République du Cameroun that was amended and debated exclusively by la République National Assembly and signed into law by its Head of State, Ahidjo who upon this amended text proclaimed himself President of the yet-to-be Federal Republic of Cameroon. Neither the Southern Cameroons Parliament nor the Head of State – who was at the time, the Representative of HM the Queen, Commissioner J. O. Field – had a hand in this constitutional affair.

Article 59 clearly states: "The present provision by which the Constitution of the Republic adopted on 21st February 1960 by the Cameroonian People is revised, shall enter into force on the 1st of October 1961. The revised Constitution shall be published in French and English, the French text being authentic."

What needs be understood is that the 1960 Constitution of la République du Cameroun was drafted by French experts in conformity with *'la mission de la civilisation Française'* which established the foundation for the French community, instrumental for the implementation of Gaullism – opposed to independence of French colonies and trust territories.

Article 77 states: "In the Community established by the present constitution the states, (overseas territories) enjoy autonomy, they administer themselves and manage their own affairs freely and democratically. There is in the Community only one citizenship. All citizens are equal before the law. Whatever their origin, race or religion they have the same duties."

The French Community, which only Sekou Toure's Guinea voted against, had overriding powers over all overseas territories. These powers – as enshrined in Article 78 of the French Fifth République – included foreign policy, defence (*'mission militaire française'*), currency, common economical and financial policy concerning strategic raw materials, higher education, and supervision of justice including external transport and telecommunication.

To hold the rising tide of the UPC anti-colonial rule in French Cameroun, France on January 1st 1960 had to grant *indépendance avec la France* to the UN Trust Territory of French Cameroun, and it was done in keeping with the philosophy of French community. It was a mere change of name, but the soul and spirit were still intact. This covert change of attitude equally applied to other French dependencies in Africa. Consequently, the leaders who emerged as the successors to the imperial thrones were those groomed within the French National Assembly – people tried, tested and found to be true disciples and defenders of French imperial interest. These were to serve as mere CEOs in the new independent states.

In this context, French letter and spirit applied the prescription of Nicola Machiavelli who in his famous book, *The Prince,* states three ways of establishing firm grip over acquired territories, namely: despoiling the territory; having your population inhabit the territory; and creating a government of die-hard faithful and loyalists who depending on you for survival will forever do your bidding. Thus, while there was Ahidjo in French Cameroun, there was Houphouët-Boigny in Ivory Coast, and Sédar Senghor in

Senegal, all having played important roles within the French National Assembly and Government. In contrast to the British who, through legislative assemblies in the respective colonies and trust territories and constitutional conferences evolved to independence, the French, who never countenanced the granting of independence never had time for such luxuries of adopting constitutions and holding elections before *indépendance avec la France*; they had prepared successors who depended on Paris rather than the people of their respective territories.

As the French supported Ahidjo against the UPC, they also supported him against the British Southern Cameroons' legitimate ambition for equal standing in a Federal Union of two states equal in status. To transplant their imperial philosophy into Southern Cameroons, nurtured under liberal political philosophy, they first made sure that the UNGA Resolution 1608 of April 21, 1961 was not implemented, thus paving the way for a bloodless annexation and assimilation. Secondly, Ahidjo enacted his annexation law under the guise of a Federal Constitution and in Article 59 by declaring the French text authentic, confining interpretation to the real authority and owner of the estate, namely, France. Southern Cameroonians unknowingly, were led like lamb into a slaughter house.

As absolute and excessive force was used to bring down the UPC, so was it equally used against British Southern Cameroons right after the declaration of the annexation law. While the annexation law was meant to cast a spell over the Southern Cameroonian people and the international community, and give annexation a semblance of legality, an army of occupation – the *'gendarmerie'* and the police with a special squad and spy network – was ready to institutionalise what had been existing in French Cameroun in this newly acquired territory. To make it convenient, the existing state of emergency was extended to cover four of the six divisions of British Southern Cameroons. Thus, Buea, the national capital and all the important towns of Victoria, Tiko, Kumba and Bamenda, amongst others, were declared zones in the state of emergency, and in Kumba and Bamenda, concentration camps of Brigade Mobile Mixtes (BMM) were quickly established.

What is spectacular about the 1996 Constitution is not only that it was crafted discretely like the 1961 and 1972 Ahidjo constitutions without Southern Cameroons' participation, but it was also crafted in the logic of the scheme hatched to expand French interest in West Africa and to transform British Southern Cameroons into an appendage and colony of France's overseas territory of French Cameroun. Thus, while the 1972-imposed constitution put an end to autonomy and gave an open cheque to French multinational oil companies like others already in place to control the black gold and other vital minerals in British Southern Cameroons, the 1996 Constitution has as its mission to nip in the bud the rising tide of Southern Cameroons nationalism and the legal and legitimate quest to restore the statehood and sovereignty of British Southern Cameroons within its international boundaries defined by treaties and under the UN Charter. It does not recognise the distinct identity of British Southern Cameroons nor does it protect the interest of the people.

This dictatorial instrument talks loosely of regional and local authorities. In Article 55(2), it is stated that the regional and local authorities are "public law corporate bodies" which "shall have administrative and financial autonomy in the management of regional and local interest. They shall be freely administered by councils elected under conditions laid down by law."

To constitutionally demonstrate the powerlessness of the Regions and that they are mere outfits of the Yaoundé kleptomaniac regime, the authoritarian instrument leaves no one in doubt. It declares:

(a) "The State shall exercise supervisory powers over regional and local authorities under conditions laid down by law" (Article 55(3)).

(b) "The organisation, functioning and financial regulations of regional and local authorities shall be defined by law" (Article 55(5)).

(c) "The rules and regulations governing councils shall be defined by law" (Article 55(6)).

To make it clear that although the Regions shall elect their representatives to regional and local councils, they have no constitutional powers to initiate and execute anything in the interest of the people and region. Article 56 states:

(a) "The State shall transfer to Regions, under conditions laid down by law, jurisdiction in areas necessary for their economic, social, health, educational, cultural and sports development.

(b) The law shall define; the sharing of powers between the State and Regions in the areas of competence so transferred.

(c) The resources of the Regions.

(d) The land and property of each Region."

Mr Biya's decentralisation is a comforting deception. The so-called Regions, like paper tigers, are huge elephants on the limbs of mosquitoes. Although each region has as its head a President elected from amongst its member councillors, they are all under the heavy hand of the Yaoundé presidential appointee.

Having made his Beti tribe the ruling clan or the super tribe, Mr Biya raises tribalism to a national ethic and religion as his authoritarian instrument: "The Regional Council shall be headed by an indigene of the Region ..." (Article 57(3)). But who is an indigene and what is the criterion for distinguishing an indigene? Why should the constitution insist that the President of the Regional Council must be an indigene while giving unlimited powers to the State President to appoint an all-powerful delegate to the region who is a stranger or non-indigene but with wide constitutional powers? It is however most instructive that the President's appointee is not accountable to the Regional Council. To prove, beyond any reasonable doubt that the President's appointee is the final authority in the Region, Article 58(1) states that he, the delegate, is "responsible for national interests, administrative controls, ensuring compliance with the laws and regulations, as well as maintaining law and order. He shall, under the authority of the Government, supervise and co-ordinate civil state services in the Region."

Although the Regional Council, its President and its Bureau have a mandate for five years, each could be suspended, dissolved or dismissed by the President of the Republic at any time. Article 59(1) states: "The Regional Council may be suspended by the President of the Republic where such organ;

(a) carries out activities contrary to the Constitution;

(b) undermines the security of the State or public law and order;

(c) endangers the State's territorial integrity."

As if these are not bad enough, it concludes: "The other cases of suspension shall be laid down by law."

In case of dissolution of the Regional Council (Article 59(2)) or dismissal of the Regional President by the President of the Republic (Article 60(2)), "automatic replacement shall be decided by the President of the Republic." And he does this without consulting anybody. If, in conformity with the constitution, the people of the region elect their Regional Council – which could be dissolved – and a President – who could be dismissed – does this not mean that the President of the Republic is above the Constitution and more powerful than the people? How can the Constitution, which is supposed to be the enabling law and supreme instrument for good governance, be sublimated to the whims and caprices of one person? Through this clause, the supreme law empowers the Presidential Monarch, who rules and reigns to bring an end to democracy, to reduce the people to consent to his will, and to mock good governance, responsible government and the rule of law.

What Southern Cameroonians have come to learn is that the Yaoundé dictatorial regime, over the years, has perfected a system under which a law is made to suit just the face and built of the victim, who prior to adopting the law, had already been pronounced guilty by the powerful. That is to say that one is not guilty for violating the tenets of a law; the powers that exist for self-perpetuation make one guilty, and the law confirms this so that the agents punish or eliminate the declared victim. This was the situation under colonial rule and it was well-perfected in apartheid South Africa. This is how non-white South Africans were easily excluded from political and economic power. This has been the lot of Southern Cameroonians since annexation and colonial occupation.

Evil, like an infant, grows once it is well nourished. Yaoundé, over the years, has tactfully and systematically reduced Southern Cameroonians to being subservient, second class citizens, and the Southern Cameroons nation, to a colonial appendage of la République du Cameroun. The mission of this "terrorist document" to quote Dr Tata Mentan, is to destroy from the subconscious of Southern Cameroonians the memories of the state of British Southern Cameroons. Consequently, this authoritarian instrument was conceived, designed and imposed to silence the clamour for the restoration of the statehood of British Southern Cameroons as defined and delimited by the colonial treaties.

To bury the distinct identity of the state of British Southern Cameroons, no reference is made in the whole text to the so-called 'unification of the two Cameroons', namely, la République du Cameroun and British Southern Cameroons. To further distort history and to conceal the truth, nothing is said of political, cultural, linguistic and juridical diversity – the dualistic Anglo-Saxon (Southern Cameroons) and Francophone (la République du Cameroun) heritage.

In the Preamble of this 1996 Constitution, it is declared:

> *"We, the people of Cameroon,*
> *Proud of our linguistic and cultural diversity; an enriching feature of our national identity ...*
> *Solemnly declare that we constitute one and the same Nation, bound by the same destiny ...*
> *Jealous of our hard-won independence and resolved to preserve same ..."*

This declaration is aimed at strengthening the false notion of one Cameroun that gained independence as one politically and legally recognised territory. Its purpose is to consolidate and seal the annexation of British Southern Cameroons and facilitate the assimilation of Southern Cameroonians to create the bilingual Francophone Cameroun nation. Right from 1961, bilingualism was not meant to be a historical inherent reality of two nations and two peoples distinct in colonial heritage, but a gift from a benevolent despot in Yaoundé. This is why bilingualism is synonymous with the frenchifying of Southern Cameroonians, and the educational system has become the logical instrument of the means to an end, namely, the assimilation of English-speaking (Southern) Cameroonians into the Francophone Cameroonians' culture where the two European languages – English and French – are spoken. Hidden in the philosophy of assimilation or in the process of frenchifying is, that la République du Cameroun – being a Francophone African country, for its international prestige – has adopted bilingualism. While the educational system has been the means to an end, the administrative system and the civil services have been the instruments of enforcing assimilation and consequently, French has become the language of command and authority: it has, for instance, been made compulsory in all Southern Cameroons schools and for any writing public examination; moreover, sign boards in the whole of Southern Cameroons are in French. The opposite has not been enforced, however, where, in Francophone la République territory or in Yaoundé, sign boards are not written in English. There is no law which makes bilingualism compulsory. This explains why texts for public examinations and from the Presidency come out only in French with translations sometimes made much later. As for sign boards, when the effort is made, the script emphasises the subordinate status of English and the translation is often defective. To crown it all, bank notes and payslips are only in French. Where then is the so-called bilingualism, when more than 95% of administrators in Southern Cameroons are Francophone, and a large part of administrative letters, circulars and notices are sent out in French?

To enforce it in administration, the Napoleonic administrative prefectural system has been imposed, and Francophones have been appointed to take charge. As for the military and police, even in the training schools, instruction manuals and imported equipment in English are translated into French (the authentic language according to Article 59 of the 1961 Constitution) even before being given out to the students. While Southern Cameroonians (Anglophone) military and police recruits are compelled to speak and answer questions only in French beginning their first day of training and throughout their life in service, Francophones do not face such a rule. Speaking English within the camp is tantamount to subversive behaviour. Having successfully and systematically moved so far, they believe annexation and assimilation have been sealed constitutionally.

This 1996 Constitution transforms the existing 10 provinces into the Regions of the Republic, as explained in Article 61(I). And in Article 61(2), it is stated: "The President of the Republic may, as and when necessary;

(a) Change the names and modify the geographical boundaries of the Regions listed in paragraph (I) above,

(b) Create other regions. In this case, he shall give them names and fix their geographical boundaries."

While this Constitution – called for through the greed of expansionism – serves to consolidate and seal the annexation of Southern Cameroons, its Articles 61 and 62 provide the instrument and strategy for the total blotting out of the distinct territory of Southern Cameroons. The President of the Republic has the powers to create new Regions and fix their geographical boundaries without the knowledge and consent of the communities so affected. Obviously, this, as it has been, will be done by presidential decree.

This can be traced back to Article 62 (2): "Without prejudice to the provisions of this Part, the law may take into consideration the specificity of certain Regions with regard to their organisation and functioning." What is meant by the "specificity of certain Regions" that will require special attention? In whose interest will this be done? Who determines the "specificity"? How are these particular Regions determined?

Memories of widely circulated rumours of efforts by the Yaoundé regime to create bilingual provinces in which parts of Southern Cameroons merged with la République du Cameroun territory are still very fresh in the minds of Southern Cameroonians. The Government has never dismissed these, which have often been met with open protests in varied ways by Southern Cameroonians who have termed these rumours as government-designed fillers sent out to measure the true feeling of Southern Cameroonians and possible reaction. To implement this diabolical design, it has now been given constitutional backing.

It is disturbing and incredible that Southern Cameroonians – whose leaders were involved in constitutional development when their country, under the trusteeship (colonial) era, was administered as part of Nigeria – have, since 1961, become perpetual subjects of imposed constitutions. Administered by the UK with the help of Nigeria for convenience, their distinct status was fully recognised, respected and defended. Southern Cameroons was a territorial and demographic minority within the Nigerian Federation, but constitutionally, its rights as a distinct territory and people under international law was respected and protected. This explains why Nigeria did not oppose UN resolution to separate British Southern Cameroons before Nigerian Independence in 1960. Nigeria supported the holding of the UN plebiscite, and did not use force to block Southern Cameroonians from expressing their inalienable right to self- determination. When the plebiscite result was endorsed by the UN, Nigeria demonstrated its readiness to cooperate in building a free world based on justice and equality by voting for the independence of Southern Cameroons. Nigeria also voted for UN Resolution 1608, for Southern Cameroons to freely form a Federal Union of two states equal in status to la République du Cameroun. But unlike Nigeria, la République du Cameroun opposed this resolution, and with France and other Francophone African nations, except Mali, walked out during the voting process for Southern Cameroons' independence. And again, this colonial bloc, except Mali, voted against UNGA Resolution 1608, to protect the legal and legitimate interests and identity of British Southern Cameroons within the UN-envisioned Federal Union. This vote against UNGA Resolution 1608 amounted to a rejection of the Federal Union.

With hindsight, the 1961 constitution, dubbed Federal Constitution, was la République du Cameroun's Constitution of February 1960, which Ahidjo amended, and in which were inserted a few clauses to placate Southern Cameroonians and mislead the world. Though some kind of constitutional talks were held in Foumban in July 1961, the meeting adjourned to be reconvened in thirty days' time – which never happened. The Foumban constitutional talks were not the UN-envisioned post-plebiscite conference as per UNGA Resolution 1608. Thus, the amendment of la République du Cameroun's Constitution was done without the knowledge of, and the adoption by, the Southern Cameroons Parliament in Buea. Without regard for the interest of the Southern Cameroonian government and people, Ahidjo promulgated his amended text on September 1, 1961, one month before the UN-prescribed date of October 1, for the termination of UN Trusteeship in British Southern Cameroons and for the formation of the Federal Union between the two distinct Cameroons. If this is not constitutional fraud, how is it that Ahidjo made himself federal president and promulgated the Federal Constitution of a federal united republic that was yet to exist? This annexation instrument was promulgated when Southern Cameroons was still a UN Trust and with HM the Queen's representative still in Buea as the Head of State.

As explained above, the formation of a Federal Union between two distinct nations and peoples was firstly a UN project to be negotiated and agreed upon under UN supervision and implementation. Secondly, it required consensus which could only happen if the supreme interest of each partner was guaranteed. Thirdly, this UN-envisioned Federal Union of two equal partners was never to be a territorial union, but an inter-parliamentary union as only eight subjects were ascribed to the Federal Government while the bulk of governmental responsibilities were the exclusive prerogatives of the states.

Given that the UN-envisioned Federal Union of its two ex-Trust territories was never legally achieved – a consequence of the non-implementation of UNGA Resolution 1608 – it is erroneous to hold that a union was formed. Its implementation, as inscribed in the UN Resolution, would have produced a Constitution for the Federal United Cameroon Republic, which should have been subjected to scrutiny and ratification by the respective parliaments of the two partners before it would have become the enabling law of the new nation. Additionally, and equally important, a union treaty should have been adopted and co-signed by J.N. Foncha for British Southern Cameroons and Ahidjo for la République du Cameroun. This union treaty, which should have protected the respective identities of the partners and their rights to freely withdraw from the union if not satisfied, would have been registered at the UN General Secretariat in conformity with Article 102(1) of the UN Charter. That no union was formed is attested to by the non-existence of a union treaty deposited with and published by the UN Secretariat.

The failure of the UN to implement Resolution 1608 – worsened with the pull out of British administrators and forces – gave la République du Cameroun the leeway to annex a UN Trust Territory that had no army of its own, by imposing its amended Constitution, the Federal Constitution. No one better explains what happened in 1961 than the representative of the French Government in Yaoundé, the Haut Commissaire, Son Excellence Pierre Mesmer, whose duty it was to ensure the extension of French neo-colonial influence in West Africa. In his book, *Les Blancs s'en Vont: Récit de Décolonisation*, written upon his leaving Cameroun, he confidently states:

> "*En exécution du référendum, une conférence constitutionnelle réunit les gouvernements à Foumban, en pays Bamoum, familier aux deux délégations, le 17 Juillet 1961. Le Président Ahmadou Ahidjo, en position de force, présenta un projet de constitution faussement fédéral, soigneusement*

préparé par ses juristes français. Ngu Foncha n'avait aucun contre-projet. En position de faiblesse puisque la population qu'il représentait ne dépassait par le quart de celle du Cameroun français et moins encore en terme économique, il acceptait sans discuter ce qui était, sauf en apparence, une annexation. La nouvelle constitution entra en vaquent le 1er Octobre 1961. Une plaisanterie circulait alors à Douala et à Yaoundé: 'Le Cameroun réunifié est un pays bilingue francophone'".

Translation: "In implementation of the referendum, a constitutional conference brought together the governments in Foumban, in Bamoum country, known to both delegations, on 17 July 1961. The President Ahmadou Ahidjo, in power, presented a deceitful draft Federal Constitution, carefully prepared by his French lawyers. Ngu Foncha had no counter-draft. Being in a weaker position, since the population that he represented did not exceed quarter that of French Cameroun and even less in economic terms, he accepted without question what was, except in appearance, an annexation. The new constitution came about on 1 October 1961. A joke was rife in Douala and Yaoundé: 'Cameroon is a reunified Francophone bilingual country'."[6]

Like any colonial authority, Pierre Mesmer is here trying to justify the annexation of Southern Cameroons by la République du Cameroun. Foumban was only an excuse in the execution of the hidden agenda which la République du Cameroun, with the help of France, had adopted upon international colonial conspiracy against the UN Trust Territory of British Southern Cameroons.

It should be noted that although the plebiscite was a UN plan, la République du Cameroun here claims the political and legal authority to implement its results. In all good conscience, how can a partner in an UN-envisioned Federal Union, claim sole right over implementation? La République du Cameroun was neither a partner nor a participant in the UN plebiscite. It was a matter between the UN and Southern Cameroons. In this inter-party dialogue, answers to the UN plebiscite questions were given directly to the UN, which had the duty to interpret and implement its outcome. It is the UN alone that has jurisdiction in matters of decolonisation as per the UN Charter and UNGA resolutions.

The plebiscite in itself was not an instrument for the formation of the Federal Union. It was an opportunity, albeit imposed, to eliminate or to choose one partner in favour of another. It was an invitation to negotiate. By design, it was a UN plan and could not be implemented by any nation, no matter how powerful. Foumban could never have been a substitute to the holding of the UN-approved post-plebiscite conference by the designated governments as spelt out in UNGA Resolution 1608 of April 21, 1961. With annexation achieved without the UN and UK raising a finger, la République du Cameroun set in motion a gradual and systematic process of occupation, colonisation and imposition of alien rule, making Southern Cameroons disappear from the map of Africa

Yaoundé faithfully and tactfully executed its hidden agenda for the annexation, colonisation and occupation of British Southern Cameroons. When the time for the next major action was ripe, in 1972, Ahidjo discretely brought in his French constitutional experts to strengthen his arm with legal documentation. When, in May, he stunned the lame-legged Parliament of the Federal Republic of Cameroon with "*J'ai décidé*" ("I have decided"), the document drafted by his French experts was handy and his subjects – who had been disempowered and disenfranchised under the one-party rule – were told to go and vote 'yes' or '*oui*' for a unitary state. Southern Cameroonians who expressed their opposition to it were bundled into various detention camps, for no one had the right to campaign against the Presidential Monarch who ruled and reigned absolutely under the one party system. The President who, in 1970 – in taking the oath of office for a new mandate – swore to uphold and defend the Federal Constitution, overthrew it instead. Of course, in a dictatorship, the constitution is mere paperwork or parchment; what counts is the will of the dictator. Consequently, in a dictatorship, all institutions and organs of government – as defined by the Constitution and the laws – exist at the convenience of the dictator, who alone incarnates the state.

The 1972 Constitution was informed by the ambition of the Presidential Monarch as with the (current) 1996 Constitution. Thus, constitutional evolution since 1961 has not been a reflection of the legitimate aspirations of the will of the people; it has been the expressed ambition of the President for the enhancement of his absolute powers. While the 1961 Constitution enhanced the President's powers, it also increased and extended demographically and spatially; that of 1972 declared British Southern Cameroons a colony and an appendage of Yaoundé. The mission of the 1996 Constitution is, simply put, to remove all traces of a distinct British Southern Cameroons nation that ever existed. The supreme law here declares the one and indivisible Cameroun Republic, a neo-colony of France. The imposed 1996 Constitution is the legal instrument to fight the right to self-determination and restoration of British Southern Cameroons statehood by Southern Cameroonians under the canopy of the Southern Cameroons National Council (SCNC), a non-violent liberation movement.

We therefore see that while in Nigeria, as a democracy, British Southern Cameroons – though spatially and demographically far smaller, was accorded full respect and protection as a territorial minority having been annexed, colonised and occupied by la République du Cameroun – has seized being a territorial minority. It is incredible that a people, who in 1954, was ruled by a democratically elected government that, as a partner in development, was sensitive to the legitimate aspirations of the people, is subjected to brutal alien rule in the third millennium, credited with ascendancy for the respect of fundamental human rights and freedoms.

Which national territory is being decentralised? Is it rational to imagine that Southern Cameroonians could have given away their distinct identity, system of administration, political system, the rule of law, judicial system, cherished cultural values, sound educational system good economic policies, freedom of speech and assembly in exchange for annexation, assimilation and dictatorial rule?

Is the notion of decentralisation – as it is preached – based on the French system of administration? If decentralisation is not a comforting deception to Southern Cameroonians, and while playing for time, sealed their fate since 1996, what evidence is there to prove that President Biya is interested in the welfare of Southern

Cameroonians? La République du Cameroun does not need decentralisation, and that is why their people are not clamouring for it. Like window dressing, decentralisation was put in the 1996 Constitution to divert the attention of Southern Cameroonians from their fundamental problem, namely, their inalienable right to self-determination and outright restoration of Southern Cameroons statehood and independence following the abysmal non-implementation of the UN experiment of independence by joining. The conception of amalgamation of two incompatible former Trust territories of British Southern Cameroons and la République du Cameroun, in an inter-parliamentary Federal Union of two states equal in status, and failing to implement the Resolution for that purpose, was a gross violation of the UN Charter. It was thus bound to crumble like the Tower of Babel.

The premise of decentralisation and the inherent weaknesses of the regional authorities render them irrelevant and meaningless in this era of democracy, and the clamour for good governance, effective separation of powers and devolution of powers for meaningful participatory democracy, accountability and transparency and the ascendancy of human freedom. All people want to participate in the decision-making process and in the governance of their society. The inherent weaknesses in the Cameroun brand of Napoleonic constitutionalism reduce the Regions to being mere colonial outposts echoing only the will of the central authority which is indeed, a one-man rule. That the Regions have no constitutional powers or defined areas of competence is proven by the fact that the issues should have been spelt out in organic law, or 'laid out by law'. And, from practice, we know the Cameroonian parliament functions like the choir of the Presidency, receiving bills from the latter, loyally dusting them up and faithfully sending back for promulgation by the Presidential Monarch who rules and reigns absolutely.

Another serious weakness of the Regions in this Constitution, as was the case with the 1961 Federal Constitution, is that there is no mention of funding or the Regions being constitutionally empowered to raise own revenue (Article 56). Everything is reduced to being 'laid down by law'. One of the greatest flaws of the 1961 Federal Constitution that kept the Federated State of West Cameroon (Southern Cameroons) on its knees until the demise in 1972 was the absence of revenue allocation in the Constitution. No tier of government can function and improve the living conditions of its citizenry without revenue. To keep the Federated State of West Cameroon impoverished, the central government took over all sources of revenue. This was done through the execution of the hidden agenda for the annexation and imposition of alien rule in British Southern Cameroons. Having annexed, colonised and occupied British Southern Cameroons, the expansionist Yaoundé state is determined to keep its colony, thus, the 1996 legal instrument.

Inherent Right Cannot be Lost:

It is pertinent to recall that until the two former UN Trust territories came together in a non-implemented UN-sponsored Federal Union or inter-parliamentary union, none was superior to the other. The two were distinct and equal in status under international law.

Firstly, each UN trust was subject to a trusteeship agreement with clearly defined boundaries. Each agreement was a treaty in itself. Though French Cameroun was larger than British Cameroons, they were equal in status and were registered under category "B" of the UN Trust Territories.

Secondly, the Anglo-French Boundary Treaty of January 1931 sealed the distinctiveness and equality of the two Cameroons.

Thirdly, each received UN Visiting Missions in its own right, the Missions serving as platform to lay out the wishes of the people's representatives, and to assess political, economic and socio-cultural development — a logical measure towards the attainment of self-government and independence, in conformity with Article 76 (b) of the UN Charter. From UN records, unification with French Cameroun was never priority; secession from Nigeria was always the key issue. Based on such reports presented at the Trusteeship

Council, the Administering Authority concerned was interrogated on the discharge of its obligations in conformity with the defined sacred trust.

Fourthly, UN instruments that declare the right to independence of dependent territories, for example, Article 76(b) of the UN Charter and Resolution 1514 of 1960, make no distinction as to size, economic development and/or potential; colonialism, in all its forms and manifestation, is vehemently condemned and declared illegal.

Southern Cameroons' association with the British colony of Nigeria for almost half a century accorded the former a lead in political development. In 1954, British Southern Cameroons attained self-governance, through election by Southern Cameroonians in their own rights, national consciousness, economic and socio-cultural development took greater strides. French Cameroun, like all other Francophone African colonies, was treated as an integral part of a multi-racial French state, with its own government and legislative house in Yaoundé since 1957. It is thus conclusive that by October 1961, when the two Cameroons came together in a supposed federal association, British Southern Cameroons, though smaller demographically and spatially, was better off in terms of having had a few more years of experience – with regard to the practice of democracy and modern governance – than la République du Cameroun.

Finally, in defending the right of each political entity in the UN-sponsored federal association, albeit unimplemented, the UN adopted Resolution 1608 of 21 April 1961 on the holding of a post-plebiscite conference in which the two partners were to attend as equals. Mindful of the trusteeship agreement, the UN approved a federal association of two states of EQUAL STATUS and christened the new nation, FEDERAL UNITED CAMEROON REPUBLIC through Article 76 of the UN Charter and Resolution 1514 of December 1960. The 4th Committee – as the political arm of the UN General Assembly on April 19, 1961 – deliberated and voted for British Southern Cameroons' independence, declaring October 1, 1961 as its Independence Day (see annex 11). It needs be pointed out that la République du Cameroun opposed the British Southern Cameroons independence and equal standing in the Federal Union. Faced with the ambiguity of independence by joining, the U. K. Government came to this conclusion:

> In order that people from the Southern Cameroons may achieve independence by joining the Republic of Cameroon, *it is necessary that the Federation should come into existence on mid-night of 1st October. At one and the same moment, there will be born the independent state of the Southern Cameroons and the Federation of the Federal United Cameroon Republic. The Federation would be a free association of independent and equal sovereign states* (British Declassified Documents). (Emphasis mine).

This explanation, given at the eleventh hour in confidential colonial records without taking judicious action to oversee the implementation of UNGA Resolution 1608, failed to nip in the bud the implementation of Ahidjo's hidden agenda. It was incumbent upon the UN to implement Resolution 1608 to take full responsibility in monitoring and ensuring that none of the parties violates the terms of the union, as would have been enshrined in the Union Treaty. Nevertheless, this failure does not nullify the inherent equality of the two former UN trust territories. However, this failure does not diminish British Southern Cameroons' right to self-determination, but it justifies and strengthens the people's legitimate struggle for national liberation and restoration. National self-determination is the eternal, inherent right of a subjugated people and nation recognised and defended by international law. This inherent right becomes a matter of urgency, the more the imperial claws and fangs are sunk deeper and deeper into the flesh and life blood of the subjugated every day of their life.

Simply put, British Southern Cameroons is a victim of annexation, colonial occupation, imposition of foreign domination and alien rule. Yaoundé, having declared Southern Cameroons an integral part of la République du Cameroun in gross violation of international law and colonial boundaries inherited at independence, becomes object of territorial dispute in international law. Consequently, it is a matter of international dimension which can only be resolved by the strict respect of international obligations governing boundaries inherited at independence. This is marked by la République du Cameroun – under international supervision – withdrawing its proconsuls and occupation forces stationed in British Southern Cameroons to its inherited borders upon attaining independence on January 1st 1960. La République du Cameroun is the successor state of le Cameroun Français.

It is in this light that the inalienable right of Southern Cameroonians to restore their statehood and sovereign independence should be understood and appreciated. As it can be deduced from the above analyses, Southern Cameroonians, although tricked, went into the UN-unimplemented federal association in total good faith and believing in the UN System, but were sacrificed and abandoned by both the UK and the UN. On the other hand, la République du Cameroun came in in bad faith, and armed with a hidden agenda, took advantage of UK's nonchalant attitude and vault face, exploited the UN's failure in implementing Resolution 1608 and the good faith of British Southern Cameroons. In 1972, with anti-constitutional tactics and force of arms, it abolished the loose federal association or co-habitation of two peoples and two nations, and annexed and occupied British Southern Cameroons – a crime in international law and a threat to world peace.

What Ahidjo did to British Southern Cameroons in 1972 has the same weight in international criminal law of foreign aggression of one state against another as what Emperor Haile Selassie did to Eritrea in 1962 or what Saddam Hussein did to Kuwait in 1989. While the rule of law in Ethiopia and Eritrea was allowed to deteriorate into a long bloody war of liberation struggle, consequent upon the East-West cold war politics that rendered the UN ineffective, it is gratifying to note that in 1990, the UN vehemently condemned Iraq for the annexation of Kuwait. Accordingly, the Gulf War which served to oust Iraq and restore Kuwait to its sovereignty by the combined forces of the USA, UK and other western nations was, with the full blessings of the UN for annexation, illegal and a threat to world peace and a crime against humanity.

The one billion dollar question is, why the annexation and brutal occupation of British Southern Cameroons by la République du Cameroun is being treated as an internal affair of la République du Cameroun. Had the UN not imposed independence by joining, and complicated it by failing to implement Resolution 1608, would la République du Cameroun have so easily annexed and occupied British Southern Cameroons? The UN meant Southern Cameroonians no ill in its envisaged experiment of a union of two states equal in status, and convincingly seeing that la République du Cameroun accepted the federal association as a ploy to annex British Southern Cameroons, should that not more than anything else prick the good conscience of the World Body to rise and defend its mission to humanity in general and Southern Cameroonians in particular as it did in Kuwait? The UN's culture of silence, in the face of the grave consequences which Southern Cameroonians have suffered since 1961, calls to question its commitment, capacity and political will to solve conflicts through preventive diplomacy.

Conclusion

It was consequent upon international colonial conspiracy against the inalienable right of Southern Cameroonians to sovereign independence as enshrined in the United Nations Charter and Resolution 1514 that the UN was manipulated to carry out independence by joining. As a step towards its accomplishment, the idea of a plebiscite was introduced, but was only a means to an end and never an end in itself. It was a process to enable Southern Cameroonians to eliminate or choose which of the two partner nations (Nigeria or la République du Cameroun) it would enjoy independence with. The plebiscite was therefore only an invitation to negotiation, and not an instrument for the implementation of the UN-envisaged experiment. This explains why, conscious of this legal implication, the UN itself went ahead to adopt Resolution 1608 on April 21, 1961 after the ratification of the plebiscite results and the vote for British Southern Cameroons' independence by the 4th Committee of the UN General Assembly.

Because the plebiscite was only an invitation to negotiate, it is undeniable that the UN's failure to implement Resolution 1608 – as a central and cardinal process for the formation of the envisioned Federal Union – means that the project was aborted by its architect. This explains why there is no treaty or instrument of union between British Southern Cameroons and la République du Cameroun registered with and published by the General Secretariat of the UN in conformity with Article 102 of the UN Charter. What gives la République du Cameroun legal title over British Southern Cameroons, which has now been reduced to two provinces and which are ruled by Francophone imposed proconsuls? Is this not evidence of annexation and colonial occupation? Does this not explain why British Southern Cameroons, as a distinct entity in international law, has disappeared from the map of Africa?

It is judicious to note the fact that la République du Cameroun with France and all Francophone African countries, except Mali, voted against forming a Federal Union with British Southern Cameroons. This explains why important UN resolutions were not implemented. Since la République du Cameroun voted against forming a Federal Union with British Southern Cameroons, why did the UN not cancel its experiment and grant independence in conformity with the UN Charter and UNGA Resolution 1514?

The Yaoundé expansionist regime has constitutionalised the annexation of British Southern Cameroons by placating the democratic world, especially the Commonwealth of Nations and its members with decentralisation and creation of so-called autonomous Regions. Accepting decentralisation, as opposed to the right to restore their statehood and sovereign independence, is tantamount to endorsing the annexation, colonisation and imposition of alien rule on British Southern Cameroons by la République du Cameroun.

No instrument recognised by international law gives la

République du Cameroun right to rule over the former UN Trust Territory of British Southern Cameroons. La République du Cameroun, by breaking international law, is a colonial power in Southern Cameroons. In nursing the ambition to colonise Southern Cameroons, la République du Cameroun's Foreign Minister, Charles Okala, opposed the vote regarding Southern Cameroons' independence. When he could not block it, and being supported by France and other French-speaking African States, he staged a walked out.[7] Consistent with their hidden agenda, la République du Cameroun and other French-speaking African countries voted against Resolution 1608.[8] Encouraged by the UN's failure to implement Resolution 1608 and UK's abrupt withdrawal of their colonial administrators and forces in the Trust Territory, la République du Cameroun's repressive forces walked in through the back door and occupied the undefended territory. Does the UK's behaviour amount to some tacit support?

La République du Cameroun is defending the merits of decentralisation as a strategy to cover up and divert international attention from its crime of annexing, colonising and imposing alien rule in the former UN Trust Territory of British Southern Cameroons. For anyone to support la République du Cameroun's decentralisation programme, they must firstly help show to the world by what internationally recognised legal instrument it (la République du Cameroun) rules British Southern Cameroons.

Men fought against slave trade and slavery not just because their masters executed the unfortunate victims at will, but because it was destructive to natural law, in the same way it is with colonialism. Colonialism is a crime against natural law. If human dignity and equality must be enjoyed by all as right – as defended by the UN Charter, the Universal Declaration of Human Rights, the African Charter on Human and Peoples' Rights and all other international organisations promoting human rights – colonialism, no matter by whom or how it is disguised, must be fought against and defeated at all cost by Man because it is modern slavery, a heinous crime against humanity.

The issue here is not about the mere ineffectiveness or the legal shortcomings of decentralisation as enshrined in Mr Biya's 1996 Constitution; it is not about good governance and development of Southern Cameroons and appointment of Southern Cameroonians into the Government of la République du Cameroun either. It is about the conspiracy to consolidate the annexation and colonisation of British Southern Cameroons. Southern Cameroonians, under the SCNC, are fighting the colonisation and occupation of their country by la République du Cameroun. Colonisation has never been reformed and should not be panel-beaten and refurbished to give it a superficial facelift in British Southern Cameroons. Even if the two Southern Cameroons provinces were given greater powers, decentralisation will never be a panacea to the struggle to decolonise and un-annex British Southern Cameroons from the crushing yoke of Napoleonic constitutionalism. As long as la République du Cameroun rules British Southern Cameroons through illegal acquisition, nothing can justify Yaoundé's imposition of its rule. Perfect decolonisation within the ambit of international law is restoring the statehood of British Southern Cameroons, and completes, under the UN Charter and Resolution 1514 of 1960, the decolonisation process by granting independence to and admitting British Southern Cameroons into the family of sovereign nations of the UN.

For the UN to condemn violation of the rights of the people of British Southern Cameroons to uphold and defend their right to self-determination, and to promote the equality of all nations and guarantee international co-operation as the foundation of world peace based on justice, it must lead its own house, namely, the former UN Trust Territory of British Southern Cameroons annexed, colonised and occupied by la République du Cameroun, another former UN Trust Territory. The UN must be fair. It must demonstrate beyond reasonable doubt that it is not an agency that allows the annexation and colonisation of smaller states by powerful, bigger states. It must insist on the respect of *uti possidetis juris*, the UN Charter and international law and obligations by all UN member nations. And, as for the British Southern Cameroons question, the UN should take necessary disposition to implement Article 76(b) of its Charter and Resolution 1514 of 1960 to achieve perfect decolonisation and admit this former UN Trust Territory into the committee of sovereign nations of the UN.

The liberation and restoration of the statehood of British Southern Cameroons will not only end annexation and colonial occupation which threatens peace and stability in West Africa, it will decolonise the Southern Cameroonian restoring its dignity, and while putting it on the path of progress, it will erase the bad memories and the scars of super power manipulation of the UN that resulted in botched decolonisation in British Southern Cameroons in 1961.

Endnotes

1. *Uti possidetis juris* is a principle of international jurisprudence that upholds the stability and immutability of territorial boundaries from the moment a colonial territory accedes to independence. By this principle, as defended by the ICJ, such territorial boundaries are inviolable. See Nfor N. Nfor, The Southern Cameroons: "The Truth of the Matter", T. Tam Printers, Bamenda, 2003, pp30 – 31.

2. Critical Date – This is a theory which holds that whatever was the situation or right of parties at the time regarded as the critical date, it remains unchanged. With reference to dates of independence it holds that the clock stops ticking from that moment the colony attains independence and whatever were rights, they remain constant.

3. Annex I Boundary Treaty Between British Southern Cameroons and French Cameroun.

4. Art. I, Constitution of the Federal Republic of Cameroon, September 1, 1961.

5. Pierre Mesmer discussed in greater detail hereafter.

6. The Two Alternatives. On page 11 of this famous UN document that served as the Manifesto of the UN-sponsored and organised plebiscite for Southern Cameroonians, the following are

listed as federal subjects; (1) public freedoms, (2) nationality, (3) national defence, (4) foreign affairs, (5) higher education, (6) immigration and emigration, (7) federal budget, and (8) posts and telecommunications.

7. Logically speaking, Foumban could only have been an opportunity for preliminary consultations on the constitution which was to-be because the final action was to be taken in the UN convened post plebiscite conference prescribed by Resolution 1608. As per discussions at Foumban, Foncha did not acquiesce, that is why the meeting was adjourned.

8. Annex II UN General Assembly 4th Committee Vote on Independence of Southern Cameroons. Fourth Committee, 1152nd Meeting, Wednesday, 19 April 1961.

9. Annex III UN General Assembly Vote on Resolution 1608 of April 21, 1961.

Chapter Five

The Two Cameroons and the Bakassi Peninsula Conflict: What Is at Stake?

Introduction

Modern African nation states are the product of European colonial interests, and the ways by which these colonial territories were brought about are bound to keep the entire continent fragile for many years to come. Asiwaju, in his well-researched paper, *The Bakassi Peninsula Crisis: An Alternative to War and Litigation*, rightly holds that, "Compared with the older parts of the nation state world, notably Western Europe and Northern America, the national state in Africa is still a relatively recent creation. Unfortunately the central concern is still with sovereignty assertions and related territorial claims and counter claims. However these assertions have continued to detract attention from the more critical projects which have become far more urgent now than ever before in view of the worsening economic crisis currently facing the individual national states on the African continent."[1]

While African modern nation states are a recent creation and a consequence of how colonialists carved out the continent, it must be understood that the artificiality of inherited boundaries has been aggravated by the unwillingness of some of the successors to the colonial thrones to abide by and respect the tenets of international law regarding territorial boundaries towards the achievement of independence. The fragility of these colonial boundaries, resulting from blatant disregard of these international instruments and accepted principles, is too rife in the Bight of Biafra with evident warnings of an outburst if quick action is not taken. But international law is not silent on this. The doctrine of *pacta sunt servanda* (Vienna Convention on the Law of Treaties, Article 26) makes it mandatory for all parties involved in a treaty, international agreement, declaration or convention to respect and defend the precepts thereof. It states: "Every treaty in force is binding upon the parties to it and must be performed by them in good faith."[2] We must admit that African modern nation states are a function of the inherited colonial boundaries as defined by treaties signed by the respective colonial powers, and on becoming a member of the UN, each is obliged to respect and defend the UN Charter, its abiding mission and international instruments.

This chapter sets out to examine the birth of the two Cameroons and it will also answer the questions: Is there a Bakassi Peninsula Conflict? Or is there some imperceptible phenomenon, in which case, the prime actor is using the Bakassi peninsula conflict as a smokescreen? Why did the flames of the conflict become so evident in the 1990's? What is the permanent solution?

The Birth of the Two Cameroons

The central issue in this chapter is the incontrovertible historical facts and legal instruments on the birth of and the existence of two Cameroons in Africa. The way in which these two countries came into being is the same as that of all other African territories that are today exercising sovereignty over their inherited territories. The two Cameroons are each an amalgamation of different kingdoms and chiefdoms that had nothing in common before the colonial era. There had never been a Cameroon kingdom or empire before the 1884/85 Berlin Conference. And the names themselves – Kamerun, Cameroons and Cameroun – given by colonial powers, namely, German, British, and French respectively without doubt eloquently depict the colonial origins of the two Cameroons.

The origin of the name dates back to the 15th century when Portuguese explorers visited the West African coast. Entering the Wouri estuary, these explorers "found a variety of prawns swarming in the region, and called the river Rio dos Camaros (River of Prawns)." In 1472, Spanish explorers also visited the coast under Fernaua do Pao and discovered the island that later came to bear his name, namely, Fernando Po. In 1494, when the New World was divided between the two major European powers namely Spain and

Portugal, and Fernando Po became Spanish possession, it was "the Spanish version of Camaroes-Camerones which gave rise to the Anglicised name of Cameroons." These Spanish explorers saw Mount Fako from the sea and named it the Chariot of the Gods.[3]

At the end of World War I, German colonies and protectorates were declared enemy territories and were taken over by the allied powers – now considered spoils of war – in the manner of the Berlin Conference of 1884, when the African continent was partitioned among European powers without the knowledge and consent of Africans. In the case of German Protectorate of Kamerun, the combined British, French and Belgian forces defeated the German forces in the territory. The UK and France, occupying the territory, then affected a provisional partition and set up administration within their respective sections of the partitioned German Kamerun before World War 1 ended.

The consequences of World War I threatened human existence and world civilisation. To put an end to any future war, the very powers, whose conflict in Europe became globalised, organised a peace conference in Paris. On January 30, 1919, it was decided in the Peace Conference that the German colonies as well as former Turkish territories were to be placed under the mandate system. US President, Woodrow Wilson, succeeded in convincing European powers "to accept a universal application of the mandates system", but he did not succeed in establishing self-determination as its basis.[4] His insistence on self-determination was to ensure that the mandate system worked towards the supreme interest of the inhabitants. Had such a system been adopted and upheld, many conflicts and bloody wars in ex-enemy territories that have bedevilled humanity would have been avoided, for the inheritor imperial states could not have treated the territories as their possessions.

Under the mandate system, "Principal Allied and Associated Powers, to whom the territory passed either by treaty, or, according to the American contention, as a result of the war, transferred the territories directly to the Mandatories, selecting generally the power in actual military occupation and following, in the main, boundaries agreed upon by them in treaties made during the war. These transfers were with the proviso that the territories should be administered as 'mandatories on behalf of the League'."[5]

The settlement of the question of provisional partitioned German Kamerun boundary took place in Paris during the spring of 1919. On March 7, Viscount Milner, Secretary of State for the Colonies of the British Empire, met with the French Colonial Minister, Henry Simon, to discuss the Cameroons and Togoland. After minor adjustments to the provisional partition of 1916, the two leading imperial powers agreed upon determining the frontier separating the territories of the Cameroons, placed respectively under the authorities of their governments as traced on the map that was attached to the signed Declaration of London, July 19, 1919.

Whatever adjustments were made to the haphazard boundaries to consolidate spheres of occupation, were in consonance with the political, administrative, economic and strategic interest of the new colonial powers. By attaching the map of each territory to the Declaration, the boundary is thus made distinct and each territory is made exclusive and permanent.

What needs to be pointed out is that the United Kingdom was interested in recovering its original territory founded by English Baptist Missionaries under Alfred Saker, who bought the land and named it after the British monarch, Queen Victoria. Between 1858 and 1885, four missionary governors administered the territory from the capital of Victoria in the name of the Queen. It must be recalled that the UK, France and Germany fought for the colonisation of this territory in the Gulf of Guinea. At the Berlin Conference, both France and the UK lost to Germany. World War I gave them an excuse to recover what they lost, thanks to their victory over Germany then.

According to the terms of Article XXII of the Covenant of the League of Nations, the mandatory system aimed at establishing a better system of administration for 'backward' peoples and communities that has existed under the regime of colonies, protectorates or spheres of influence. It deemed to be better in the sense that "it would more effectively secure the liberty, material welfare and opportunity for development of the native inhabitants and that would...secure the opportunity of all states of the world to equal participation in the trade and resources of these areas." [6]

One essential point in Article XXII that must be emphasised is the premium laid on "the well-being and development of such peoples" which was seen as a "sacred trust of civilisation." The peoples and territories placed under the mandate were entrusted into the care of 'advanced' nations. In this regard, the League of Nations was the embodiment of a sort of world conscience, which ought to promote civilisation in 'backward' societies and the world in general, without discrimination with regard to race, culture or religion.

Both the UK and France were thus charged with the task of ensuring the well-being and development of inhabitants in their territories, each remaining accountable to the League. 'Baby territories' were administered on behalf of the League and the mandatory powers were never to treat the territories the same as their colonies.

Ensuring that the inhabitants had inalienable right to their land and natural resources, and that they were to never be deprived of their essential identity, being in a mandated territory, they were never to become nationals of the mandatory power, whose duty it was to preserve fiscal autonomy in the mandated area, utilise all revenues for its benefit and not transfer its administration.[7]

It is thus clear that Article XXII of the League of Nations' Covenant – coming after the Anglo-French Agreement of 1919 – constitutes the second legal instrument to the existence of two distinct Cameroons and the first international instrument duly agreed upon by sovereign nations in a world body. As per Article XXII, the League of Nations ended the German Protectorate of Kamerun after Germany renounced to its rights on overseas territories. By endorsing the Franco-British Declaration of July 10, 1919, the League of Nations gave international legal status to the existence of the British mandate of Cameroon and the French mandate of Cameroun. France and the UK, unwilling to return the territory to Germany because disagreeing with the latter's colonial philosophy and values, established a political, administrative, legal and educational system aimed at erasing the memories of German rule.[8] With this aggressive approach, British Cameroons was as far and remote from French Cameroun as the French colony of Niger was from the British colony of Nigeria. The two mandated territories were respectively registered as class B mandates.

For administrative purposes, on June 26, 1923, pursuant to a British order in Council, the British mandated territory of the Cameroon was divided into Southern Cameroons and Northern Cameroons. While Southern Cameroons was administered as a separate province with Nigeria's group of southern provinces, Northern Cameroons, being non-contiguous, was further fragmented and administered as the provinces of Benue, Adamawa and Bornu of Northern Nigeria.

With the demise of the League of Nations following its inability to avert the World War II, the United Nations Organisation was set up in 1945. The UN established the Trusteeship Council, which replaced the mandate system. Article 75 of the UN Charter states:

> "The United Nations shall establish under its authority an international trusteeship system for the administration and supervision of such territories as may be placed hereunder by subsequent individual agreements. These territories are hereunder referred to as trust territories."

Following the formation of the Trusteeship Council on January 17, 1946, the British Foreign Secretary, Ernest Bevin, announced to the UNGA that the UK was willing to place its mandated territories of Tanganyika, the Cameroons and Togoland under UN Trusteeship. This move was followed by Australia placing New Guinea and Nauru Islands under Trusteeship, as did New Zealand with Western Samoa, Belgium with Rwanda/Urundi and France – announced by Foreign Minister Georges Bidault – with Togoland and Cameroun.

Mandated territories, under the Trusteeship Council became

trust territories, and the mandatory powers became the administering authorities, each signing a Trusteeship Agreement with the UN. Article 3 of the United Kingdom Trusteeship Agreement approved by the UN General Assembly on 13 December 1946, states:

> "The Administering Authority undertakes to administer the Territory in such a manner as to achieve the basic objectives of the international trusteeship system laid down in Article 76 of the United Nations Charter. The Administering Authority further undertakes to collaborate fully with the General Assembly of the United Nations and the Trusteeship Council in the discharge of all their functions …"

Although Article XXII of the League's Covenant mentioned the autonomy of the inhabitants and their collective full right to development, it is evident that the Trusteeship system was an improvement. The fundamental objective of the Trusteeship system was:

> "To promote the political, economic, social and educational advancement of the inhabitants of the trust territories, and their progressive development towards self-government or independence …" (Article 76(b)).

Here, the right to self-determination, freedom, justice and equality of all peoples and territories is explicitly defended.

Under the International Trusteeship system, the two Cameroons, one Anglo-Saxon and the other Francophone, were distinct Trust Territories equal in status. Each was registered under category B Trust Territory and was entitled to independence in their own right.

For administrative convenience, the UK continued to administer its Trust Territory as part of Nigeria which was under the mandate system of the League of Nations. However, through its association with Nigeria, British Southern Cameroons tremendously gained from the latter's evolution – politically and constitutionally – and thus, made progress in the art of constitutional democracy, the rule of law, human freedom and freedom of the press better than French Cameroun. In line with such development, British Southern Cameroons achieved self-government in 1954. With a new Constitution in 1957, in addition to the House of Assembly, it was also granted a House of Chiefs and a full ministerial government. It was only in 1957 that French Cameroun attained self-governance. British Southern Cameroons' progress towards independence was assured when its Parliament adopted, in 1960, its own Constitution and became a distinct state with a democratically elected functioning government in between independent Nigeria to the west and independent la République du Cameroun to the east. Neither Nigeria nor la République du Cameroun contested the distinct existence of British Southern Cameroons.

But, through colonial conspiracy, the UN was manipulated to impose a plebiscite in British Southern Cameroons. Instead of outright independence, as specified in Article 76 of the UN Charter and UNGA Resolution 1514 of 1960, the plebiscite was imposed to bring about independence by joining either Nigeria or la République du Cameroun.[9] Although the vote favoured a Federal Union with la République du Cameroun, and the UNGA adopted Resolution 1608 of April 21, 1961 on a post-plebiscite conference to adopt modalities for the formation of the UN-envisioned Federal Union of two states of equal status, the UN failed in its obligations to implement this landmark resolution. The consequences of this were bound to be grave. La République du Cameroun exploited this failure and annexed the British Southern Cameroons.

The Bakassi Peninsula Conflict

With the mandate and Trusteeship Agreements, treaties in their own rights and the Anglo-French Boundary Treaty of January 9, 1931, the Bakassi Peninsula has become an integral part of the British Southern Cameroons territory. Since on the premise of international law, British Southern Cameroons is a separate nation, how is it that la République du Cameroun, which by the Anglo-French Boundary Treaty of 1931 does not share maritime boundary with Nigeria, is in dispute with Nigeria over the ownership of Bakassi?

The expansionist la République du Cameroun, not respecting international treaties, paints and projects the false identity of being the successor state of German Kamerun, which legally, no longer existed since the Versailles Peace Treaty. This false image seems to have been accepted even by Nigeria, which was dragged to the International Court of Justice at The Hague by the false claimant, la République du Cameroun.

From point of fact of history and law, the Nigeria-la République du Cameroun conflict over Bakassi Peninsula is indeed a question of British Southern Cameroons' identity. Since the flawed decolonisation process in British Southern Cameroons ends in annexation by la République du Cameroun, one can talk of the British Southern Cameroons factor in the Nigeria-la République du Cameroun relationship. This British Southern Cameroons factor manifests itself in overt and covert in-built hostility, distrust, suspicion, conflict, open clashes between the patrolling troops and frequent loss of lives between Nigeria and la République du Cameroun. This being an international conflict with grave consequences, the solution lies only in respecting international treaties and obligations, making right the wrongs of 1961, and restoring the statehood of British Southern Cameroons. To attain the goal of lasting peace, the UN must live up to the defined wisdom that informed its founding.

To establish which country has sovereignty over Bakassi Peninsula, it is logical we turn to the colonial treaties in force. It should also be understood that according to the principle of international jurisprudence of *uti possidetis juris* and the critical date, from the moment a dependent country attains independence, its international boundaries become immutable, inviolable and permanently fixed.

According to the Anglo-German treaty of 1913, paragraph XX, "Should the lower course of the Akwayafe so change its mouth as to transfer it to the Rio del Rey, it is agreed that the area now known as the Bakassi Peninsula shall still remain German territory."

Going further in its delimitation, Article XXI states: "From the centre of the navigable channel, on a line joining Bakassi Point and King Point, the boundary shall follow the centre of the navigable channel of the Akwayafe River as far as the 3-mile limit of territorial jurisdiction. For the purpose of defining this boundary, the navigable channel of the Akwayafe River shall be considered to lie wholly to the east of the navigable channel of the Cross and Calabar Rivers."

According to this treaty, it is conclusive that while the British Southern Cameroons-Nigeria, international boundary is consequent upon the 1913 Anglo-German treaty, the British Southern Cameroons-la République du Cameroun international boundary has triple international enforcement instruments, namely, the mandate agreement as explained herein above, the Anglo-French agreements of 1919 and Boundary Treaty of 1931, and the Trusteeship Agreement, each complementing the other.

The border skirmishes, which, in the past were always handled bilaterally, assumed a completely different dimension in the 1990s. When the matter was brought to the Committee on Conflict Management and Resolution of the Organisation for African Unity (OAU), a resolution calling for respect of inherited colonial boundaries was adopted. It called for parties to discuss how to restrain and withdraw their troops from the Peninsula. The failure of the Committee to declare Nigeria as the aggressor and demand unconditional withdrawal fails short of la République du Cameroun's expectation. Losing faith in the OAU's mediation, President Paul Biya of la République du Cameroun sent out envoys on an extensive diplomatic offensive which covered USA, Canada, France, Germany, the European Community Headquarters in Brussels, the ICJ at The Hague, China, as well as East and Southern Africa in a bid to mobilise world opinion in favour of a proposed UN Security Council Session on the Bakassi crisis.[10]

In defence of his resolve to project Nigeria as the aggressor, President Biya, in an address to the nation on March 23, 1994, declared that Cameroon would not relinquish any part of its territory. As opposed to Nigeria's insistence for bilateral talks to resolve the crisis, Biya, pushing to the wall Nigeria's military ruler, General Sani Abacha, placed as pre-condition for any summit meeting, Nigeria's unconditional withdrawal from the Peninsula.

Hopes were kindled when bilateral talks were fixed for Maiduguri and Nigeria. However, Mr Biya dashed all hopes when he brought in French paratroopers and a warship in the dispute area. Southern Cameroonians interpreted this as Biya acting in conformity with his cherished philosophy of 'he who wants peace must prepare for war', which certainly raised doubts as to his commitment to a peaceful resolve of the conflict. They also saw in this hardening of position, grounds for their fears that Yaoundé may be out to provoke war with Nigeria in order to transform their annexed territory into a battleground, and under the cover of prosecuting war against an external enemy – Nigeria – seek to crush the independentists and bury their legitimate aspirations for restoration of their sovereign statehood – British Southern Cameroons. Although the presence of French paratroopers and the warship, which was confirmed by the French Ambassador to Nigeria, was no strange act as la République du Cameroun has a defence pact with France, Southern Cameroonians' fears were legitimate and they did not take this war-like stance lightly and kindly.

The All-Anglophone Conference (AAC) – parent body of the Southern Cameroons National Council (SCNC) – under two months of the eruption of the Bakassi crisis, challenged on February 21, 1994, Yaoundé's reference to the intangibility of frontiers arising from the 1961 plebiscite attaching the Southern Cameroons to East Cameroon. The AAC, speaking for Southern Cameroonians, saw in Yaoundé's use of the word 'attaching', la République du Cameroun's scouting for international legitimacy as well as pride in having annexed and occupied the former UN Trust Territory of Southern Cameroons. President Paul Biya, in ignoring the UN-envisioned Federal Union of two states equal in status, though unimplemented, referred to Southern Cameroons as if it was a territory without international legal status, indeed, no man's land.

To President Paul Biya, the internationalisation of the conflict was an absolute for survival. Having rigged the 1992 presidential elections, and counting only on the loyalty of the military of which he is the Commander-in-Chief and on the judiciary of which he is the Chief Magistrate, he needed some magic force to turn his illegitimacy, as declared by the opposition, to legitimacy. Although he won substantial votes in la République du Cameroun, Southern Cameroonians, beyond any doubt, showed to Biya that he was held in contempt. For giving more than 85% of their votes to John Fru Ndi instead, Southern Cameroonians were heavily punished with a state of emergency and an economic blockade during which lives were lost and a lot of Nigerian goods were publicly destroyed. It was during this 1993 economic blockade – named 'Operation Dorade' – that the Bakassi conflict was aggravated. This further estranged the Southern Cameroonian people. Biya used the Bakassi Peninsula conflict against Nigeria, whose ten thousand citizens were said to have matched in Bamenda during the launching of the SDF in 1990 and whose government was accused of supporting Ni John Fru Ndi, as a life boat for his regime. He hoped that with diplomatic victories, the people of la République du Cameroun seeing him as a strong, decisive and capable leader enjoying international legitimacy, will turn their total support to him. Biya's appeal for national solidarity against a common enemy, namely Nigeria, could not be taken kindly by the people of Southern Cameroon, treated like a conquered people and often mockingly referred to as 'Nigerians', 'Biafrans', 'Anglos', and 'anglofools', not only by street boys and the low in ranks but even by high ranking officials in ministries and in the National Assembly. To the people of British Southern Cameroons To them, it was the constant *gendarme* brutality that they are subjected to and that was extended to Nigerians residents in Bakassi Peninsula that sparked the heightened crisis.

The Hidden Truth

Nigerian claims to the Bakassi Peninsula are based on traditional ties and lay with the inhabitants of the island. Some Nigerians maintain that the inhabitants are the Efik and Ibibios, and that Bakassi was Efik Kingdom, under the rule of the Calabar King. The defenders of Nigerian sovereignty over Bakassi argue that the Anglo-German Treaty of 1913 violated an earlier agreement between the British Crown and the Obong of Calabar of September 10, 1884. This agreement between Old Calabar and the Queen of England, they explain, concluded that no part of the territory was ever to be ceded.

On the topic of effective occupation and cultural links, the argument is also that more than 90% of the inhabitants are Nigerians who carry on the fishing industry. The Efiks, claiming to be the first settlers of the Peninsula, are said to be the extension of those in Nigeria. Inhabiting the coastal region, fishing is their main occupation. The only challenge to the inhabitants is on the question of sovereignty as defined by treaties inherited at independence. Mindful of the consequences of tampering with the artificial boundaries inherited on attainment of independence, the OAU, at its Cairo Summit of 1964, declared:

> "Considering that border disputes are a serious permanent source of conflict",
>
> "Considering moreover that the boundaries of African States as established on the day of their independence constitute a tangible reality..."[2]
>
> "Solemnly declare that all member states are committed to respecting the boundaries which were in existence at the time they attained independence."[11]

From the 1964 OAU Resolution, the AU Constitutive Act, Article 4(b) has come to reaffirm the position of member nations of the continental body, which in conformity with the principle of international jurisprudence of *uti possidetis juris* and the critical date, respects boundaries inherited at independence, binding all member nations towards peace, stability and development in Africa. Judging from this standpoint, the fundamental question here is: Who had sovereignty over Bakassi when la République du Cameroun and Nigeria attained independence on January 1st 1960 and October 1st 1960 respectively? Which country exercised sovereignty over Bakassi Peninsula by 1960 when these two nations joined UN membership that same year?

La République du Cameroun claiming to be the successor state of German Kamerun and dwelling on the 1913 Treaty holds that Bakassi is Cameroon's territory. It is known that all modern African states are based on colonial treaties and boundaries inherited on attainment of independence, and that la République du Cameroun had no maritime boundary with Nigeria at independence, nor was any territorial claim made.

The fundamental problem is that the right question is never asked. Nigeria has failed to defend the obvious. In la République du Cameroun's submission to the ICJ, it is clearly stated that Bakassi is Southern Cameroons territory. But under imperial cloak, it is la République du Cameroun that has sovereignty over this former UN Trust Territory, Southern Cameroons having been transferred to la République du Cameroun through the decolonisation process following the plebiscite of 1961.

Transferred by whom? What is the international legal instrument of transfer? How could the decolonisation process, disregarding Article 76 of the UN Charter and the 1960 Resolution 1514, as well as prescribing independence without preconditions to all dependent territories, become a means by which Southern Cameroons surrendered its inalienable right to national self-determination and self-existence, and was consequently transferred to another territory? How it is that la République du Cameroun presented the UN – whose founding mission is to guarantee respect for international obligations, equality of all nations and international cooperation amongst nations, large and small, as precondition for world peace based on justice – as the agency for annexation and colonisation through which it acquired Southern

Cameroons. This is a paradox.

We should recall that the plebiscite was an act of self-determination for British Southern Cameroons, and that a federation between the British Southern Cameroons and la République du Cameroun was to be formed under the UN supervision and under international instruments. Moreover, the UN General Assembly, of which Nigeria and la République du Cameroun were members at the time, adopted UN Resolution 1608(XV) on April 21, 1961 approving a post-plebiscite conference to work out modalities on the formation of the UN-sponsored Federal United Cameroon Republic of two states of EQUAL STATUS, but this UN Resolution was never implemented. It is worth pointing out that, while Nigeria voted in favour of Resolution 1608, la République du Cameroun and France and other Francophone African countries, except Mali, voted against it (See Appendix 111 for details). Cognisant of the plebiscite's results, the powerful 4th Committee (Political Committee) of UN General Assembly voted on April 19, 1961 for the independence of Southern Cameroons, declaring 1st October 1961 as Independence Day. Faithful to its hidden agenda against the Southern Cameroonian people, and failing to block the vote, la République du Cameroun's Foreign Minister, Charles Okala, supported by France and some Francophone African countries, walked out of the meeting. But Nigeria, recognising Southern Cameroonians as a people and believing in their inalienable right to be masters of their own destiny, and defending the international system as the guarantor of world peace based on justice, was among the 50 UN member nations that overwhelmingly voted for the independence of Southern Cameroons. The total vote cast was 2 'no', 12 abstentions and 50 'yes' by the UK, USA, USSR, South Africa, Ghana, Nigeria, Canada, Australia, Sweden, Mexico, Libya, Ethiopia, among others. When these 50 UN Member Nations voted for Southern Cameroonians to form an independent state, the people called Southern Cameroonians included Bakassians and the Bakassi Peninsula as an integral part of the territory of British Southern Cameroons.

In the conduct of the plebiscite organised by the UN, the people of Bakassi Peninsula, now an integral part of the UN Trust Territory of British Southern Cameroons, voted. The Peninsula constituted part of one of the 26 plebiscite districts of Southern Cameroons. Since this plebiscite was conducted by the UN, it is obvious that the conclusive details are in the archives of the UN, and the ICJ should have privileged access.

Nigeria ignored what should have brought the Southern Cameroons question on the table of the ICJ, and dwelled on traditional links which colonial treaties buried in Africa. This explains the artificiality of African boundaries. The Southern Cameroons question – an issue of international concern and a threat to peace and stability in the West African sub-region – is the real thing at stake, the bone of contention between Nigeria and la République du Cameroun. The Bakassi Peninsula is a diversion, a cover up, and until the real problem is solved, we beckon only the worsening of hostility ending up in blood bath. In the Nigeria-la République du Cameroun conflict, British Southern Cameroons is the victim, and Bakassi Peninsula is the smokescreen which la République du Cameroun is using to cover up where Yaoundé presents Nigeria as the aggressor violating the territorial integrity of la République du Cameroun. However, based on boundaries inherited at independence, the two stand guilty before international law.

In 1972, in a letter to Nigeria's Minister of External Affairs, Dr T. O. Elias the Attorney General who was later attorney general of the Federation of Nigeria, citing relevant colonial texts to prove that Bakassi peninsula is not Nigerian territory, wrote that, "According to the information received from the Federal Directorate of Surveys, the Bakassi Peninsula" was never included as part of Nigeria in the administrative maps of Nigeria since Southern Camerouns (*sic*) ceased to be part of Nigeria in 1961. Furthermore, the Northern, Western and Eastern Regions (Definition of Boundaries) Proclamation 1954 (L.N. 126 of 1954) showed the Bakassi Peninsula as forming part of what then was Southern Camerouns (sic).[12]

If, upon attainment of independence, there was no dispute of territorial claims, what has been responsible for the genesis of the hostile relationship in the following years?

The origin of hostile relationship, aggressive tendency, distrust and suspicion of one another can be traced to bungled decolonisation in British Southern Cameroons. Nothing can better explain the validity of this conclusion than the report by K. Lees, Plebiscite Supervisory Officer after his first Enlightenment Campaign of October 28, 1960 to the Deputy Plebiscite Administrator, Buea. In the field, he was faced with the following baffling questions: "Why have we not had a third choice? Why can we not stand alone? Why should a poor man sell his independence to join with bigger and richer men?" He concludes: "There was wide spread ignorance of what exactly the Republic of Cameroon was particularly in the remote area."[13]

Going further, colonial authorities affirmed that, "Most people in the Southern Cameroons do not want to be administered by the Republic; they do not want to have anything to do with French army or police (which they fear). They do not want a French system of law, they do not want the French language, they do not want to risk being pushed around by French officials, and they do not want policy dictated to them by Republic politicians. Least of all they do not want the British connection to be completely severed or to be cut off from British help…They fear being pushed into Nigeria as much as they fear being pushed into the Republic."[14]

Like a decaying and painful tooth that must be extracted — else the victim knows no peace, can neither eat, drink nor sleep — the problem created by UN experiment of independence by joining and the abysmal failure to implement UNGA Resolution 1608 should be corrected, and the statehood and sovereign independence of British Southern Cameroons re-established as voted for by the UN General Assembly's 4th Committee, on April 19,1961 in conformity with the UN Charter and UNGA Resolution 1514 and the expressed wish of the people of British Southern Cameroons..

With greed and ambition for territorial expansion, la République du Cameroun — an equal partner of British Southern Cameroons in the UN-envisioned Federal Union that was never implemented – violated all international laws, conventions and annexed Southern Cameroons. It is by force of annexation and occupation of British Southern Cameroons, what the people feared as expressed above, that la République du Cameroun claims maritime boundary with the Federal Republic of Nigeria. This claim is a gigantic fraud, illegal and *ab initio*. Fraud vitiates all that springs from it. Something acquired fraudulently can never gain legitimacy and legality and become a right. The passage of time changes nothing. Time does not expire fraud. Thus, la République du Cameroun, by annexing and imposing colonial administration on British Southern Cameroons and getting into border conflict with Nigeria, is only compounding its criminal act and aggravating the threat to peace in the sub-region.

Fuelling the Flames

The Bakassi Peninsula and the estuarine waters of this region have always been a bone of contention. Between 1885 and 1891, the British and German colonial powers put in a lot of effort to resolve the battle over who owns Bakassi. It was in the act of instituting a definitive settlement that the Anglo-German Treaty of 1913 was realised. The British, describing it as a 'worthless zone of contention', ceded Bakassi Peninsula to Germany. Bakassi Peninsula then became an integral part of German Kamerun and colonial Nigeria's eastern neighbour. Unfortunately, WWI broke out in 1914, ending with the defeat of Germany and partition of German Kamerun as spoils of war by the UK and France. As pointed out above, the UK, after regaining its territory founded by English Baptist missionaries, administered its regained territory, for purposes of administrative convenience, as part of Nigeria. Thus, the coastward demarcation of the Anglo-German boundary as per the 1913 Treaty halted by WWI, was not raised again since it was the UK exercising sovereignty over the colony of Nigeria and the UN Trust Territory of British Southern Cameroons – formerly part of Germany Kamerun that ceased being after the war.

When time came for Nigeria to attain independence on October 1, 1960, the UN, respecting the distinct identity of British Southern Cameroons within its international boundaries, separated the latter from Nigeria. As per the 1913 Treaty, Bakassi remained an integral territory of British Southern Cameroons. In 1961, the Bakassi people voted in the UN-sponsored detachment and conducted a plebiscite without Nigerian protest, and Nigeria consequently also gained independence within its defined international boundaries.

As British Southern Cameroons was no longer part of independent Nigeria from 1960, it was obvious that the definitive boundary demarcation further southwards into the sea halted by WWI would have to reopen. Sovereignty over Bakassi from the formation of the loose federal association between British Southern Cameroons and la République du Cameroun passed to the government of the Federal Republic of Cameroon, which in international affairs exercised it on behalf of the Federated State of West (Southern) Cameroons. The point being emphasised here is that, unlike the Nigerian Federation, in which all parts were one national territory under British colonial rule and attained independence as such, the Federal Republic of Cameroon was a loose inter-governmental union and never a territorial union. Above all, there was never a treaty of union duly signed and registered with the General Secretariat of the UN in conformity with Article 102(1) of the Charter. This inter-governmental union was made up of two distinct nations and peoples inheriting different colonial territories and coming into the loose federal association with specific characteristics which they were determined to guard jealously. Consequently, while the federation lasted, the Federal Government played the role of custodian of international relations for the two equal partners in the loose federation.

Thus, in 1965, when the urgency for the delimitation and surveying of boundary to the sea was opened, it was the Government of the Federal Republic of Cameroon that handled the matter with the Federal Government of Nigeria. The work went on smoothly. But, in 1967, the Nigerian civil war broke and the Bakassi Peninsula became the most dangerous zone of the region, having to receive special security attention. Although France supported Ojukwu's secessionist Biafra, the Southern Cameroons factor prevented Ahidjo from taking public stand behind President de Gaulle as Bongo and Houphouët-Boigny of Gabon and Ivory Coast respectively did. The strong historical and cultural ties between British Southern Cameroons and Nigeria convinced Ahidjo that any support for Biafra would be too risky because many Southern Cameroonians were beginning to see their hopes dashed as Yaoundé was stealthily eroding their autonomy. Ahidjo's support for Nigeria was to placate Southern Cameroonians and avoid the inevitable. Worthy of note is the fact that it was the Federal Republic of Cameroon, and not la République du Cameroun, which supported Nigeria. Were it not for the Southern Cameroons factor, the defence pact and co-operation agreement that Ahidjo signed with France before flag independence in 1960 would have dictated otherwise as it will be shown below.

The other issue aggravating the hostility and increasing the vulnerability of the zone is its economic potential and strategic location and importance. The Peninsula is rich in natural resources; fish, noodles, oil and gas. Oil companies granted authorisation by both Cameroun and Nigeria are engaged in oil exploitation close to the zone. Due to the endemic nature of the problem, and conscious of the grave consequences of any war between the two countries, a communiqué was issued on September 2, 1974, establishing a moratorium on oil extraction in a 2 km corridor on both side of the line, dividing the territorial waters of the estuarine waters and islands in the Cross River area.

How far has this bilateral act of understanding been respected? If it was, would there have been any clashes or legal battle at the ICJ, especially when the Border Co-operation Agreement between Nigeria and Cameroon held that any "infringement shall as far as possible be resolved locally and ultimately through diplomatic channel?"

In 1981, a serious clash causing the death of five Nigerian soldiers at the hands of *gendarmes* of Cameroon, almost started a war between the two countries. Nigeria imposed harsh conditions and issued an ultimatum to the rulers in Yaoundé. The military government of General Obasanjo had, only two years prior, shifted to a civilian government under President Shehu Shagari, a Muslim from the north, Sokoto, whose ancestors spread Islam to all of northern Cameroun. To avert a war, Ahidjo, also a Muslim from the north of Cameroun, respected the ultimatum.

Since 1990, the clashes have been too frequent, with accusations and counter accusations from each country. Nigerians have accused la République du Cameroun's *gendarmes* of brutality, extortion and killing of civilians. Between 1991 and 1992, there were six clashes which rose to thirteen by September 1994. Between December 1993 and February 1994, Nigeria alleged that 30 Nigerian fishermen were killed, and properties were destroyed "while millions of Naira worth of goods had been lost to Cameroonian *gendarmes*."[15]

Because of frequent clashes, Bakassi became a territory occupied by two countries, with many inhabitants displaced. While those who claim Nigerian citizenship have moved into neighbouring states of the Federation, those claiming Cameroonian citizenship have moved into the hinterland of Southern Cameroons. With the Peninsula occupied by hostile military forces, elections could not be conducted in the zone, and Biya claimed victory for his party even though the mayors, councillors or the proconsuls – Francophone *sous-préfet* – reside in Bakassi. The clashes of the early 1990s registered greater calamities, and Biya did not only reinforce the Cameroon military presence, but to dramatise the conflict, brought in French troops. The military and civilians of both sides did not take this kindly. While some Nigerians saw it as a provocation, it was general consensus that Biya's action that only confirmed the neo-colonial status of la République du Cameroun and that it was not independent of France.

As stated above, while the loose federation between Southern Cameroons and la République du Cameroun lasted, there was consistent effort to contend any conflict with Nigeria through cordial bilateral relations and contacts. However, with the annexation of Southern Cameroons, hostility has heightened. If during the Nigerian civil war, Yaoundé and Paris were on parallel lines, and in 1981 Ahidjo had preferred bowing to Shagari's ultimatum, it must be noted that even when less severe clashes occurred in the 1990s, commitment to bilateral talks for a peaceful settlement lacked seriousness and sincerity. Mediation within the auspices of the OAU, under President Eyadema of Togo, was aborted due to lack of co-operation on the part of President Biya. In addition to French military presence on behalf of Yaoundé in keeping with the defence pact, la République du Cameroun along with its colonial master (France), and Paul Biya, who replaced Ahidjo on November 6th, 1982, took Nigeria to the ICJ at The Hague. This heightened hostility and internationalised the Bakassi Peninsula conflict after the failure of the OAU to bring the two to an amicable settlement.

With economic decline in both countries, lesser known Bakassi Peninsula – abounding in rich economic potential – could salvage and panel beat to acceptable shape, the battered image of any of the states if the Peninsula was exclusively controlled and its natural resources exploited by their rightful owner. Southern Cameroonians and the Southern Cameroons National Council, embarking on the restoration of the statehood and sovereignty of British Southern Cameroons, see the conflict differently. The light must be on why President Paul Biya decided to internationalise the conflict over the question of sovereignty over Bakassi Peninsula by suing Nigeria at the ICJ. Until this question is answered, treaties in force and in defence of justice for all, Bakassi will remain an open sore, sapping away the energies of the two nations and perpetually threatening peace and stability in the whole west and central African sub-regions.

For a Permanent Solution

Having annexed British Southern Cameroons in violation of international law and the UN Resolution 2625(XXV) of October 1970, la République du Cameroun needs a legal document as cover. To seal its expansionist tendency, Bakassi Peninsula is an excuse, and Nigeria has been dragged in as an accomplice to this violation. Although la République du Cameroun admits in its memoriam to the ICJ16 that Bakassi Peninsula is Southern Cameroonian territory to mislead and confuse the ICJ to rule in its favour, it declares that (British) Southern Cameroons was transferred to it (la République du Cameroun) by way of the plebiscite.

Nigeria's silence – by not insisting on la République du Cameroun to submit the instrument by which a nation and a people were transferred to it (la République du Cameroun) – misled the ICJ to rule in favour of la République du Cameroun by using the Anglo-German Treaty of 1913 instead of the Anglo-French Treaty of 1931.This gave the impression to la République du Cameroun that its claim of being the successor state of German Kamerun is valid. Nothing could be further from the legal truth than this.

How is it that Nigeria, which was among the 50 UN member nations that, in the powerful 4th Committee of the UNGA, voted for the independence of (British) Southern Cameroons on April 19, 1961, declaring 1st October 1961 the Independence Day of Southern Cameroons, forgot this historical reality? How is it possible that Nigeria forgot that la République du Cameroun and France led other Francophone African countries to walk out after they failed in their bid to block the vote for Southern Cameroons' independence? Why has Nigeria also forgotten that on April 21, 1961, upon adoption of the Resolution 1608 on the post-plebiscite conference for the implementation of the UN-envisioned federal union of two states of EQUAL STATUS, la République du Cameroun and France led other French-speaking African nations to vote against it? Without any doubt, having rejected the UN-envisioned federal union, they worked to ensure that the UN never implemented this resolution. Did Nigeria and la République du Cameroun share a maritime boundary when they respectively achieved independence in 1960 and joined UN Membership that same year? What seriously accounts for la République du Cameroun's hostility towards Nigeria in the 1990s, as compared with that of the immediate post-independence era, other than the Southern Cameroons factor?

The failure to face the law and truth, as it ought to be, led Nigerian authorities and even some intellectuals to forget the following facts:

(a) There are two Cameroons, one Anglo-Saxon and the other, Francophone, in Africa.

(b) By the Anglo-French Treaty of 1931, Nigeria shares almost 1700km along the eastern border with the two Cameroons, and the maritime and vital section is to (British) Southern Cameroons and not la République du Cameroun.

This disregard of history and legality led those who should shape public opinion to mislead the people of Bakassi, including some older inhabitants who, as Southern Cameroonians, voted in the plebiscite of February 1961, to protest against being forced to become le Camerounais Français. They cannot consider surviving under the brutality of the *gendarmes*. Determined to not being subject to perpetual tyranny and reign of terror, they have called for a referendum so as to choose between Nigeria and la République du Cameroun.

It is the failure to face reality and to guarantee the reign of justice and fair play for all that has led to the change of attitude in la République du Cameroun towards Nigeria after 1972, when the Cameroonian loose federation was abolished, and British Southern Cameroons was annexed and reduced to two provinces of la République du Cameroun. This disregard of history and legality governing international boundaries has made T. O Elias to state: "The principle of good faith in international relations demands that Nigeria should not disavow her word of honour as evidenced by the note of 1962. Every effort should be exerted on our side to ensure that Nigeria does not show ingratitude to a sister country that stood by us during the civil war."[17]

Southern Cameroonians support that la République du Cameroun's strategy of dragging Nigeria to the ICJ is to enable the former to obtain international legal ruling, granting it sovereignty over Bakassi, and maintain that with the demise of the Federal Republic of Cameroon, each partner in the defunct loose association has the legal and legitimate right to pull back with its territory and maintain its identity as inherited at independence. Consequently, la République du Cameroun, with no stretch of imagination, can suppress the Anglo-French Treaty of 1931, manufacture a territorial dispute with Nigeria in order to annex British Southern Cameroons, and hold on to the 1913 Anglo-German Treaty. It will be scandalous and an act of betrayal for Nigeria to take this into account, it will have to collaborate with la République du Cameroun in the annexation and colonial occupation of British Southern Cameroons, whose territorial boundaries, as a fact of history and international law, are well known to Nigeria.

Nigeria had one trump card at the ICJ to insist that la République du Cameroun submits the instrument by which Southern Cameroons was transferred to it. But Nigeria erred by dwelling on the traditional and cultural ties of the old Calabar Kingdom and Bakassi Peninsula and the agreement sealed between the Queen of England and Obong of Calabar. Are modern African nations not the product of treaties reached between the colonial powers without the knowledge and consent of Africans? It is these treaties – defining colonial boundaries – which the OAU declared inviolable and immutable in 1964 and reaffirmed in the AU Constitutive Act. Nigeria missed the finest hour to make history. Although this is not irredeemable for Southern Cameroonians, they are not ready to surrender to be the footstool of la République du Cameroun.

As the regional power which should defend the continental body's resolve to guarantee peace and stability – a vital ingredient of development – Nigeria, which has spent so much in peacekeeping and in fighting white colonialism should oppose all acts of illegal territorial acquisition. As a regional power, Nigeria should understand that its interest, stability and development are predicated upon its ability and resolve regarding the respect of the AU Charter, Resolutions and shared values by all members of the regional organisation. Nigeria's role in insisting on the respect for the sanctity of boundaries inherited at independence and the prevention of extra-territorial acquisition by any African state is the insurance for African stability, democracy, economic development, the rule of law, and the enhancement of Nigeria's leadership on the continent. This should be central to Nigeria's foreign policy. Based on colonial heritage, Nigeria and British Southern Cameroons have more in common than the latter has with la République du Cameroun. Nigeria cannot forget that it voted for the independence of Southern Cameroons. It is bound to respect its duty to defend its vote at the UN for Southern Cameroons' independence.

The Enrolment Order by the Abuja Federal High Court Ruling of March 5, 2002 (suit number FHC/ABJ/CS/30/2002) – the peoples of Southern Cameroons versus Attorney General of the Federal Republic of Nigeria stated:

"A PERPETUAL INJUNCTION restraining the Government of the Federal Republic of Nigeria whether by herself, her servants, agents and or representatives or otherwise howsoever from treating or continuing to treat or regard the Southern Cameroons and the peoples of the territory as an integral part of la République du Cameroun."

In conclusion, after taking judicious notice of the non-implementation of UNGA Resolution 1608, it declared:

> "The Federal Republic of Nigeria shall take any other measures as may be necessary to place the case of the peoples of the geographical territory known as of 1st October 1960 as Southern Cameroons for self-determination before the United Nations General Assembly and any other relevant International Organisation."

It is only through positive action in accordance with the Abuja Federal High Court ruling, and through the pursuit by the Southern Cameroons National Council, that peace and stability can be enjoyed in this sub-region? The way peaceful resolution of the conflict must be pursued for any war of liberation will firstly destabilise Nigeria and secondly, too costly for the flash point will be the inherited colonial linguistic divide, Anglophone vs.

Francophone, Africa. Every effort must be exerted to avoid such a calamity.

The Abuja Federal High Court ruling defends the right to self-determination of the Southern Cameroonian people. It upholds their right to defend the territorial unity of British Southern Cameroons as well as the principle of international jurisprudence of *uti possidetis juris* and the critical date. It respects the AU Constitutive Act, Article 4(b), defending the immutability of boundaries inherited at independence.

What must be stated, as a point of principle and without mincing words, is that the function of a court is to defend rights, guarantee justice and ensure that violation is punished according to the law. No court of law or tribunal has as mission to transform illegality into legality. By dwelling on the Anglo-German Treaty, the ICJ erred in its ruling when, as a point of fact of history and law by the Versailles Peace Treaty, German Kamerun ceased to be and the Anglo-French Treaty and the Trusteeship Agreements gave rise to the two Cameroons under new imperial powers. It may be Nigeria's silence on certain fundamental facts that was responsible or that contributed to this misrule. But onus lies on the ICJ and the UN, which has the ultimate responsibility with regard to decolonisation and the independence of former colonies and Trust Territories, and guaranteeing international cooperation and world peace.

As far as the Bakassi peninsula is concerned, the SCNC and Southern Cameroonians hold la République du Cameroun and Nigeria guilty of violating the territorial integrity of British Southern Cameroons. Neither the map of la République du Cameroun at independence, on January 1, 1960, included British Southern Cameroons nor did the map of Nigeria include Bakassi peninsula on October 1, 1960.

In respect of the principle of *uti possidetis juris*, Brownlie states: "The general principle that pre-independence boundaries of former colonial administrative divisions all subject to the same sovereign remain being, is in accordance with good policy and has been adopted by governments and tribunals concerned with boundaries in Asia and Africa."[18] The ICJ holds: "The territorial boundaries which are to be respected can also stem from international borders which separated a colony from the territory of an independent state or a state under protectorate but which had preserved its international legal personality."[19] The status of British Southern Cameroons aptly fits into this definition, for it was not in dispute when Nigeria and la République du Cameroun respectively became independent in 1960 and joined the UN.

It was based on the strength of the distinct identity of British Southern Cameroons, as governed by colonial treaties, that the SCNC filed its interpleader to the ICJ at The Hague against the annexation and occupation of Southern Cameroons. Although the SCNC complaint has not yet been considered by the ICJ, which, according to Article 35(1) of the UN Charter, handles only matters brought before it by UN member nations. But the UN Charter declares in its Preamble,

> "We the people..." and not, 'we, the nations'. And above all, British Southern Cameroons is a UN Trust that suffered botched decolonisation.

The inalienable rights of British Southern Cameroons to exist as a distinct sovereign nation under international law cannot be compromised by fraud by an expansionist power. East Timor never lost its right when it was annexed and occupied by Indonesia. So, even if the current ICJ ruling was to compel Nigeria to withdraw from Bakassi in favour of la République du Cameroun, this act changes nothing.

Pope John Paul II, addressing the UN General Assembly on the occasion of its 50th anniversary in 1995, drew the attention of the world body to an incontrovertible reality of our time. He declared:

> On the threshold of a new millennium we are witnessing an extraordinary global acceleration of the quest for freedom which is one of the great dynamics of human history. This phenomenon is not limited to any one part of the world; nor is it the expression of any culture. Men and women throughout

the world, even threatened by violence, have taken the risk of freedom, asking to be given a place in social, political and economic life which is commensurate with their dignity as free human beings. This universal longing for freedom is truly one of the distinguishing marks of our time.

In conclusion, he reminded the international community:

> A presupposition of a nation's right is certainly its right to exist therefore no one-neither a state nor another nation, nor an international organization is ever justified in asserting that an individual nation is not worthy of existence.

That same session of the UNGA adopted the declaration contained in document A/AC240/1995/CPR.1VRev.1, reaffirming "…the right to self-determination of all peoples taking into account the particular situation of people under colonial or other forms of alien domination or foreign occupation, and recognizing the right of peoples to take legitimate action in accordance with the Charter of the United Nations to realize their inalienable right of self-determination."

The British Southern Cameroons case against la République du Cameroun at the African Commission on Human and Peoples' Rights (ACHPR) in Banjul, The Gambia, is about the entire territory of Southern Cameroons as per the treaties in force. As Southern Cameroons won the Abuja Federal High Court ruling against Nigeria, so will ACHPR against la République du Cameroun. Once the Southern Cameroons identity question or inalienable right to sovereignty is solved, the Bakassi matter would have automatically been resolved.

Conclusion

The right to self-determination of any people held together by a common culture and history, and belonging to the same defined and recognised territory under international law, is a highly rated principle of international law. Self-determination, which expresses the will of the people, must be seen as the other side of the cherished coin of democratic principle. It is not a destabilising force but an engine of stability, confidence building and the means to the social and economic development of the peoples and nations concerned. In his *Why Division?* (1998), Nadesan Satyendra, in defence of the right to self- determination of all distinct peoples, makes this soul searching declaration: "If democracy means the government of the people, by the people, for the people, then the principle of self- determination secures that no one people may rule another."

Southern Cameroonians are not citizens of la République du Cameroun and cannot be made so by presidential decree or by the constant use and waving of the gun and constant release of mortal bullets into their skulls and stomachs when peacefully protesting. They are a distinct people by history and colonial heritage – the yardstick that defines and makes all other African nation states separate from one another. Why then, should the right to self-determination be denied Southern Cameroonians who attained self-government in 1954 as a British Trust Territory, and was from 1960 until 1961, a separate state between the two newly independent nations of Nigeria (to the west) and la République du Cameroun (to the east)?

Southern Cameroons, victim of imperfect decolonisation, has become a colony of la République du Cameroun consequent upon annexation, occupation and imposition of alien rule. This has undermined stability, peace and democracy in the sub-region. The Bakassi Peninsula conflict is consequent upon imperfect decolonisation in British Southern Cameroons, kindled by République du Cameroun which is exploiting it to legalise its annexation, colonisation and brutal occupation of Southern Cameroons.

Like la République du Cameroun and Nigeria, British Southern Cameroons is entitled to effective decolonisation and independence within the ambit of international law, the UN Charter and resolutions to enable the people to shape their destiny under their democratically-elected government. Finally, effective decolonisation will enable the sovereign independent state of Southern Cameroons to assume its deserved seat at the UN and other international forums, and contribute to the building of democracy, peace-based justice, and development, a free world and greater humanity. The UN is duly bound to complete the decolonisation process that it started – and abandoned midstream, which facilitated the annexation of a UN Trust Territory.

Endnotes

1. Asiwaju, Anthony I. The Bakassi Peninsula Crisis: An Alternative to War and Litigation, in Boundaries and Energy Problems and Prospects.

2. Shirley V. Scott, (editor) International Law & Politics, Lynne Rienner Publishers, Inc., London, 2006, p.66.

3. Eyongetah R. Brain, A History of the Cameroon, Longman Group Limited, London, 1974, p.53.

4. Wm Roger Louis, Great Britain and the African Peace Settlement of 1919 in American Historical Review, Vol.61, 1966, p.881.

5. *Ibid*, p.885

6. Quincy Wright, Sovereignty of the Mandates in the American Journal of International Law, Vol. XVII, October 1923, p.691

7. *Ibid*, p.695. The question that readily comes to mind is, how far did the UK honour this obligation as far as the administration of British Cameroon was concerned?

8. Determined never to return the acquired territories to Germany and to keep each as distinct, exclusive systems were introduced. As for the British it was a question of revamping what had been introduced in 1958. There are recorded reports of people welcoming British forces, complaining of several murders by German forces and one of the Reports to the Colonial Office concludes " from these statements it will very plainly be seen the awe in which the native held the German; and also the universal

dread of the German's return to this country." P. V. YOUNG, Resident, Cameroons Province, 17th June, 1918.

9. It must be remarked that in signing the Trusteeship Agreement in 1946, HM Government in Article 3 (quoted here above), pledged to honour and respect the obligations of the Administering Authority as enshrined in Article 76(b) of the UN Charter. The issue of a plebiscite as a means to accomplish independence by joining was a colonial construct in total violation of the UN Charter, and the will and legitimate aspirations of the people, made known both to HM Government and the UN.

10. Quincy Wright, Op. cit. p.697

11. The News, 21 March 1994, p.25

12. Cameroon Life, April/May 1994, p.14

13. Ndi Anthony, Southern/West Cameroon Revisited, 1950-1972: Unveiling Inescapable Traps, Volume One, Paul's Press, Bamenda, 2013, p.343.

Special note should be taken of the fact that Lees' report covers the Grassland region from which Foncha comes. This does not only dismiss the empty propaganda being peddled by la République and the agents that unification was cherished and that Foncha and the Grass landers carried/sold people to la République du Cameroun, it proves beyond any reasonable doubt that international colonial conspiracy pushed British Southern Cameroons into a trap and Foncha coincidentally happened to have been the unwilling shepherd.

14. *Ibid*, p.350

15. Cameroon Life, April/May 1994, p.14

16. Memoriam: Submission of la République du Cameroun to the ICJ on Land Dispute with the Federal Republic of Nigeria, 1994, par. 2, 143, p. 107.

17. The News, op cit.

18. Ian Brownlie, Principles of Public International Law, Claredon Press, Oxford, 4th Edition 1990, p.135.

19. ICJ Ruling of 22nd December 1986, Boundary Dispute case, Rec.1986, p.566.

Part III

In Defence of Identity

Chapter Six

Recurrent Fractured Foundation

On October 1, 1961 the hastily-crafted Federal Republic of Cameroon, Cameroon, without legal anchor and instrument or treaty of union, binding a culture and common language, without a common history, political philosophy and administrative system, without a common value system and world view and shared aspirations of the two peoples and two nations, stood like a a giant on clay feet. The two nations, two peoples, one Anglo-Saxon, and the other, Francophone, were strangers to each other. Both the leaders and the masses could only communicate through an interpreter. There was no sense of belonging; nothing binding them together in respect of the foundation of modern African nation states, namely, colonial heritage. For distinct peoples to forge a common destiny, there must be common aspirations and common interests to preserve, develop and promote the common good. For a people to claim a common identity, they must be held together by a common culture built over the years by the same historical experiences. A common culture that holds and binds a people together is woven by shared experiences, beliefs and core values. These constitute the foundation of an evolving national personality and consciousness, giving those who hold common beliefs and core values, their concept of man and his mission, society, social relationships, ethical values, beliefs, common aspirations and world view. Language plays an important role in national personality as it is the vehicle and storehouse of shared ideas and values, which must be preserved as well as marketed to project the worth and identity of the people within the cosmos.

All these were absent in this federal republic of strangers, with no commitment to what was professed publicly. To hold the parts together, no matter the length of time, it was obvious that some key greedy players were bound to adopt unorthodox means to satisfy their self-interests.

Nation-building must have a foundation, and there is no foundation that will hold together and serve as a reference point outside culture.

This chapter aims at demonstrating that in the absence of a unifying culture to hold the two distinct Cameroons together, and that le Cameroun Français, which came into being upon a hidden agenda, has annexed and colonised British Southern Cameroons, which under the circumstance, has every right under international instruments to seek external self-determination, and that this cannot be realised without fighting the erosion of its own cultural values and the imposition of Francophonism via assimilation and domination.

What is Culture? And why is it important and central to national liberation?

The Chambers Universal Learners Dictionary defines culture as "a form or type of civilisation of a certain race or nation and the customs associated with it."

For example, you can talk of African, American or Arab culture in the same manner as you would of Kenyan or Senegalese culture, each nation having its own, distinct culture through which it expresses itself and by which it is recognised. Serving as the soul of the nation, it is equally important to understand that as a nation cannot exist without culture, culture itself has no fertile ground from which to grow and propagate if without a nation, and the state gives it form and self-expression.

Frantz Fanon maintains that "...culture is first the expression of a nation, the expression of its preferences, of its taboos and of its patterns. It is at every stage of the whole of society that other taboos, values and patterns are formed. A national culture is the sum total of all these appraisals; it is the result of internal and external extensions exerted over society as a whole and also at every level of that society. In the colonial situation, culture, which is doubly deprived of the support of the nation and of the state, falls away and dies. The condition for its existence is therefore national liberation and the renaissance of the state."[1]

According to Dr Bernard Fonlon, "...culture is to a country what a soul is to a man, that is the principle of life, of unity and continuity; and therefore, that a nation is not just merely so many millions of people living on the same land or stemming from the same ancestral origin, but that a nation, thanks to its culture, is essentially a unit of thought and feeling, and will and action."

Culture is not static; it is dynamic and evolves as the people's capacity and mastery of their environment and social condition progress. It is not culture that creates a people. On the contrary, it is the people that build their culture. Through their specific civilisation, they defend, preserve, promote and protect their common identity. Man's insatiable quest to improve his living condition, to produce for himself and more, to understand his physical and social environment, to reach out and interact with his fellow man, to explore even the unknown and to understand his origin, provides the material content of his culture or civilisation.

Patrick F. Wilmot says: "Culture is the total self-expression of a people, through which a people reflects on its destiny as a people, and becomes conscious of itself as a people. By thus reflecting on itself, by becoming aware of its achievements and failures, a people can chart a course of action based on a realistic consciousness of its own strength."[2] Quite often, culture is limited to dances, modes of dressing, carved stools and brass heads, tools, hair styles and language, amongst others. As important as these are, it is clear that culture shapes the mode of social relationships, determines and directs economic, scientific, technological development and the political life of the given people.

From these definitions, it is explicit that the culture of a people or national culture is alive and waxing strong when the nation is on firm feet, and not a victim of foreign domination and alien rule, which cannot thrive if the culture of the dominated is left intact or if and force and laws are used to disrupt and kill what gives the people a sense of distinct identity. Frantz Fanon declares: "Colonial domination, because it is total and tends to over-simplify, very soon manages to disrupt in spectacular fashion the cultural life of a conquered people. This cultural obliteration is made possible by the negation of national reality, by new legal relations introduced by the occupying power, by the banishment of the natives and their customs to outlying districts by colonial society, by expropriation, and by the systematic enslaving of men and women."[3]

Colonial Imprint: The Building of the Two Distinct Cameroons

To subjugate and weaken the power of resistance, colonialism imposed western cultures in Africa: each colonial power implanted in its colony the culture of the metropolis. Everything indigenous to Africa was considered primitive, barbaric and had to be put away or destroyed. However, some works of art, condemned by anthropologists and missionaries as the idols or the gods of primitive Africans, were carted away into and remain confiscated until today by western museums as objects of great value, serving as attractions to tourists and sources of income.

From 1916, after the defeat of German forces, the great empire builders of Europe, the UK and France partitioned and occupied what hitherto was referred to as the German Protectorate of Kamerun. At the founding of the League of Nations at the end of WWI, what was ratified in 1884/5 during the Berlin Conference as German possessions was declared spoils of war and Germany, was made to renounce all claims and rights over its overseas territories. Though enemy territories were not to become integral parts of the existing colonial empires of the time, they were subjected to the same political philosophy and administered by same colonial administrator, under the same colonial administrative systems. The administrators were either posted from the metropolitan capital or transferred from another colony. Their mission in the ex-enemy territory was the promotion of the Administering Authority's interest, namely, economic benefit and political prestige.

After the WWII, these ex-enemy territories became Trust Territories. Although the Trusteeship Council obtained periodic reports through the UN Visiting Missions, Trust territories in practical terms were not treated better than colonies and were made to benefit from the overloaded notion of 'sacred trust'. The consequent failure of the UK Government to accord British Cameroons preferential treatment as expected under the sacred trust fared worse than in all other British colonies in West Africa.

The emergence of two Cameroons is understood firstly through the physical partition that took place in 1916 and was ratified by the Versailles Peace Treaty and the League of Nations in 1922. Secondly, after WWII, the two Cameroons became Trust Territories of the UN, and the Trusteeship Agreements signed respectively with the two Administering Authorities – France for French Cameroun and the UK for British Cameroons – maintained their exclusiveness. Thirdly, this partition sustained to this day, gives the two distinct territories contrasting personalities and visions, thanks to the philosophies and cultural building blocks of the two European powers that occupied divided German Protectorate of Kamerun. Through their administrative, legal, educational systems and socio-cultural values, these European powers imbued their respective civilisations and personalities into their territories thus, moulding the distinct two Cameroons.

In French Cameroun, France planted the seed of French culture. The overriding interest of the French colonial mission was to spread French culture as a logical means of making overseas territories, colonies and Trust Territories alike, integral parts of France. Central to the French colonial philosophy were two images which were of 'prestige' and 'grandeur'. France saw Africa as the means of making France a super power in the world. The apostles of French imperialism held that the duty of the metropolitan France was to "transform, according to her image, the people over which she has extended her sovereignty, to imbue them with her spirit, her heart and her faith."[4] Jules Ferry, a leading supporter of the colonial mission during the Third Republic, boldly set the seal for the harmonisation of the notions of wealth and prestige as two sides of the same imperialist coin. He argued that France "cannot be resigned to playing only the role of a second-ranked nation in the world" and that France must do wherever she can and spread "her language, her customs, her flag, her weapons, her genius."[5]

French statesmen were committed to building a multi-continental French state, and (theoretically) propagated the idea of equal citizenship to all, irrespective of colour. In the building of a French multi-continental state or Greater France, assimilation was exported to the overseas territories evenly with no distinction between colony and Trust Territory. To acquire French citizenship and enjoy full rights and privileges, one was expected to have been imbibed with French culture and to master the French language. The political elite did everything possible to enforce these conditions. France and the French culture were universal standard. And to succeed in this enterprise, the superiority of the French culture – the civilising mission – was systematically established while erasing all remnants of German culture and notion of German Kamerun. The reality painted was that of le Cameroun Français as imbued with a personality by France, to which it must remain attached.

All these shaped the position of the inhabitants of French colonies and Trust territories under French Administration. France set standards for them, which they endeavoured to reach. The elite glorified everything French and could never assert their own separate worth as they became dependent on France. Those who sat in the French National Assembly, such as Houphouët-Boigny or Senghor, were even opposed to African independence when anti-colonialist movements were sweeping across British colonies and North Africa. When it could no longer be denied, France granted flag independence or *indépendance avec la France*. A black Frenchman inherited the throne vacated by a white Frenchman – the true master – in the overseas territory. While France is saved from direct responsibility, with co-operation agreements (Pact Colonial), such as what Ahidjo signed with President de Gaulle in November 1959 with the assistance of a multitude of technical advisers in all domains, the heir to the throne is meant to protect, preserve and promote French interests in the Francophone African nation state. Treating France Outremer as part of the multi-racial French state, Frenchmen were encouraged to invest and settle in overseas

French territories, which considerably accounted for economic and infrastructural development in French Cameroun. Paris, to this day still guides major policies, and decides who manages its affairs and promotes the interests of France in Yaoundé.

Unlike that of France, the political philosophy that influenced English nationalism is committed to liberty based on Christianity and moral ethics. English nationalism, like French nationalism, was also the mother of imperial expansion, and English political philosophy puts great emphasis on the individual and the community. There is no question of detaching an individual from their root. Respecting their culture, as long as it did not contradict the colonial system in place and posed no problem to British colonial philosophy and interest, both the indigenous cultural values and the imported one co-existed.

Consequently, the colonies were never seen and treated as an integral part of the UK nor did representatives from the colonies and Trust territories ever sit in the House of Commons or House of Lords. There was a clear distinction between the UK and France as far as colonial philosophy was concerned. Assimilation, as a means of creating an elite class, was not practiced in British colonies and Trust Territories.

As British Southern Cameroons was administered as part of Nigeria, colonial administrators posted to the Trust Territory had a free hand in the adoption of an administrative system suited to local realities. Thus, the indirect rule system was adopted, and this gave rise to the use of local human resource. While the French direct rule system interfered, and in some cases even destroyed the indigenous political system and institutions, the British indirect rule system recognised, sustained and used the same to administer the people: "The indirect rule system was a policy, which allowed the powers of traditional rulers to remain intact to the maximum degree consistent with imperial rule."[6]

Since there was no notion of building a multi-racial British state, thus making the overseas territories integral parts of the UK, few British men went out to administer the colonies. Although primarily based on economic interests, British colonisation however necessitated the training of indigenes, for a start, to take over the lower jobs. The colonies were expected to be self-sustaining. Treated as a small and valueless territory, which was described as dispensable, British Southern Cameroons was paid little attention in terms of economic development. This explains why British Southern Cameroons remained, for almost half a century, underdeveloped and the most 'backward' area of British West Africa.

The direct involvement of the local elite in modern or democratic governance such as the traditional rulers and the few educated elite, and especially those who returned from the two world wars, gave rise to the building of national consciousness. To their credit, the colonial policy made it mandatory for recruited Africans to work only within the territorial boundaries of their homeland. Nationalism and the spirit of self-determination sprang in British colonies and Trust Territories, bringing benefits to the natives earlier than it did in French colonies and Trust Territories. Comparably, the UK developed a more progressive colonial policy and granted self-government to its colonies much earlier than France, Belgium, Portugal and Spain. While France dismissed self-rule by 1946, India attained independence in 1947, and in 1957, Gold Coast in West Africa, became independent Ghana, these two latter countries being ex-British colonies.[7]

British Southern Cameroons, although much smaller and underdeveloped than French Cameroun, had achieved self-governance with a constitutionally elected government in 1954, while French Cameroun attained the same status with an elected government in 1957. In this same year, British Southern Cameroons moved one more step further in its march towards independence, when a House of Chiefs was constitutionally created, enhancing the role of traditional rulers, the custodians of native or indigenous laws and customs. Such an institution never existed in French Cameroun as Paris was interested in the co-opted elite whose mission was to drag it into the embrace of France. Thus, while there was no House of Chiefs in French Cameroun, an important step towards modernising the indigenous institution of governance was constitutionalised in British Southern Cameroons which, like The UK, administered a parliamentary system of government, had a bicameral legislature with the House of Chiefs holding a similar position of honour like the British House of Lords.

Another area worth examining is the significant role the imported metropolitan languages played in the scheme of things. While the use of French was a necessary instrument to implant the French rigid centralised system and culture and the moulding of dependent elite in French Cameroun, the liberal policy of British Southern Cameroons permitted the teaching of local languages – the storehouse of the people's cultural heritage. The result obtained in Southern Cameroons was the same in Nigeria and other British-administered territories. This encouraged the development of local languages, and in British West Africa, this freedom led to the development of an English-based pidgin. It still serves as a lingua-franca in British West Africa, with a few variations. The pidgin in British Southern Cameroons developed as well as it did due to the plantation agricultural system that led to urbanisation in the coast and spread into French Cameroonian towns such as Douala and Nkongsamba. It was thus easier in Douala, for example, to have an elder express himself in a smattering of pidgin than in French, the policy of assimilation.[8]

The British stood clean of acculturation or assimilation. Nevertheless, to the French, this was central to the colonial policy of building a multiracial super power European state as the colonies were tied to the apron strings of Paris. British colonial policy measured its success in the spread of commerce and acceptance of British laws, which emphasised human freedom and dignity. The French saw success in the adoption of French culture and in the subordination of the colonies to the complete and eternal dominance of France.

The classic contrasts between the colonial policies of these two leading African colonial powers – UK and France – and how they shaped the two Cameroons, one Anglo-Saxon, and the other Francophone, are indeed revealing. While British paternalism took the form of pressures to preserve custom and maintain distance between the UK and Southern Cameroons and between the British and Southern Cameroonians, French paternalism held the '*évolué*' to bring le Cameroun Français into the full grip of France as a means of sustaining French prestige and grandeur. French paternalism had "No room for the primitive chief but the *évolué*, graduate of a French University, denizen of a Paris Salon, the African who had thoroughly imbibed French culture."[9] In other words, British colonial policy was "empirical, commercial, practicing indirect rule, keeping Africans at a distance, verging on racism", while that of the French was "Cartesian in its logic, seeking glory, practicing direct administration, acting as apostles of fraternity and anti-racism"[10], albeit theoretically, for the maximum benefit of the system.

But this was practiced because it gave the imperial nation the desired advantage and explains why, despite French imperial philosophy of a multi-racial French nation, black Africans never enjoyed the same status as French citizens. Recruits from Algeria, Senegal and Mali were sent off to France to provide slave labour in the development of the railway system, for example. No white French citizens were subjected to such type of physical labour – the unpleasant jobs set aside for subjects from the black continent who were deemed to have the type of physical energy and strength required for these. On the other hand, while such modern railway system (including the underground one) was developed in France to ease the movement of goods and services, no such thing was done in the colonies; any such development was substandard and limited to moving goods to the ports for export to Europe and to bring manufactured goods from the ports to the colonial capital from where transportation to natives was done with extreme difficulties due to poor infrastructure. Everything was exploitative to maximise gain for the benefit of France.

Thus, while the British left behind them the legacy of self-consciousness and pride in one's roots, the French, through assimilation, uprooted the Francophone Cameroon elite and made the latter dependent on France for the realisation of their personal worth. On March 4, 1916, these two colonial powers did to German Kamerun what Europe did to Africa in 1884. Through the partition and in keeping with their respective avowed colonial policies, they have effectively nurtured two Cameroons, two peoples with two distinct cultures. With diametrically opposed world views and concepts of the state and common good, the more the Francophone ruing class – which has monopolised political, military, economic and judicial power – has tried to impose what it inherited, namely, assimilation, on Southern Cameroonians, the more the latter rejects it and defends instead, their distinctiveness. Between the two, distrust, bitter memories and ill-feeling are recurrent and threateningly explosive. The more le Cameroun Français uses force, assimilation, patronage, corruption and other tactics to subject British Southern Cameroonians to consent to French ways being superior and should be accepted for their personal transformation, the more the latter, so as to remain masters of their destiny, reject these and hold on tenaciously to their values and use reason and the law to win the war against annexation, colonial domination and alien rule by Yaoundé.

The Fault Line

Every human being is born into a family, and each family belongs to a community of human beings that has built a history, culture, a consciousness and a personality. The consciousness of belonging to your own family and kind is equally strong among animals. Ducks, fowls, cats, dogs, goats and sheep may belong to one farmer and co-habit but each knows and defends its kind. Even the chicks of a hen will not stray to the duck nor will the young lamb stray to the goat for milk. If animals and birds are so rational in judgement when it concerns defending identity, should human beings – rational – not be more aggressive in such defence and do much better? Is it a crime to do so?

The question of identity, or 'who one is', is natural to all human beings. What it seeks to achieve is to distinguish and separate 'we' from 'them' in terms of genealogy, tribe, history, culture, language, religion, values and institutions or nations. Each people seeks to define its place within humanity, and above all strives to be recognised, accepted and respected as the equal of other human beings and communities. What must be accepted as reality that the politics of identity is the dominant issue for a people's survival in dignity. No people wants to be subordinated to foreign domination, and each wants to occupy its equal political space in world affairs and make its legitimate contribution toward a better world. It is in the nature of man to be his own master, and a people, to be their own master. This explains why people fought against foreign domination and alien rule of the white. No people in human history have ever willingly surrendered their place to outsiders.

When different cultures meet, be it for mutual benefit or otherwise, the point at which they converge is a "fault line."[11] When the meeting is mutual, there is respect, confidence is built, social interaction is generated and sustained, and there is cohesion as the spirit of give and take enhances the identity of each, facilitating the cross-fertilisation of cultural values.

But when differences are not natural, there is something fundamentally wrong with the coming together of distinct groups. If society A sees it as their right to treat B as inferior for the mere reason that they are different and therefore deficient, the latter is placed in a vulnerable position, one which is worse than when the latter surrenders to A. In such circumstances, the relationship lacks cordiality: there is no thread of fairness, trust and an environment conducive for growth and development. When recognition, acceptance, respect and tolerance are absent, when hostility reigns and when domination and assimilation are the policy of the stronger, the victim is bound to resist and to develop a withdrawn posture, causing distrust and conflict between the two, leading to disintegration. This has been a permanent feature of human history, and most wars are consequent on a clash of cultures because each culture is unique. Culture, a storehouse of a peoples' rich heritage, is not only unique, but it is equally dynamic, exporting, as well as receiving of what it finds from other people, to be of fundamental value. It has the capacity to both accept and reject anything found to stand against its nature and identity.

As each culture is unique, each community of human beings is unique and rejects any act that forces their subordination. No people and no culture duplicate the other, and no two peoples share the same historical experiences. To avoid conflict over geographical space, God – the Creator – gave to each people their eternal inheritance on Earth. To avoid that people enter conflict consequent upon expansionist tendencies, God also gave the eternal law: "Do not remove the ancient landmarks…" (Prov. 23:10). It should be pointed that the clash of cultures, which is responsible for most wars in history, is the consequence of expansionism by greedy, powerful states that violate this divine law.

One distinguishing aspect of the modern age is the increasing sense of self-consciousness made possible by the explosion of knowledge and easy communication. The world today is a global village of distinct cultures, peoples and nations, with each stressing the importance of self-preservation and self-identity. Struggles for the defence of self-identity, in any part of the world, are known even by people in remote areas, owing to advancement in communication and technology. People are bound to compare, contrast, ask questions and find solutions to problems.

Change is an inevitable phenomenon in any society and is most compelling in one under foreign domination and colonial occupation. It is the vehicle of human progress, and the more people of any given society are innovative, creative, hardworking, are united and patriotic, the faster and more sustaining their level of development.

Martin Luther King Jr declares: "Change, does not roll in on the wheels of inevitability but comes through continuous struggle. And so we must straighten our backs and work for our freedom. A man cannot ride you unless your back is bent."

Change in society comes by disapproval and rejection of injustice and the strife for justice and freedom as inherent human rights. In seeking to overcome evil, people create the primary condition for development. Once people believe they are worth more than what they are made to believe or what they are experiencing – an unwholesome state of affairs in which they find themselves – they must disapprove of their current state and cherish what their status and the condition in which they find themselves have denied them. When they do so, they must, by natural and international law, be determined to go for that which will bestow upon them their true and respectable worth and identity. Unless a people hate what they are not, they cannot love what they are. The force in shaping the world in the post-Cold War era is that of "culture and cultural identities, which at the broadest level are civilisation identities." Huntington maintains that people who ignore this reality "deny their family, their heritage, their culture, their birth right, their very selves. They will not lightly be forgiven"[12], for, to stand against change is to betray the people by denying them their rightful place of honour in history.

British Southern Cameroons today stands at the crossroads of history. After forty-five years under British administration as a UN Trust, it finds itself under black colonialism or neo-apartheid, comparable only to apartheid in old South Africa. What is mind-boggling and unexplainable, is that the less powerful la République du Cameroun aspires to swallow British Southern Cameroons, a task which was impossible for Nigeria, a greater, more powerful country. At the dawn of the third millennium, it is taboo to pronounce or write 'Southern Cameroons' for others to hear or read. It is sacrilege to draw the map of Southern Cameroons. And it is treacherous to convene a meeting on such a subject on Southern Cameroonian soil. Many have gone to prison for wearing t-shirts with inscriptions such as 'FREE SOUTHERN CAMEROONS'. Some have disappeared, never to be heard of again, while others have been brutally murdered by the forces of occupation for countering the make-belief that Cameroun is one and indivisible. Arbitrary arrests, torture, detentions are so frequent to the point that activists and the faithful eulogise release from detention as "Baptism of fire" which purifies and hardens and raises the individual to a hero. Consequently, those who miss an arrest opportunity regret and lament it. What the authorities defend so eloquently and shamelessly is that this Cameroun includes what came to be known and identified as British Southern Cameroons after WWI. What these neo-African imperialists fail to explain is the need for an enlarged la République du Cameroun, former le Cameroun Français, at the cost of a sovereign independent Southern Cameroons. For Southern Cameroons to surrender to imperialism is to betray humanity and the cause of FREEDOM and HUMAN EQUALITY, as ordained by the MOST HIGH from Creation and defended by international law and conventions.

In the struggle for the Southern Cameroonian identity and sovereign independence, primacy must be given to defining and accepting who Southern Cameroonians truly are and who they are not. The boundaries that separate Southern Cameroonians from Francophone Cameroonians or *les Camerounais français* must be clear. What makes one different from the other is natural and not a simple matter of discrimination and marginalisation. This cannot be without consequences. But this struggle in defence of TRUTH, LEGALITY and JUSTICE should be recorded as natural because it is a noble cause. That Southern Cameroonians are not French Cameroonians, or *les Camerounais français*, is a fact of natural law and not hatred. The sun rising in the east, no matter where you stand, is a law of nature which man does not have the power to modify or change in the same manner as Southern Cameroons having the right to exist as a separate nation. It is disadvantageous to human beings to not recognise and accept cultural differences, and to cover up and pretend that they do not exist or that one can be superimposed on the other on grounds that the one is superior to the other. This is what breeds conflict between peoples of different cultural backgrounds and delays human progress since time and resources are wasted on solving avoidable problems instead of investing in human development for universal peace and greater humanity. The genesis of most human conflicts and wars that have threatened to shatter the hopes of humanity and reverse human history can be traced to a clash of different cultures, with the one claiming superiority and imposing itself onto the other, considered to be inferior. What humankind has come to learn and accept is that no culture and people will ever surrender to extinction. All strive to maintain their boundaries and preserve their identity for posterity. Who are we and who does not belong are questions constant in human history. Huntington maintains that, "we know who we are only when we know who we are not and often only when we know who we are against."[13]

To maintain the annexed colony by portraying a false image in defence of the much vaunted and indivisible Cameroun is deliberate cultural pollution and dilution on the one hand and cultural emasculation on the other. Through the confiscation of political, military, judicial and economic power, Southern Cameroons is flooded with Francophone administrators, civil servants, military and judicial authorities. Even the wardens who control traffic in the towns of Southern Cameroons are Francophone. Not only is admission into higher institutions controlled by the Francophone ministers in Yaoundé, but the few institutions which Southern Cameroonians got – at great cost to their persons and dignity – are also dominated by Francophone lecturers and students. In business, they dominate the economy not only in the sectors where Southern Cameroonians lack capital but even in petty trade. During weekends and holidays, the streets in the big towns are invaded by Bamilike teenagers selling all kinds of goods. The old cry of Ibo domination, which served as the battle cry for secession is indeed child's play. While the old cry was a problem relating to the character of the individual, be it a Bamilike, a Bassa, a Beti, a Douala, the current is institutionalised, supported and defended by the establishment. With ready capital, and strong ties with the administration, wretched Southern Cameroonians are selling their land, including ancestral graves, to the Francophone at an alarming rate. While the ordinary Francophone is getting the land at give-away price, the Francophone administrators use their overwhelming powers and privileged positions to get what they want, and through corruption and embezzlement, build the mansions they want.

With the glaring lack of opportunities for employment, many young Southern Cameroonian are forced to move to the towns of Yaoundé, Douala, Edea, Garoua, Nkongsamba or Kribi for greener pastures. These young people, like their counterparts in institutions of higher learning for survival instinct, become victims of cultural emasculation, consequent upon intensified assimilation. The picture painted here can only be experienced, for there is no language that can better explain the situation to an outsider.

From whichever angle, this is a deliberate policy of Francophone population implantation in Southern Cameroons, emasculating Southern Cameroonians of their cultural heritage and brainwashing them with a slave mentality to water down the struggle for liberation and restoration of British Southern Cameroons statehood.

To defend identity is to look and move inward, anchor in your roots, hold unto the roots of your natural identity and to love and cherish what means much and accounts for your being. This is the evidence of your knowing and cherishing to preserve and in honour, defending and being proud of who you are. Self-love leads to self-will to protect and defend. To love who you are implies to hate who you are not. Until you hate what imposes a false consciousness and personality on you, you cannot truly love, cherish, defend and promote who truly you are created to be – a free and equal being. Politics is an instrument man uses to defend the 'we' as opposed to the 'them'. This helps to distinguish those outside from the 'we' inside, thus enhancing collective self-identity. This does not mean closing the door, but being who you are in order to better open up and interact with your fellows as equals for the onward match of human civilisation; you cannot impact the world from an inferior or slave position.

Once a foreign culture is imposed on another, it registers a crack in the fault line, demanding the defence of exclusive identity, which can only be reinstated by separation or disintegration of the two or more societies held together by force. This separation is absolute to conform to the natural order of things; it is to respect and maintain the boundary line that separates the one from the other. This separation is to restore the boundary line of mutual respect and not hatred. The laws of nature stand for cooperation based on mutual respect, tolerance and a shared spirit, and not intolerance and imposition. People resist and fight psychologically, then physically for what distorts their history, personality and vision of the cosmos, and makes them inferior to the people of the imposed culture. It must be understood that man is firstly a cultural man before being anything else. Nothing binds people together better than the culture that shapes their individual and collective being. Ideologies and religion may cut across and bring people of different cultures together, but culture maintains its boundaries. It is an enduring cementing force for those inside, or who belong, as opposed to those outside the culture boundary who, by the natural order of things, do not belong.

Culture and National Restoration:

Culture is defined as the "core element of the distinctiveness of peoples and other communities is often at the centre of the claim for self-determination when the cultural identity and expression of a community is suppressed or threatened."[14] The binding and generative force of cultural values on a people, under foreign domination and occupation, is fundamental to the notion of and claim of the right to self-determination. It is this consciousness of avoiding the inevitable that pushes a colonial regime to desperately engage in cultural genocide and the policy of divide and rule to weaken the colonised and keep them as the footstool of the coloniser. But, culture assuming the force of the living spirit of any given people, cannot so easily be broken, killed or set aside. The more the colonised are oppressed and brutalised, the more hatred against the coloniser intensifies and forces the oppressed to look inward. The scars of merciless brutalisation, a broken spirit caused by systematic repression as well as mental agony confirm that they are treated as sub-humans because they are different, because they have lost control over their land and natural resources, which are exploited for the benefit of the coloniser, and because they do not exercise political and legal authority over their land. They are poor, wretched, oppressed and treated disdainfully because their fate is in the hands of foreign rulers. The one who controls your land dominates you, imposes his laws, culture and history, and as the victim, you cease to be his equal for he dictates your actions at will.

Judging from the lifestyle of the people of British Southern Cameroons and their attachment to their ancestral lands, it is conclusive that the people draw their "spiritual, cultural or economic strength and vitality from the land"[15] and their natural environment. Conscious of the natural bond that exists between a people and their land, the UNGA proclaimed in its in Resolution 1803 (XVII) the "right of peoples and nations to permanent sovereignty over their natural wealth and resources." The political and cultural development of a people is predicated on the independence a people exercise to exploit their natural wealth for their own benefit. But, a people subjugated loses all rights to the control of their land and natural resources, which are plundered to weaken the basis of reawakening and resistance.

It is a fact that each modern African nation state is a product of its colonial history. If from 1916 to 1961, British Southern Cameroons and French Cameroun (modern la République du Cameroun) were respectively ruled by two distinct colonial European powers, namely, UK and France, and within this period of separate existence, each gained independence as a territorial, legal, cultural, economic and historical reality, what then justifies the disappearance of British Southern Cameroons, and by what instrument of international law does la République du Cameroun exercise sovereignty over Southern Cameroons other than by annexing and occupying this former UN Trust Territory? In comforting deception, la République du Cameroun lays claim to being the successor state of German Kamerun. But German Kamerun ceased to exist at the Peace Treaty of Versailles, and it was within the Trusteeship period from 1945 to 1960 that anti-colonialist movements took the upper hand in shaping national consciousness and institutions of statehood developed in the two distinct Cameroons, and in January 1960, French Cameroun gained independence from France. But the character of anti-colonialist movement adopted in British Southern Cameroons differed from that in French Cameroun, which was violently suppressed by French colonial forces. The two were never one Trust Territory under one Administering Authority, and the two never gained independence as one sovereign nation state.

The incontrovertible evidence before us, as painful as it is, is that la République du Cameroun, by force of annexation and occupation, exercises full sovereignty over Southern Cameroons land and resources at the expense of the true owners of the territory. While British Southern Cameroons was, under trusteeship rule, a territorial unit under international supervision, the situation under la République du Cameroun is worse: la République du Cameroun rule in British Southern Cameroons is not governed by any law. This is done in violation of international law and norms governing peaceful co-operation among nations and peoples.

Consequent upon the imposition of Francophone centralist political power and culture in Southern Cameroons, the foundation of the Anglo-Saxon liberal political culture cracked upon the abolition of the political institutions that were established to defend and promote values. This dealt a deathblow to the blossoming of constitutional democracy, the rule of law, freedom of assembly and expression, freedom of the press, free market economy, balanced development and equal opportunity for all the citizens. The disruptive effect of annexation and assimilation as well as the imposition of foreign culture are seen in the enslavement of the people and are visible everywhere in Southern Cameroons in stagnation, economic rape, abandonment and decay, and the development of underdevelopment. For Southern Cameroons to share in the hope of a free people, enjoy the benefits of democracy, and reap the fruits of the abundance of their natural endowments, radical change to oust foreign domination and alien rule is a prerequisite.

For the culture of an annexed people to be relevant to or become the engine of national rebirth and positive change, it must reject foreign domination; it must be built around the social conditions of the people. This is "culture which eschews nostalgia and sentimentality, effeminacy and illusion. Such a culture is part of the rhythm of the life of the people tapping the most vital sources of their repressed historical development."[16] Translated in music, art, literature and science, it must be a mirror of the people's true social condition. Such is culture that is a binding, mobilising and is an invigorating force that serves as the sustaining engine of national rebirth.

Every people or every state, to be relevant in world affairs and dynamically play a meaningful role in the furtherance of human civilisation, democracy, freedom, equality and world peace based on justice, must fight to conquer foreign domination and alien rule. The history of an enslaved people — a nation that is the footstool of another nation — cannot contribute to human civilisation and human dignity. People trampled upon have no history of their own. Their history is distorted or declared irrelevant, and history taught to their children is made-up stories that glorify their oppressors and the imposed system. Every distinct people, every nation, big or small, must strive to occupy its deserved position in world history. To be relevant and impact, is to actively be involved in shaping and contributing positively to world affairs. Huntington observes that the demise of the Cold War has created a new phenomenon, "the eruption of global identity crisis".

People are anxious to know their place in history. Pushed out of centre-stage, they are forced to look inward and then, look across, see the occupiers of the centre-stage and ask: Who are we; where do we belong; and who is not 'us'.[17] Wherever peoples of different civilisations have been co-existing under one national roof, such as Czechoslovakia and Yugoslavia in the former USSR, identity issues were bound to become quite intense. This resulted in the cracking of the fault line, and the emergence of separate nations along cultural civilisation lines. In the developing world of Africa and Asia, the situation is bound to be far more disturbing because colonial empire builders, to sustain their interests, dislocated genuine decolonisation forces when handing power over to their own agents. This meant that genuine decolonisation, crucial to the guarantee of freedom, equality, dignity, the blooming of genuine democratic process, enduring peace and sustainable development for the wellbeing and happiness of the people, was postponed.

Southern Rhodesia became Zimbabwe under Robert Mugabe, after ousting the white settler regime of Ian Smith which imposed itself on the majority Africans. Other similar African cases are these of Namibia, which the white apartheid regime in South Africa annexed; South Africa under a minority white regime that instituted the heinous apartheid rule; Eritrea which, through the help of Western interest was annexed by old Ethiopia under Emperor Haile Selassie; Western Sahara annexed by Morocco; and British Southern Cameroons annexed by la République du Cameroun with the help of international colonial conspiracy against the sovereign will of the people of Southern Cameroons.

The plebiscite of February 1961 in Southern Cameroons could never have been a logical means to an end because the options were imposed and therefore, were not options per se, and the third option, namely, sovereign independence, was denied to the people. Was the holding of a plebiscite, for the purpose of attempting independence by joining that denied outright independence in a self-governing UN Trust Territory, not a violation of the UN Charter, UN Resolution 1514, the fundamental human rights and the right to self-determination of the people of the Southern Cameroons?

Western colonial powers connived against the supreme interest of Southern Cameroonians, and exploiting the inherent weakness of the UN, made it play the role of a facilitator for the re-colonisation of Southern Cameroons by la République du Cameroun. Both Article 76(b) of the UN Charter and Resolution 1514 of 1960, which makes inalienable the right of all peoples and territories under colonial rule to freedom and independence unconditional, were ignored and violated. The plebiscite therefore, was not a genuine democratic instrument for Southern Cameroonians as a people to shape their destiny in view of the fact that the free exercise of their sovereign will was denied: they were called to run with their feet put in concrete. The exercise of political rights must not be tied to strings and must be without obstruction, control and external negative influences and manipulation. The history of mankind teaches that no people, no nation has ever freely voted for extinction. But, once an aggressor succeeds in his diabolic enterprise, he distorts and misrepresents the history of the subjugated people. Things only change for good when the people re-discover themselves, and know who their true friends and true enemies are. This explains why love and hate, and trust and distrust are natural and recurrent in human history.

The scientific analysis of the past and the clear understanding of the present, buried in hopelessness, must give birth to full resistance to the Yaoundé colonial regime. We must understand that colonialism, like a parasite, thrives and succeeds by means of the treacherous submissiveness of the intellectuals; the betrayal of the political elite who are contented with crumbs that fall from the colonial master's table; the detachment of the traditional rulers from their custodian roles to become rotten bananas in the hands of the colonial proconsuls for the mere glory of being called 'auxiliary of the administration'; the subservience of exploited women and youth; and the de-empowerment of the masses who become irrelevant to the political equation of the ruling clan. But the hope for a new dawn begins with a crop of patriotic intellectuals who, believing in the people, interact with the masses, and galvanising them, transform them into a formidable force whose united and patriotic actions ought to reverse the imposed evil system for the shaping and mastery of their legitimate destiny.

The unity of the politically-conscious intellectuals with the masses, and the giving of political education to and mobilisation of the masses for national rebirth is, in itself, transformational and gives birth to national culture. Culture, as a uniting force, is a necessity in the struggle for national existence which sets culture moving, and opens to it the doors of creation. Later, it is the nation which will ensure the conditions and framework necessary to culture. The nation gathers the various elements necessary for the creation of a culture – those elements, which alone, can give it credibility, validity, life and creative power. In the same way, it is its national character that will make such a culture open to other cultures, and enable it to influence and permeate other cultures. A non-existent culture can hardly be expected to have bearing on reality, or to influence reality. The first necessity is the reestablishment of the nation in order to give life to national culture in the strictly biological sense of the phrase.[18]

The coloniser dreads nothing as much as a politically-conscious people who have been mobilised, organised and empowered to fight foreign domination and alien rule. The unity of the patriotic intellectual and the masses heralds the inevitable downfall of colonial rule. No mistake should ever be made to ignore the role of the masses in anti-colonial struggle or any struggle to put down tyranny, and bring about democratic rule that should herald freedom, justice and sustainable development for all. Genuine and enduring change comes from transforming the minds and consciousness of the subjugated people. They must be made to see their poor condition as a direct consequence of their subjugation. Once a people are annexed, and their land occupied through brazen exploitation, systematic torture and enslavement of their minds, their creative powers are held hostage. Political education, effective mobilisation and organisation of the masses release the creative talents and transform a people's power into the key to unlock their right to freedom, development, dignity, equality and justice. The struggle to re-establish their national sovereignty is a concrete manifestation of cultural nationalism which assumes new dynamism, new forms, new strengths and progressions.

For the transformation of the exploited and disempowered masses into an invulnerable force, the latter must first undergo mental decolonisation that empowers them with the consciousness of self-worth and dignity. They must be made to believe in themselves as the equals of their oppressors and as the rightful owners of their land and all its endowments. Once the mind is decolonised, the physical body, soul and spirit, which were weakened, broken and conditioned to accept colonial laws, as well as divine precept become repulsive. It must not be forgotten that the driving force of colonialism is the profit margin, which accrues from economic plunder and cheap labour extracted without commensurate compensation from the colonised masses. If the worth of a man is measured by his genuine contribution to transform life and improve the living conditions of his people, it is thus conclusive that the most urgent thing for the Southern Cameroonian intellectual of today is to invest his genius in the liberation and building of his nation, British Southern Cameroons.

The decolonisation of Southern Cameroons, which means in reality, making Southern Cameroonians know who they are and who they are not, making them know the facts, reject falsehood and make them understand and believe in the truism that the sustainable development of a people is firmly anchored on their freedom, is not mere sentimental issue. The upsurge of national rebirth is absolute, genuine and natural, indeed a logical and enduring foundation of national development. It is in respect of history and legality; it is in defence of the duty of Southern Cameroonians of this generation accepting responsibility to bequeath a rich legacy to the unborn by contributing to human civilisation and freedom by fighting injustice, illegality and falsehood so that justice, legality and truth may reign in their land and become a right for all. The urgency of Southern Cameroons' national rebirth is further strengthened and springs from mass poverty in the midst of plenty, the agony of joblessness, squalid life after wasted years to acquire education and skills, the humiliation of being tortured to unconsciousness, spat in the face by agents of the occupation force, the constant reign of terror through imposition of states of emergency, curfews, kale-kales, constant bloody repressions amounting to silent genocide, economic plunder, cultural desolation and the constant reminder that, as long as the land is occupied, you and your kind will be treated as an endangered species. It is revolting to go through this, day in and day out, thus making life meaningless, short and brutish.

Scientific analysis of the past, married with clear understanding of the present buried in hopelessness and haplessness should give rise to collective resistance against the colonial regime. This deliberate action to shape the destiny of the people marks the beginning of a new era in which Southern Cameroonians themselves, not external forces, become the makers of their history, which will become the material content of their dynamic heritage. Here, the consciousness of 'we' and 'us' as opposed to 'they' and 'them' must be illuminated by hopes of a brighter future through overcoming subjugation. To strengthen the people's hopes for a brighter future, their repressed historical, political, economic and cultural development must be understood as a consequence of foreign domination and alien rule, which has resulted in the plunder of their wealth, silent genocide against their people, their inherent dignity, the distortion of their history and their true culture.

For Southern Cameroonians to become masters of their own destiny, they must sink and bury their petty differences and jealousy brought upon them by their coloniser. With pride, they must rehearse the great days of 'Benevolent Neutrality' under the leadership of E.M.L. Endeley, S.A. George, J.N. Foncha and J.T. Ndze, amongst others. These great patriots uncompromisingly identified and defended the Fatherland, Southern Cameroons. When the challenging moment came to choose between self-interest and collective interest, they opted for the latter, and the meeting of Mamfe in 1953, marked the beginning of the history of Southern Cameroonian nationalism. The consciousness of 'we' and 'us' as opposed to 'they' and 'them', which started in the 1940s, was strengthened. In an evolving nation state emerging from colonial dictatorship, such as Southern Cameroons, it should never be expected that in striving for nationhood, there will be no challenges, petty differences and internal conflicts. Conflicts are part of the dynamics of growth when positively analysed. But what must be understood is that, for purposes of collective defence and survival in dignity, group cohesion, solidarity, commitment, loyalty and vigilance are necessary to withstand aggressive external forces and for the projection of collective heritage. Bonds that unite the Southern Cameroonian people must be emphasised to tilt the scale in favour of 'us' as opposed to 'them'. It must be understood that in all situations, group survival in dignity and security is predicated on the collective capacity to confront, withstand and get rid of the enemy and diabolic tactics that tear the group apart and keep them weak and exploited.

The fault line has absolutely failed to provide security, safety and well-being for Southern Cameroonians because la République du Cameroun's culture of annexation and assimilation has given birth to a dynamic of hatred. Since the fault line is beyond repairs, Southern Cameroonians have only one option: the reassertion of their self-existence and independence, which will constitute the foundation and enduring driving force of their freedom, prosperity, dignity within the family of free peoples and sovereign nations. The spotlight must be put on the self-evident fact that, without emboldening Southern Cameroons national consciousness and making it a living reality in the council of the free, the Southern Cameroonian politico-intellectual elite pays lip service to African consciousness, liberation, freedom, economic development and independence. Where is his platform, solid background? The existence of Southern Cameroonian national consciousness gives impetus to African consciousness and universal consciousness. The world is for the free, and not those in bondage or those vegetating in the backwoods of the pretenders to democracy and universal values.

Conclusion

The African continent is in large part divided into Francophone and Anglo-Saxon states as a legacy of two of the main colonial powers that dominated Africa and that imposed their civilisations, which even in Europe, stand in constant rivalry; none can surrender to the other. If it were not a question of using Africans as guinea pigs, it is incontestable that an experiment of building a supranational Francophone-Anglo-Saxon state would ever have been contemplated. As the two could not co-exist as equals, the pro-annexationist and assimilationist la République du Cameroun has extended its sovereignty over and reduced Southern Cameroons into two provinces of its territory. Although this has been done in blatant violation of the rights and fundamental freedoms of the people of Southern Cameroons, it has been maintained through the constant use of brute force and international propaganda to deceive and mislead the international community. Restoration of statehood and sovereign independence is the only means by which the Southern Cameroons people can pick the pieces, mend their lives and broken hopes, and obtain and enjoy the level of freedom and security, and meaningful lives which human beings are worthy of.

Southern Cameroons − based on colonial heritage, which is the foundation of all modern African states − is as distinct from la République du Cameroun as Ghana is from Ivory Coast or as Nigeria is from Niger and as The Gambia is from Senegal. Their distinctiveness is a reflection of that of their creators, the UK and France, and the respective political philosophies and cultural building blocks which they respectively imposed in colonial Africa. It is not a question of wishing otherwise. Southern Cameroons and la République du Cameroun, based on their respective colonial evolutions, are two distinct countries with internationally-recognised boundaries that attest to their separateness, distinct national cultures and separate inherited colonial languages. The Anglo-French Boundary Treaty of 1931 and the different Trusteeship Agreements are Boundary Treaties in their own rights, contrasting colonial histories that vividly establish their distinctiveness − two different independence dates, two distinct peoples with contrasting ways of life, world view, vision and aspirations.

On the basis of social evolution, self-awareness or consciousness, the two peoples do not share the same experiences and concepts of state and governance. To fuse them with a dominating and oppressing people is to set a time bomb soon to explode with far reaching consequences than could be imagined.

The restoration of the statehood and sovereign independence of Southern Cameroons is a logical solution because the UN experiment, like that between Eritrea and Ethiopia, has failed beyond repair. Restoration will not deprive la République du Cameroun or any institution or organisation of anything, and it will instead save the UN another dark spot in its history of failures to use preventive diplomacy as well as mankind from the horrors of war and tragedy.

Finally, it should be pointed out that imposed presidential decrees erasing historically documented names and the constant and systematic use of bullets to silence peaceful protests cannot take a people away from their true nature or make from them two different peoples. Consequently, although la République du Cameroun has annexed Southern Cameroons and imposed the rigid Francophone centralised system of administration and its administrators − the occupation forces, part of which cannot communicate using the pidgin, the dreaded policy of divide and rule to fragment the people and keep them weak − the distinctiveness of Southern Cameroons as a common historical and legal entity, its colonial cultural heritage and linguistic unity, common economic life seriously ruined by Francophone exploitation and abandonment, and the people's commitment to democracy and probity still distinguish them as a separate people. If there can be "no two nations, no two peoples, for which this consciousness enjoys identical expression,"[19] how do we expect the two distinct Cameroons to co-exist − under one national roof − in any other manner than as coloniser and colonised? And this evil, like slavery and servitude, has been banned by the civilised world.

Each nation, each people shares and enjoys a specific cultural history, cultural identity and collective heritage. In Africa, while the roots are buried deep in the African soil, colonial heritage came to define exclusive international boundaries. Once the rhythm of these experiences is allowed to blossom without disruptive impositions from outside, the forward march of the people is assured and smooth. The common anchor of each nation and each people is their history and their culture, identified as distinct from one another.

Southern Cameroons is after all, the collective heritage of the Southern Cameroonian people.

The evil twin of annexation and colonialism in all its forms and manifestations having been outlawed, la République du Cameroun should withdraw from the territory of Southern Cameroons as has its mentor, France, withdrew from Guinea Conakry in 1958. What la République du Cameroun has done is what international law proscribes as crime against humanity and a threat to world peace, and the democratic world must not turn a blind eye to what is taking place in Southern Cameroons.

While it was a violation of Article 76(b) of the UN Charter and UNGA Resolution 1514 of 14th December 1960, which proclaim complete independence the inalienable right of all peoples and dependent territories, it is evident that la République du Cameroun exploited the weaknesses of independence by joining, and annexed and occupied the Southern Cameroons. As defined by international law and Resolution 1514, the provisions of international law cover all the people of Southern Cameroons and the territory. Because there was no legal and legitimate foundation for the UN experiment, it cracked beyond repair and is a threat to peace and security in the West African sub-region. The solution lies in the right to self-determination of the people of Southern Cameroons, who are resolved to peacefully restore the statehood and sovereign independence of their Fatherland. Self-determination is an eternal principle of international law, with universal application. The democratic world and the international system committed to global peace based on justice cannot afford to treat the people of Southern Cameroons as sub-humans.

Endnotes

1. Frantz Fanon, Reciprocal Bases of National Culture and the Fight for Freedom, speech presented at the Congress of Black African Writers, 1959, Reproduced from *Wretched of the Earth* (1959) publ. Pelican, p.4

2. Patrick F. Wilmot; In Search of Nationhood: The Theory and Practice of Nationalism in Africa, Lantern Books, Ibadan, 1979, p.186

3. Frantz Fanon, op. cit. p.1

4. Quoted in Richard Joseph, (Ed) Gaullist Africa: Cameroun under Ahmadou Ahidjo, Fourth Dimension Publishers, Enugu, 1978, p.6

5. Ibid.

6. Immanuel Wallenstein, Africa; The Politics of Independence, Vintage Books, New York, 1961, p.65.

7. By 1957 Houphouët-Boigny and Leopold Sedar Senghor of Ivory Coast and Senegal respectively were members of the French Government in Paris defending the grandeur of the multi-continental French state. In 1958 they voted overwhelmingly for the French Community while only Guinea (Conakry) under Sekou Toure voted against and became the first French colony to gain independence in West Africa.

8. With heavy repression, forced labour and harsh economic life many indigenes of French Cameroun escaped into British Southern Cameroons. Some settled permanently, thanks to Southern Cameroons legendary hospitality, and gained employment in the civil service and the CDC plantations. These French Cameroun citizens became the Pidgin language – carriers.

9. Richard Joseph, op.cit.p.192

10. Ibid. p. 66

11. For detail discussions, read Samuel P. Huntington, The Clash of Civilizations and The Making of World Order, Simon and Schuster, London, 1997 PP 207-8, 246-65.

12. Ibid. P.20

13. Ibid. p. 21.

14. Report of the International Conference of Experts on the Implementation of the Right to Self Determination as A contribution to Conflict Prevention, Held in Barcelona, from 21-27 November 1998, and P.12

15. Ibid.

16. Wilmot, Op. Cit. P.192. s

17. Huntington, Op. Cit. 125

18. Frantz Fanon, op. cit. p.5

19. Abdullahi Mahadi, George Kwanashie and Alhaji Mahmood Yakubu (eds) Nigeria: The State of the Nation and The Way Forward, Arewa House, Kaduna, 1994 P. 61

Chapter Seven

For National Renascence

To take Southern Cameroons out of the current political quagmire, the struggle for restoration must embrace strategies for economic emancipation to free our people from a short and cruel life. These are strategies for achieving self-reliant and self-sustaining development. It is the foundation of reversing the ills of annexation, colonial occupation, imposed alien rule and the deliberate plunder of the economy and natural wealth of the land by foreign vampires, which alienates the people, reducing them to slaves on their land. What is central here is the capacity of building or empowering the citizens for self-fulfilment through individual and collective positive action.

To bring meaning to Man, development must be Man-centred, that is, it must put people first because Man is the agent of the ultimate purpose of development, which is to improve on his living condition and guarantee his well-being and happiness. This demands that services, such as education, health, good road network and easy communication system, and the effective development of the agricultural sector into the mainstay of the Southern Cameroonian economy, should receive prime attention rather than military might and prestige and projects that glorify the ruling elite and their external partners. Governmental policy must be aimed at drastically reducing the current mass unemployment through meaningful education that empowers the individual with skills, and through the improvement of the industrial sector, which under the current dispensation, has deliberately been made non-existent. We must not forever remain producers of raw materials which are taken away at cheaper prices by producers of processed goods that are sold to us at cut throat prices.

Southern Cameroons is primarily an agricultural country, and even this sector suffers neglect and underdevelopment. Despite the preponderance of natural resources, there are no industries in the territory to transform raw materials into finished products, both for local consumption and for export. If Southern Cameroons is deliberately starved of industries which process natural resources, Biya's policy of subjugation and de-empowerment has given the northern part of Southern Cameroons – regarded as a rebellious province – its infamous industry, which consists of six prisons that are found in almost every County (administrative division).

Strategies for economic development demand a structural transformation which will engineer the diversification of production through the creation of an industrial sector. This will lead to a rise in production and improvement in the quality of goods, and an introduction of a variety of finished goods in the market that is growing ever more competitive, and will improve the general quality of life of the citizens as well as raise life expectancy.

Economic development should not just be understood to mean an increase in the Gross Domestic Product (GDP) or Gross National Income (GNI) of a country. As important as these indicators are, they could be misleading. They are capitalist indicators used by external forces to divert attention from the critical problems that developing nations face. While the GDP of a country may point to the evidence of economic growth, it does not translate into economic development, which must have a transforming effect on the individual and the greater majority of the given society. The target in economic development should be creating greater opportunities, and inspiring the masses for creativity, initiative, partnerships, healthy competition and achievement.

For restoration to bring meaning to Southern Cameroonians, economic development must lead to "improvements in material welfare, especially for persons with the lowest incomes; the eradication of mass poverty with its correlates of illiteracy, disease and early death, changes in the composition of inputs and outputs that generally include shifts in the underlying structure of production away from agriculture towards industrial activities, the organisation of the economy in such a way that productive employment is general among the working-age population rather than the situation of a privileged minority."[1]

The policy of economic development must aim at ending glaring disparities between the rural and urban centres; it must engineer equality by ending the concentration of wealth in the hands of a tiny few of the population; it must guarantee the efficient distribution of goods and services for the benefit of all the regions and citizens; and it must develop an effective and efficient, cheap means of transportation and communication throughout the country. To this effect, the development of the energy sector must receive due attention, for without energy, industrialisation, which can radically transform a society that depends on mass importation of its basic needs to an economy capable of competing favourably with the industrialised societies, will remain an illusion.

Special attention must be given to education – which is a human right – to make citizens conscious, patriotic and assertive. For a healthy and productive citizenry, medical care should also be accessible and affordable to all. In health-care delivery, prevention and sanitation should be given priority. Cheap and easy means of transportation and communication, and easy access to goods and services throughout the national territory will greatly enhance national unity and build greater sense of belonging in citizens as well as boost individual well-being and freedom.

According to Adebayo Adedeji, to achieve self-reliant and self-sustaining development or "self-centred development", the following conditions must be fulfilled:

(a) The democratisation of the development process;
(b) The initiation of a process of de-alienation;
(c) The creation of the right political and social environment;
(d) iv)The recovery of self-confidence by the people...[2]

As the restoration struggle requires the mass mobilisation of the people for popular positive political action, economic development, which will serve as the sustaining cushion of political power, equally requires the mobilisation of all the energies and talents of the citizens of the nation. The masses are mobilised to invest in economic development for their own self-development. Through mobilisation and capacity building, the latent energies are released by interacting with the available material resources in the application of the technology that must be adapted to the environment.

British Southern Cameroons is trapped today in a paradox of growing energetic young people with skills and anxious to work, but who cannot find jobs. The consequences of this are mass poverty, frustration and despair. This situation, as alarming as it is, exists in a country endowed with abundant natural resources. The problem is simple: Southern Cameroons has been annexed, colonised and occupied by la République du Cameroun, and to keep the citizens subservient, weak and polarised, economic development of the territory has deliberately been ruled out. The poor have no power, and they are exploited or are uneducated, explaining why skilful and educated Southern Cameroonians, who cannot stand the heat of the problem, bear the crushing hammer of annexation, and because they are not ready to fight from within, are escaping from the country. The coloniser is pleased to see them leave the shores of its acquired colony. British Southern Cameroons suffers a tragic brain drain. To reverse this situation and bring about purposeful change, the legitimate struggle for liberation and restoration anchored on legality must be led by single-minded, development-oriented leadership with a mission of engineering socio-economic transformation in the new British Southern Cameroons. Such leadership must see the restoration of the statehood of British Southern Cameroons as the evidence of their patriotism and an indispensable road map, the genuine power of the people as the masters of national economic development, and the engine of their right to collective existence in dignity as a people and a nation. No people and territory, under foreign domination, have ever developed. Economic plunder and brutal repression are the evil twins of any people under foreign occupation, domination and alien rule, until the subjugated rise up and overthrow the expansionist power.

Thus, Nfor concludes: "The Southern Cameroons Question isn't mere marginalization, deprivation, neglect or lack of people in strategic positions. It is annexation while marginalization, exploitation, among others, is the manifestation and consequences of a chronic disease. It is a political question..."[3]. It is one of imperial dimension.

The evidence of annexation and colonial occupation has led Mukong, in the characteristic language of an advocate of anti-imperialism and colonialism, and an unquestionable defender of human freedom and victim of Yaoundé dictatorship, to conclude: "...Instead of government by dialogue, we have government by terror. Instead of legislation by debate we have legislation by ambush. Instead of law and order by persuasion, we have law and order by banditry and piracy. He, Ahidjo himself has been referring to it as a peaceful revolution."[4]

To forge ahead with resilience and zeal, patriotism, and a sense of purpose and meaningfulness, Southern Cameroonians must deal with reality and understand that the task of state restoration, or in other words, national reconstruction, is far more demanding, challenging and inspiring, and calls for greater sacrifices and hard work. We must know from where we are taking off, and with vision, properly define our strategy to attain ultimate national goals on a short-term and long-term basis. This must start with regaining the reins of political power, which will enable Southern Cameroonians to become masters of their destiny.

The glaring facts are:

(a) British Southern Cameroons has been annexed and recolonised by la République du Cameroun.

(b) To keep Southern Cameroons subservient and an appendage, its economic infrastructures have been destroyed, financial institutions liquidated, and its natural resources are exploited without redress.

(c) To sustain this relationship of dependence, no meaningful investment is encouraged in British Southern Cameroons.

(d) As an occupied colony of la République du Cameroun, it supplies cheap labour and raw materials such as oil, cocoa, coffee, tea, palm kernel, rubber, timber and banana, which are only exported from the metropolitan sea port of Douala as the Tiko and Victoria natural deep sea ports in Southern Cameroons have been abandoned. Linked to la République du Cameroun by assimilationist umbilical cords, British Southern Cameroons receives all its manufactured goods and services from and through la République du Cameroun. Even the brewing of beer is forbidden in the Southern Cameroonian territory. Everything must be brought in from the metropolitan la République du Cameroun. With the people stripped of their government, and their inherent rights to their natural resources weakened through the policy of divide and rule, naked exploitation and plunder will be sustained.

Southern Cameroonians must recognise themselves as a colonised, assimilated and oppressed people – as a people under foreign occupation because la République du Cameroun, by the force of arms, abolished their government and state institutions, and has imposed Napoleonic constitutionalism and Gaullist administration in their country. People under foreign occupation and domination lose the right to rule and shape their own destiny; they are disenfranchised. Consequently, the first task facing the Southern Cameroonian people is the necessity to mobilise themselves for the historic fight to dispossess the aggressor of the (political) power that they acquired illegally. Once Southern Cameroonians regain the power that they lost, which made them into subjects of a foreign power, they will capture and control state power. Until this is done, Southern Cameroonians will know no freedom, let alone live in freedom, and enjoy justice, peace and prosperity.

To regain power, which guarantees the people's freedom and progress, a subjugated people must confront the enemy until it is knocked down and chased out of the monopolistic control of political power. The engagement of the people in popular political action is legitimate because nothing acquired illegally can become legal by the passage of time. In Southern Cameroons, the brutal exploitation of the masses is sustained through the aggressive and monopolistic control of the army, the police, the courts and the educational system. The foreign imposed system, manned by proconsuls and trigger-happy occupation forces which are heavily dominated by Francophones, are completely oriented to serve the foreign ruling class.

The task of the moment is to better understand our condition, and be well organised to confront the enemy by being assertive. To do this effectively, Southern Cameroonians must join the national resistance movement, namely, the Southern Cameroons National Council, to get rid of annexation and foreign domination.

All human beings are equal before the law, and as Trust Territories of the international system, British Southern Cameroons and French Cameroun were equal too. But, as different peoples and Trust territories under different Administering authorities, British Southern Cameroonians and French Cameroonians were respectively imbued with different political philosophies of life with regard to the state, legal, educational and cultural systems. British Southern Cameroonians and *les Camerounais français* are different from each other. Being different is neither a crime nor does that make one inferior to the other; being different does not make one a lower human being than the other. Foreign domination has its roots in the erroneous notion of the superiority of one group because they have what others do not have, forgetting that each person or people have something unique. Each people and territory under international law has the inalienable right to self-existence and independence. This is why self-determination is a high principle of international law, and annexation and imposition of alien rule are a crime against humanity and a threat to world peace. It must be understood that individual self-survival in freedom and dignity is intrinsically linked to and guaranteed by the collective survival of each people. And this cannot be realised without an independent homeland. It is national sovereignty that guarantees and promotes individual and collective freedom. It justifies the inalienable right of people under foreign domination and alien rule to fight for their freedom and independence.

'Never kneel down! Never surrender! Never retreat! Never compromise with the oppressor! Never be contented with the crumbs!' These should be the watchwords ringing ceaselessly in the subconscious of every patriotic Southern Cameroonian mind and every people under foreign domination and alien rule. To compromise and collaborate with the annexationist is to betray yourself and the inalienable right of your people to freedom and sovereignty which guarantee the people's dignity and their territorial integrity. This land belongs to British Southern Cameroonians and no one else. It is the heritage of Southern Cameroonians; it is theirs to love and cherish. And to love and cherish is to defend what accounts for your being and contributes to your identity as the equal of other people. It is a historic duty without which you have nothing to be proud of and to finally bequeath as a rich legacy to your descendants.

Roads and railway lines were constructed from the hinterland to the seaport on the coast in colonial Africa for the purpose of evacuation of raw materials. But this privilege is not even enjoyed in the annexed and recolonised British Southern Cameroons, which explains why the Victoria and Tiko seaports, and Mamfe river port have been abandoned in favour of the Douala seaport. To transform British Southern Cameroons as a whole into a mere reservoir of raw materials and to facilitate transport thereof, Southern Cameroons is linked to la République du Cameroun via the Bamenda-Bafoussam and Tiko-Douala tarred road and the Kumba-Mbanga-Douala railway. Southern Cameroons also serves as the market for the supply of manufactured goods from la République du Cameroun, transported with extreme difficulties on very bad seasonal roads and/or carried on the head to the remote villages. No airport exists in British Southern Cameroons whereas there was an international airport in Tiko and three inland airports before the total annexation and occupation. To move from the north to the south, and vice-versa, you must cross two provinces of la République du Cameroun because the Nkambe-Bamenda-Mamfe-Kumba-Buea trunk road has been abandoned. The Bamenda Ring road, which Biya pledged to the population in

September 1990 while on official visit to Bamenda to personally supervise its tarring, is yet to be realised. This explains why a direct journey from Wum to Nkambe, which used to take two hours on a well-maintained earth road in the 1960s, is now a forgotten issue as the trip can only be made via Bamenda-Kumbo, then Nkambe. This makes the journey at least three times longer.

In the struggle for national rebirth, patriotic Southern Cameroonians must see the empowerment of the individual as an urgent task. Those of the Diaspora should commit themselves to the restoration of the nation of Southern Cameroons. Individual students and those working abroad should make it a duty to acquire knowledge and skills, which tomorrow, will be transposed or imported into Southern Cameroons. Southern Cameroonians should form interest and professional groups that cut across ethnic communities, and should go into partnership with foreign companies and investors, with the sole purpose of transferring acquired technology and businesses into Southern Cameroons. Capital and technology are fundamental to the transformation of a 'backward' society into a fast developing economy. For such development to be self-reliant and self-sustaining, the society in need of transformation must not solely depend on the importation of foreign capital and technology, which consequently sustains dependence instead. Southern Cameroonians must see their stay in foreign lands − consequent upon the hostile political, economic and cultural climate at home due to annexation and brutal occupation − as a period of inoculation with a strong patriotic spirit and a development-oriented mind. It must be understood that the developed nations of the west were developed by the citizens themselves, thanks to the nationalistic and people-centred policies of their respective governments. Also, what needs to be emphasised is that, not only did the west develop with wealth from Africa and the third world in general, but imperial agents, on an individual basis, brought the looted capital back to their nations too, never wasting nor concealing it in banks outside their respective countries. Southern Cameroonians must be determined to be the prime movers of the development of their nation.

With a clear understanding, Southern Cameroonians should be spartanly prepared to serve their people and Fatherland. The ultimate goal of development is to eliminate poverty, mass suffering, drudgery, illiteracy, inequality and mass unemployment, and guarantee well-being and happiness for the large majority. For development to be all-inclusive and sustaining, equal opportunities should be provided for all and no discrimination of any kind allowed. This action is geared towards restoring the Southern Cameroons nation to its legal and legitimate status as the guarantor of individual and collective freedom and dignity to the citizens, and as an effective player in world affairs.

For development strategy and policy to be people-centred, the individual in the remotest village in British Southern Cameroons – be it in faraway Akwaya or Nwa – must be the focus. The demanding task should not be to give a fish and make him look up to and glorify his giver; it is to teach him to be conscious and proud of his personality, endowed with rich potential and skills which should be developed for self-fulfilment and national development. Every citizen should be trained and inspired to become the agent of positive change. The individual should be taught how to catch not only a fish for himself but for many, and how to process, preserve and use the excess as medium of exchange, to generate income to satisfy other needs, and for investment. He should also be trained to form partnership with others, and how they can diversify and maximise production and profit in-groups. This is the development, which put simply, is that of the people by the people and for the people. What must be emphasised is, by making the individual the focal point of development, all the different districts and villages of the nation will receive due attention. We must first see and reach the village before dreaming of going to the moon. With such a people-centred orientation, the capitalist system, with its reliance on the GDP and GNI as the determinant of economic development in which the individual is not only avoided but gets lost and his interests are never considered, will have no place in the Southern Cameroonian socio-economic reconstruction and development process. If the ultimate goal of national economic development is the well-being and happiness of the individual citizen, and not to make a tiny elite rich and powerful, the policy must be Man-centred or Man-focused. The empowerment and development of all citizens result from individual capacity building. One becomes assertive and progressive as the consciousness of self grows stronger, and the capacity to master one's condition and environment becomes a reality.

As pointed above, national reconstruction is far demanding, and the take off point for the rebirth of the Southern Cameroonian state is far more disheartening today than in 1961, when Southern Cameroons had its seaports and airports, its electricity corporation and other economic and financial institutions such as the PMB, the Cameroon Development Co-operation (CDC), CamBank which served as a national bank, the Development Agency, Santa Coffee Estate and its factory for coffee processing, The Ntem Palm plantation, the Buea Prison Farm, and many thriving small scale industries and businesses owned by nationals and foreigners. Towns such as Mamfe, Kumba, Tiko and Victoria were real commercial centres, visited by large numbers of citizens of la République du Cameroun, to buy imported goods including cars and cement which cost less than in their own country. But today, these towns lie in ruins and dormant as if they were devastated by war. The rehabilitation and improvement of these economic infrastructures and institutions should be seen as top priority before new ones are ever initiated to meet growing needs.

To engineer the socio-economic transformation of Southern Cameroons, a high premium must be placed on education and the acquisition of skills and technology for national reconstruction and development. The educational policy should aim at inculcating values of self-esteem, integrity, honesty, discipline, self-confidence, national consciousness and commitment to the defence of the common good. Southern Cameroonians must believe themselves to be the equals of any other human being, and should know that their dignity and individual self-worth are tied to the sovereignty of their Fatherland, British Southern Cameroons, without which they are worthless. Above all, the citizens should be educated to know that, by their hard work combined with their patriotism, they will become a prosperous and great nation, and that they will be respected by other peoples and nations.

To encourage creativity – inventiveness in the individual – it will be incumbent upon the government to protect and defend the individual citizen, guarantee his security, and create such institutions that encourage partnership and team spirit, and facilitate and promote initiative and reward excellence. Remuneration should discourage brain drain, a factor which currently deprives Africa of its high skilled manpower, thus keeping the most endowed continent industrially underdeveloped.

The second important factor necessary for sustainable socio-economic development is the building of a stable, open and liberal society that encourages and promotes healthy competition and companionship. Southern Cameroons, it must be pointed out, thrived in this manner until the dawn of the Dark Age in 1961. A stable, open and liberal society is one in which the citizens enjoy equal opportunities, social justice and the equitable distribution of income, and enjoy freedom of movement, association and speech, and are protected by the law. The democratisation of the development process encourages healthy competition and free flow of goods, services, information, and attracts foreign investors, because no capital goes into an uncertain environment tarnished by bureaucratic bottle-necks, bribery and corruption in the civil service and courts. The independence of the judiciary must be guaranteed. Wealth and materialism should not determine the worth of man. To discourage the craving for materialism at all cost, those who acquire wealth illegally must be investigated immediately, and once found guilty by the court of law, must be punished, and the ill-gotten wealth, confiscated by the state.

The third factor that will create an enabling environment for development and progress is the capacity for efficient and effective economic management. When a society is endangered by a propensity for mismanagement, investors run away or withdraw their capital. The immediate victims who bear the brunt of this withdrawal are the consumers and producers of commodities and services. While moral and ethical values must be inculcated in the citizen right from childhood in the family and in school, society should have in-built mechanisms for checks and balances so as to discourage violation and violators of norms and laws, and for these mechanisms to be seen as effective, the guilty must be punished. This is where the courts of law and tribunals play vital roles. For them to be effective and unbiased, the judiciary must be independent of the executive and the lawmakers, and all must be equal before the law. Moreover, effective investigations must be carried out and dealt with expeditiously. The current situation in which adjournments are done at the instance of the big man, the powerful in society and the holy cows of the state to further suffer the little man, widow, the poor and the innocent must not be tolerated in the new Southern Cameroons. The courts must treat all equally, and must dispense with justice quickly for justice delayed is justice denied.

The psychological factor is also important here. The individual citizen is both the creator and consumer of the benefits of development. For him to play this dual role efficiently and effectively, he must be equipped with knowledge and skills, enjoy self-mastery, he must be empowered, he must be inspired, motivated and be achievement-oriented. Each individual must see himself as part of the whole and as belonging to the larger society of Southern Cameroons, which is in need of development for self-preservation and protection in order to assert itself and play its deserved role in the group of sovereign nations. If Southern Cameroons remains the footstool of la République du Cameroun, the Southern Cameroonian identity will become irrelevant or non-existent and cannot be claimed as proudly as are the American, a British, a Dutch, Ghanaian, Namibian, Senegalese or South African ones. The Creator made no mistake in making the Bafaw, Bakweri, Banwa, Mankon, Bambalang, Kom, Nso, Wimbum or Bayangi, among others, who, by colonial construct and international law, today constitute the nation of British Southern Cameroons. By the endowed potential and ordained gift of God, we have the capacity to make Southern Cameroons great, and why not God's nation in

Africa for the service of man and for glory of God.

Southern Cameroonians must develop and combine the values of individual self-reliance with collective or national self-reliance and collective-self-esteem, for the whole is stronger and greater than its parts. By history and colonial heritage and international law, Southern Cameroons is a nation distinct from la République du Cameroun in the same manner as it is from Nigeria. This explains why Southern Cameroons did not become an integral part of Nigeria despite being administered by it for forty-five years (1916 to 1961) under colonial rule, and English, common law as well as the political, administrative system, socio-cultural and educational system being the common British heritage of the two countries and peoples.

The mentality of worshipping the boss, the officer, *le chef, Monsieur le Directeur*, copied from la République du Cameroun, which saps away one's sense of worth and equality, and stifles creative initiative that leads to mastery imposing dependence complex, should be purged out from every Southern Cameroonian. The restoration struggle demands that we retrace our routes while judiciously learning from others, such as Namibians, Eritreans, East Timorese, South Africans, Estonians, Czechs and South Koreans who, though were once annexed and subjected to foreign domination, fought and regained their freedom. Self-determination, through rebellion against foreign rule, alien domination and exploitation, is legitimate and is protected and defended by international law. But to compromise with the annexationist or aggressor is a crime whose punishment hangs even on the neck of the innocent descendants of the traitor. To rebel against gross injustice is not a crime punishable under any law, be it divine, local or international. Instead, it is a right protected by all laws and good conscience. It is killing a monstrous virus in the supreme interest of humanity.

The ultimate goal of the state is to guarantee the well-being and happiness of its citizens. To this end, the exploitation of the natural resources of the country must be towards the good of the citizens. It is the translation of development into concrete meaning and collective benefit. Development should be understood as a means that enhances and expands human freedom – a call for the elimination of social factors that restrain man from exercising and enjoying his humanity; things that hold him back from exploring his social and physical environment.

Amartya Sen, the 1998 Nobel Laureate in Economic Science, defines development as the "removal of major sources of unfreedom: poverty as well as tyranny, poor economic opportunities as well as systematic social deprivation, neglect of public facilities as well as intolerance or over activity of repressive states."[5] As experienced in British Southern Cameroons, the fundamental problem has been the exclusion of Southern Cameroonians from effective participation in political and economic spheres. As such, they did not develop, aggravating their subjugation. Economic opportunities expand the frontiers of each human being. In light of this, Amartya Sen declares: "What people can positively achieve is influenced by economic opportunities, political liberties, social powers, and the encouragement and cultivation of initiatives. This institutional arrangement for these opportunities are also influenced by the exercise of people's freedoms, through the liberty to participate in social choice and in the making of public decisions that impel the progress of these opportunities."[6]

Individual human freedom is enhanced when the capability to avoid starvation, poor or lack of accommodation, illiteracy, morbidity and premature mortality and exclusion from political participation – which should not be understood in the narrow sense of casting a ballot of paper in an election – is expanded. In the dictatorial states of Africa, witnessed in Cameroon, for instance, elections are mere window dressing and results are often predetermined in favour of the incumbent candidate. But periodically, people are raided to the polls, like cows to the stream have a taste of clean water with salt. As experienced in Cameroun under the Presidential Monarchies of Ahidjo and Biya, while at the stream, a cow could exercise its right of choice to drink the water; however, the voters have no choice with regard to the results of the election since these are predetermined in favour of the ruling oligarchy. This is electoral terrorism at its best, as with time, the disenfranchised are threatened by statesmen with sanctions if they fail to register and cast the ballot of paper thrust into their hands for them to vote in favour of those ordained to rule and reign.

For Southern Cameroonians to fear the bull because of its horns, and surrender to foreign domination and alien rule of la République du Cameroun is an act of self-treachery and denial to their descendants of their right to freedom, independence, dignity and a worthy inheritance. As courageously demonstrated in 1953 by Dr Endeley and his fellow compatriots who rejected UK's policy of administrative convenience – whose end was to deny Southern Cameroons its legitimate and legal right to self-existence as a nation state by integration into Nigeria – the compelling task for patriotic Southern Cameroonians of this age is to reject the concocted and imposed independence by joining, which has facilitated annexation and colonial occupation by la République du Cameroun, and denied Southern Cameroons its inherent and inalienable right to sovereign independence and equal standing with other UN Trust Territories and former colonies that attained sovereign independence in accordance with UN Charter and their legitimate will. When Endeley and his team saw the imperial evil in administrative convenience, they declared Benevolent Neutrality in Nigerian politics and returned home. Upon re-uniting with their people, they called for secession from Nigeria, and recognising their right under the UN Charter, demanded the creation of the Southern Cameroons Government. Independence by joining, which has facilitated annexation and colonial occupation, and transformed la République du Cameroun into an imperial power, permitting the abolishment of the Southern Cameroons Government in Buea with grave consequences, should spur Southern Cameroonians toward the restoration of their statehood as the only positive action to redeeming their lost identity and equality with la République du Cameroun and other sovereign nations of the world.

Political freedom, which should enhance political participation, effective and efficient decision-making and development, is the outgrowth of social engineering and the empowerment of the people enabling them to freely determine who governs them and based on what principles and programmes. In a democracy, those who rule govern by the consent of those who are ruled; those in authority and the people are held together by a social contract of trust in which the former do not impose their will nor do they manipulate the latter through corruption or coercive use of state institutions. The people, on the other hand, do not surrender their inalienable right to their rulers. It is partnership for nation-building, and development is a collective and continuous process. This takes place in a society in which people enjoy their civil rights and are ruled by the law, and not by the whims and caprices of dictators who are more powerful than state institutions. In such societies, the citizens have the right to criticise those in authority who, in turn, listen to the cries and suggestions of the people. By respecting the social contract, they remain sensitive, responsible and accountable to the ruled. The citizens have the right to express their political voice and enjoy freedom of the press, and have multiple parties espousing different ideologies and programmes which they choose to endorse freely. In a genuine democracy, people live under the rule of law; dialogue is accepted as an instrument by which differences are negotiated and resolved; citizens reserve the full right to dissent without being subjected to brutal repression; and those in authority submit to the will of the people through the ballot box. It is in such a state that Man finds self-fulfilment.

This should be the vision for, and mission of, the SCNC for the new Southern Cameroons and its citizens.

Endnotes

1. Charles Kindleberger & Bruce Herrick (1977) quoted in Emmanuel A. Aka, The British Southern Cameroons 1922-1916: A study in colonialism and underdevelopment, Platteville, Madison, 2002, p.1.
2. Adebayo Adedeji, Towards a Dynamic African Economy, (selected Speeches and Lectures, 1975-1986, compiled and arranged

by Jeggan C. Senghor, Frank Cass, 1989, p.81.

3. Nfor, N. Nfor. The Southern Cameroons: The Truth of the Matter, Quality Printers, Bamenda, 2002, p.4.

4. Mukong, Albert W. (ed.) The Case for the Southern Cameroons, CAMFECO, USA, 1990, 95.

5. Amartya Sen, Development as Freedom, Oxford University Press, Oxford, 1999 p.3

6. Ibid,

Chapter Eight

The Winning Spirit

Once, a preacher's sermon shown on television made a lasting impact on me. He told a short story about two patients, James and Simon, needing special care in the Intensive Care Unit (ICU). They were bed-ridden and received no visitors from outside. James' bed was by the window and Simon's was far from it, at the other end of the room.

The two did not know each other before becoming roommates. However, in this isolated ward of the hospital, two things united them. First, they were well-educated and English was their common language of communication. Second, they were both in the same situation, both bed-ridden and in ICU, and none was therefore superior to the other.

There, they were disconnected from the larger world. They were in a world of their own.

As if to constantly replace what their condition had deprived them of, James would turn and look outside every morning, pretending to make a film of what was happening outside. Turning to his friend Simon, he told stories about the weather, the beauty of the rising sun, the blue sky, happy kids playing and others dancing, market women dressed in exquisite clothes with their goods on their heads, wonderful cars in the streets, birds singing in the woods and others flying high in the sky, and many other wonderful stories. Simon listened to them intently and they shared jokes together. These stories were like a spiritual, psychological and physical tonic that lifted their spirits and brightened their day, making them part of the larger world outside.

Unfortunately, James' health suddenly deteriorated and he passed away, worsening without any doubt, Simon's affliction. The physical absence of James was more painful to the latter than the sickness that kept him bed-ridden. To overcome his isolation and loneliness, he requested after three days of mourning, that his bed be moved so that he was by the window. He believed seeing the scenery outside would cheer his spirits and mind. The nurse, understanding his condition and state of mind, did as he requested.

As soon as his bed was moved, he turned to the window to see the world outside. What did he see? A huge, black wall stretching parallel to his room, as far as his eyes could see. He could not help it. He turned to the nurse. "What am I seeing? Where is this huge wall from?" he asked in despair.

The nurse answered: "That wall has been there before this ward was built."

Stunned, Simon retorted: "But my late friend, James, used to tell me many wonderful things, beautiful blue skies, bright sunshine, and other things that he used to see. With this huge dark wall, how was he seeing those beautiful things?"

The nurse, beamed with a smile and answered: "Simon, James was seeing those beautiful things from the inside."

Yes, from the inside!

The winning Spirit – the spirit that inspires people to overcome afflictions, the conquering spirit that triumphs – is from the inside. Yes, from the inside! It could be said that the physical frame called the body is the house of the real Man. We are told in the scriptures that God created man in His own image. I believe that it is not the physical body which He formed from the dust of the Earth. The God-like part of Man is the spirit which God breathed into him so that he becomes the kind of living being that he is. I believe that it is the God-spirit in Man that makes him a moral, spiritual and rational being, which endowed him with the capacity to know God and the difference between good and evil, and the right to choose and strive towards excellence. This explains why Man is always reaching out for what is ideal, which will give him mastery over his environment and so that he is never held in chains by any force, visible or invisible. The drive of Man is to be free, toward self-actualisation and self-fulfilment.

From the story of the two patients, we learn a lot about life. The first lesson can be summarised as follows:

(a) Believe in yourself as being equal to other human beings.
(b) Believe in others as worthy beings like yourself.
(c) Build bridges.
(d) Be a positivist.

The second inescapable lesson which we get from their story is that life is full of challenges. It is short and irreplaceable, and whatever the situation we are in, our physical condition should not dominate the spirit. The spirit being in charge should lift you higher to make the best of your circumstance. The worth of human life is not measured in the length of days on Earth, but in what was achieved on Earth within the given time and circumstance. Moreover, our achievements are not measured in the context of self-aggrandisement or personal satisfaction, but rather in the degree to which they impact others, influence society and transform the human condition. When we are in isolation, life is wasted and meaningless. In community, in service, and in sharing and caring, Man finds self-fulfilment and the purpose for which the Creator sent him on Earth.

The third lesson we learn is that, with the right attitude, you win or lead a victorious life. It is called the winning spirit. In the story, James won the friendship and admiration of Simon because, irrespective of his condition, he had the right attitude and spirit. To him, life was not just the physical and the material. To James, it was his physical body that was sick and bed-ridden; not his spirit, not his mind; and not the humaneness in him. That is why he continued to see, admire and enjoy God's creation, and still loved and cherished humanity, believed in others, did not accept that he was in an isolated ward, did not give way to defeat, did not give in to his condition as a bed-ridden patient, and instead shared his perception of the world around him with his friend, Simon. James believed in possibilities; not impossibilities. He lived from the inside and not just from the outside. As a positivist, he was a man who would bring sunshine into the dark spaces of any human mind.

Man is not only a physical being; he is a moral, spiritual and intellectual social being. These attributes are what make him more advanced than other animals. Using these, especially his intellect, combined with his spiritual being and physical energy which he applies in his quest to master his environment and relate with other peoples, he builds his culture and history. The urge to reach out, explore, understand and overcome negativity that keeps him in chains make Man strive for excellence. These higher attributes make him hate evil. To attain self-fulfilment, he navigates towards what is good, upright – the ideal that lifts the spirit and makes him happy. He cherishes and believes in dialogue as a medium for reaching consensus. He resists imposition and domination, which are unworthy of him. Self-fulfilment is attained within and not outside him. Man lives in society and through social interaction builds bridges with others for mutual benefit and societal growth and development. As an agent of change, and knowing fully well that his society is part of the world community, his society interacts with other societies to contribute to the building of a better world for mankind.

Man is a community man. In his community, the urge and aspiration for self-fulfilment translates itself into community, or collective self-fulfilment or the greater good for the larger man and posterity. In community, Man does not see self-fulfilment outside collective interest and the natural urgency of collective defence, preservation, promotion and perpetuation of the entity held together by history, culture, ethos and experiences – good or bad – which they have in common.

In 1953, Southern Cameroonian leaders in Nigerian colonial legislatures and government demonstrated this winning spirit when they looked inward, and analysing the state of affairs affecting their country and people, came to the conclusion that Southern Cameroons and Southern Cameroonians were discriminated against, and toward the collective interest, reacted by declaring Benevolent Neutrality in Nigerian politics. It can be reckoned that this was the first effective use of the force of argument in Southern Cameroonian politics, and it worked. While violence may start and end with an individual, the force of argument, which is built on truth for the sake of justice and human excellence, draws inspiration and strength from the people. Consequently, Endeley had to lead his fellow parliamentarians back to Southern Cameroons, where the first conference on the destiny of Southern Cameroons was held in Mamfe. Endeley led a delegation to London, where a collective decision would be made in this regard. The will of the people was the petition demanding for a separate region for British Southern Cameroons in recognition of its international status. Based on the facts of history and international law, they argued that British Southern Cameroons was not an integral territory of Nigeria, but a distinct UN Trust with equal rights to self-existence and self-determination. This was a historical and legal fact which the British Government could not argue against, and the demand of the British Southern Cameroonian demand was granted in 1954, thanks to the adoption of a new constitution for Nigeria.

It shows that truth is infinite and absolute, and will come to be accepted as an irrefutable reality respected with time.

The challenge goes to the few to whom truth is first revealed, to speak out and defend it uncompromisingly, whatever the challenges may be and the odds they face. The stiffer the opposition, the greater the evidence that they are on the right path, and the higher the degree of benefits they will get. Truth does not wither or diminish in the face of opposition. Instead, it becomes stronger and self-evident then. But the more the apostles of truth propagate and open it up to the masses hungry for the change they need the most, the more opponents – unable to defend their criminal acts – will be forced to revise their tactics. The defenders of truth in a society in absolute need of change are often ridiculed, given awful names, despised and ignored by those benefiting from the decadent system. When this does not work, the defenders of the status quo will embark on the persecution of the apostles of the truth whom the masses, gagged as they are, see as their saviours. "All truth," declares Arthur Schopenhauer (1788-1860), "passes through three stages. First, it is ridiculed. Second, it is violently opposed. Third, it is accepted as being self-evident."

History teaches us that the more truth is opposed and ridiculed, and its apostles persecuted, the more those for whom it is meant become very inquisitive, and even secretively try to find out more of it. Inherent in truth is the power of self-multiplication. The more truth is defended by its apostles, the more it grows because its followers, in escaping from persecution, carry it with them.

The struggle for the restoration of the statehood of British Southern Cameroons is based on the following facts:

(a) British Southern Cameroons, in respect of inherited colonial boundaries that constitute the foundation stone of African modern nation states, is a nation distinct from la République du Cameroun. Under international law, it is entitled to national self-existence and sovereign independence.

(b) In conformity with Article 102 of the UN Charter, there is no legal instrument binding British Southern Cameroons to la République du Cameroun. In view of the non-implementation of UNGA Resolution 1608 of April 21, 1961 la République du Cameroun's exercise of sovereign power in British Southern Cameroons is consequent upon its annexation, a crime according to international law. La République du Cameroun is a colonial power in British Southern Cameroons.

(c) The SCNC, championing the struggle, is not committing any crime. Under the UN Charter and international law, it is instead helping to erase the ugly scar of the failure of the UN system to respect its own Charter and Resolutions in the Trust territory of British Southern Cameroons. The UN failed in implementing its mission of promoting world peace and democracy, and defending and supporting human freedom, dignity and the equality of all nations, whether large or small, to national self-existence in the case of the decolonisation process in British Southern Cameroons.

'The Force of Argument, Not the Argument of Force', which is the SCNC's motto, is Southern Cameroons' form of Gandhi's philosophy of non-violence. The force of argument has as top priority, the building, preservation and promotion of internal cohesion against the common enemy. It is known that some of the characteristics of colonial rule are the policy of divide and rule, corruption of the elite and traditional rulers, exploitation, patronage and mass poverty. Through diabolic plots, the unity between the educated elite and the masses is deliberately punctured and prevented, and the masses, under the constant use of brute force by the colonial repressive force, are treated as an imperilled species while the elite are dosed into slumber with sinecure positions and crumbs that fall from the master's table. Such an elite, lacking in self-esteem and self-worth, betray their people, and led by spineless self-seeking politicians, become collaborators. The fragmentation of the colonised society is to keep it weak, fragile and perpetually dependent on the metropolis. This makes the rule of the whip and gun easy, and as the reign of terror makes the mobilisation of the masses a herculean task for the few patriots, the urgency of collective and effective resistance against oppressive colonial rule is painful and delays fulfilment at their own peril. Nevertheless, by natural law, it can only be temporary since truth must always triumph. The masses will carry the day. Collective self-defence is not only the right of the people; it is their fortress for survival in dignity.

At another level, some among the educated elite, bereft of nationalistic spirit, assist in entrenching the colonial policy of divide and rule as they embark on building tribal and ethnic loyalties. This is not to say that the existing ethnic groups or nationalities are inherently bad. When these tribal configurations are formed to sustain and push forward a limited agenda; when such associations are lacking in the overall national agenda; when they lack an inclusive nationalistic agenda of liberation, freedom and independence; and when this elite core fail to inspire their allies to understand the reality on the ground, and to appreciate the fact that a fragmented people will forever remain weak, oppressed and exploited, contrary to their privileged position in society, they are playing the colonial game of pent-up prejudices and divisionism.

For self-seeking benefits, the elite declare that their cultural associations are apolitical. If Man is a political animal, how does he create an association with other political animals that is apolitical? True patriots should transform these associations into vital organs and agents of effective political education for national liberation.

Let these associations be mission-oriented, and focused on the greater good which will bring happiness, well-being and self-fulfilment to all citizens. By plunging to these low self-seeking agendas at the expense of the broad-based national agenda, the educated elite make the coloniser much at ease, and encourage the colonial policy of divide and rule.

On the contrary, the political consciousness of educated elite must revolutionise their attitude, behaviour, perception and orientation, thus, transforming them from being the exclusive members of a clan or tribe to being citizens of a nation. This, in the least, does not mean turning their back on the members of the clan or tribe but, that they must see the progress and prosperity of the tribe as being intrinsically welded in that of the nation. Therefore, the tribe becomes the nation in microcosm while the nation is the tribe in macrocosm. The translation of national ideals, hopes, values and legitimate aspirations to the comprehension, appreciation and empowerment of those at the grassroots is the bounding duty of the politically-conscious intellectuals who purposefully identify with the people. How can they inculcate national ideals, values and hopes of a better future if they turn their back on the people of their village or tribe? Preaching and defending their nationality does not nullify their roots as Nwe Mbum, Bafaw, Bakweri or Bafut. It is a question of striving and defending the loftier ideals of belonging to a larger community. As for collective survival in dignity: yesterday, we defended the tribe (today's micro- nation) against invaders, exploiters and foreign oppressors; today, primacy must be given to defending the nation state for our collective survival in dignity.

The history of our society imposes on the educated elite a heavy, challenging duty – the urgency of positive change to enable the masses of our people to escape misery, want, disease and ignorance. The educated elite imbued with revolutionary ideas of positive change must nourish that change in the masses so that it blossoms, and finally frees our nation from the shackles of annexation, colonial occupation and alien rule to enable British Southern Cameroons to assume its rightful place among the free nations of the world.

The SCNC, seeing an instrument of national liberation in the act of countering violence with violence, will only transform it into second nature or a norm of our society. Violence begets violence, and once entrenched as part of national culture, it becomes difficult to erase from the sub-conscience of man. Is it not said that habit is man's second nature? We have a very clean case well anchored in history, culture and legality of a distinct territory defined by inherited colonial treaties and distinct political and administrative system that the occupier of our land cannot counter. What we urgently need is for national consciousness and solidarity invigorated by patriotism to divest the illegal occupant, la République du Cameroun, of the cruel control and exploitation of our land.

With the application of the force of argument, which is reason based on facts of history, culture, law and the mind are the tools to prove who is right or wrong. Such exchange of ideas, facts and knowledge takes place freely anywhere and at any time, even with the enemy. The force of argument is the controlled and rational use of force. It gives no room whatsoever to any Southern Cameroonian to use violence against his fellow compatriot under the pretext of fighting the enemy. Non-violence is the rational use of force to defeat the enemy without compromising your ultimate objective or giving any excuse to your enemy to cause greater destruction of human and material resources of the land. It should be pointed out that even without counter application of instruments of violence by the SCNC, Southern Cameroonians have witnessed much loss of human and material resources during imposed states of emergency and economic blockade, code named Operation Dorade. With counter-violence as instrument, the liberation of la République du Cameroun will have justifiable cause to place the whole territory of Southern Cameroons under martial law, and under the cover of darkness of the reign of evil, intensify the maximum use of instruments of violence and destruction on a larger scale. This rational use of force helps in maintaining and strengthening internal bonds of unity among Southern Cameroonians. Non-violence or the rational use of force is the greatest source of strength which the barbaric regime has found difficult to defeat.

The SCNC, in the application of this rational use of force, exposes the enemy, la République du Cameroun, as a foreign colonial aggressor who is wicked, blood thirsty, a violator of international law and norms, and an inherently evil regime. La République du Cameroun, represented by its gun-toting *gendarmes* or trigger-happy police whose brutality and dictatorial arrogance is household and the overzealous proconsuls and administrators who, in behaving like lords of a conquered land, are answerable to no one in Southern Cameroons, which is the annexed territory they rule with a heavy hand and which they exploit mercilessly. They compete with no one in their perpetration of atrocities against Southern Cameroonians and the Southern Cameroonian nation, which they have reduced to an appendage of la République du Cameroun. They have instituted violence as an article of faith for the perpetuation of colonial rule and imposition of the policy of assimilation.

Take, for example, the abrupt imposition of the CFA franc in 1962, to replace the British Pound Sterling (GBP), which was legal tender in British Southern Cameroons, and caused enormous losses including the deliberate destruction of Mamfe and Kumba as booming commercial centres; the closure of the Tiko and Victoria seaports and the Tiko, Besong Abang, Bali and Weh airports; the closure of the Mamfe River port and the Produce Marketing Board, whose headquarters were transferred to Douala and a huge part of its farmers' stabilisation fund was confiscated; the closure of the financial institutions set up by the Southern Cameroons Government for economic take-off such as the CamBank, Development Agency, Yoke PowerCam, Government Printing Press, Buea, Santa Coffee Estate, and Ntem Palm Plantation, were all carried out by the coloniser to impoverish Southern Cameroonians and deny the Southern Cameroonian youth, opportunities for employment. These economic infrastructures and financial institutions were not destroyed or closed because they were unviable but, simply for political and economic reasons, which would serve erase the historical and legal identity of the Southern Cameroons nation, and to transform the territory into a limping economic appendage of la République du Cameroun. Such acts of vandalism were necessary instruments to render the Southern Cameroonians subservient: the poor are weak and powerless; they have no voice.

To destroy a collective voice and justify the notion of a one and indivisible Cameroon Republic, the Southern Cameroonian government in Buea and all political and state institutions were abolished under the false notion of national unity and national integration. With this achieved, Francophone proconsuls are forced to rule with the whip and gun. National integration and national unity are euphemisms for annexation, colonial occupation, assimilation and uniformity and conformity for the enhancement of the one and indivisible la République du Cameroun.

With the rule of the whip and gun, a new culture of governance was imposed. This started with the infamous kale-kales into towns, villages or plantation camps, the introduction of the laissez-passer or Yaoundé's version of the Apartheid Pass, the establishment of BMM torture centres, the Ebubu, Tombel killings of 1962, the brutal murder of youths in Bamenda in 1990, Ndu in 1992, organised state terrorism of 1997, gruesome murders in Kumbo in 2001, systematic and constant use of excessive force at the slightest pretext to teach the anglofools an unforgettable lesson, and general and systematic gross violation of human rights, just to name but a few. All these atrocities, which are never due to provocation, are seen as premeditated acts by an external enemy against a people subjected to foreign domination and alien rule. While Southern Cameroonians mourn the murder of their compatriots and lament the violation of their basic human rights, la République du Cameroun stands guilty in the eyes of humanity in general. It cannot accuse the SCNC of any such crimes, either against Southern Cameroonians or citizens of la République du Cameroun.

By adopting the force of argument or the Gandhian stance of non-violence, we are fighting injustice, annexation, colonialism, expansionism, foreign domination and alien rule; a threat to world peace, and a crime against humanity. We are not fighting citizens of la République du Cameroun. If only the SCNC's message and mission were understood, people would have joined in fighting against this enemy of Man. But how can they, when they have been disorientated and given a negative picture of Southern Cameroons? Above all, the two peoples and two nations have never been one, and consequent upon their colonial backgrounds, they inherited different cultures, political philosophies and languages that have imbued them with contrasting personalities and visions of the state, common good and world view. It is not an issue of physical consciousness, but their beliefs, self and collective worth make each distinct, and no imperial decrees or erasure of distinct names and imposition of one common name can make the two peoples one and indivisible. The problem is far deeper rooted than the make-believe and political slogans they have imposed on people to cover the revolting conflict.

The force of argument or non-violence is not a philosophy of the weak and stupid. It should not be misconstrued to mean the catch phrase or ideology of the coward who has nothing to offer to a fast changing world. It does not mean the lack of courage to hit back at the enemy, or lack of a sense of direction and ambition. On the contrary, it implies the self-consciousness of the right and ability to fight back. But, endowed with a strong spiritual and moral principle, and committed to teaching an eternal truth, namely, that violence and counter-violence never work towards a better humanity, but destroys and slows human progress. Standing on this eternal truth and high ground of moral authority, we have abhorred aggression and violence. Violence does not depict the true nature of Man. Non-violence is not synonymous with pacifism.

Violence distorts the beauty and rhythm of life, be it human, animal and plant. To human life, it is like the unmasking of the sacred juju in the market place – an abomination. Violence, once begun, knows no limits, for even perpetrators are not free of its consequences, nor are they safe while conflict lasts. Violence does not operate on any time-honoured rules. Coming from the lower instinct of Man, it is not governed by any checks and balances, any sense of decency. It leaves perpetrators of atrocities with dented images of life to haunt them and more things to be ashamed of and hide than to be proud of and talk about for the common good. Dictators and despots promote violence for self-perpetuation, which is against the nature of Man and not in the best interest of the immediate society and the larger human community.

Non-violence sets out to correct all these, and inculcate in the minds of the agents of the despotic regime the message of eternal truth, which is that violence is anti-humanity, and in the long run works even against its apostles. Violence limits human freedom while non-violence opens limitless opportunities for Man. Aggression is the method of the despot who believes in the idea that 'might is right', for he has something to hide and thus, hates resolution of conflict through the application of reason and dialogue based on truth, legality and good conscience for the blooming of the creative powers of Man.

Non-violence is the philosophy of the courageous, the rational and the upright who has nothing to hide. It is built on the sustaining strength of truth while violence is built on the diminishing power of weapons and destructive ideology of might is right. While the force of argument or non-violence transmits words, ideas and ideals that are potent seeds for a better humanity and better world based on human freedom, justice, the rule of law, government at the service of Man: the power of weapons threaten human existence. In non-violence, freedom and justice are sought as an inherent right of man without resorting to aggression and violence, in other words, without destroying Man. It is not to say that by so doing, Southern Cameroonians are not conscious of the crimes against them and have forgiven the state of la République du Cameroun. How do you forgive someone who has killed your loved ones and robbed you of your humanity and dignity for so long without becoming repentant, and apologising? Non-violence takes stock of yesterday but, using the past and present as a launching pad, builds, preserves and promotes for the future rather than destroys it because of the unfortunate past. Conscious of the fact that today is the father of tomorrow, non-violence operates on the premise that without preserving what is worth preserving today we cannot have a better tomorrow.

In building bonds of unity and solidarity for national rebirth and freedom among citizens subjugated to annexation and colonial occupation, non-violence harnesses human and material resources, which, consequent upon brutal repression, exploitation, neglect, marginalisation and deprivation are in extreme short supply. Proverbially, it is said: when spiders unite, they have the capacity and willpower to strangle an elephant with their cobwebs. Unity and solidarity, which make the people invulnerable have led the Wimbum to hold as article of faith that '*Abee yu ngir*', translated literally to mean 'unity is strength'.

The power of non-violence is building a unifying force through systematic political education against the enemy of the people. It is translating the consciousness of 'we' versus 'them' into an active force of collective self-defence. This consciousness manifests itself in the readiness and willingness to face and confront the enemy, not in the sense of conventional war or guerrilla battles, but reason and facts to let them understand their crimes, and that they are oppressors, killers and plunderers. It is being proactive and never allowing the thief to steal, and get away, unchallenged.

In non-violence, the people are empowered with sound knowledge and skills to take their destiny into their own hands. It creates opportunities for capacity building so that the subjugated and exploited of yesterday acquire knowledge and skills, and collectively become the engine of their own development. It creates broad-based opportunities for dialogue, consultation and proper understanding of society. Through dialogue and consultation with the masses, which builds the spirit of tolerance and give and take, the leaders are better positioned to articulate and aggregate the aspirations and needs of the masses, and thereby plan and identify the priorities comprehensively.

Non-violence transmits to people fighting for their rights, thanks to political consciousness which the down-trodden come to acquire through training and interaction with leaders, that political power, which the oppressors wield, is not an exclusive preserve of the rulers and enemy of the people. They come to understand that those who rule depend on their subjects to wield and exercise political power. Although despots try to create a myth about their source of authority, they inwardly seek acknowledgement and acceptance by the people to give meaning to their right to rule. They cannot rule the gods. They cannot contend themselves with ruling animals and plants. They cannot rule in a void. They cannot be contented in ruling themselves or in ruling just a section of the population. They can only find contentment in ruling the entire people, and such a people must first submit to their right to rule. Through systematic political education, the subjugated come to the understanding that to submit to illegality is to compromise their inherent right to freedom and dignity. To their credit, they come to the knowledge that rejecting and challenging foreign domination and alien rule in all facets, is to advance the cause of the freedom of the oppressed and contribute to world democracy and human progress. By consistently and systematically rejecting and challenging foreign domination and alien rule, the dictators' right and rule are challenged and weakened.

Consequently, once the masses understand how much power they have at their disposal, with proper orientation, organisation, coordination and management of this essential resource, they can deprive the unjust rulers of the power they need to continue oppressing the people. They divest the latter through non-cooperation, by withholding loyalty and not respecting the unjust and oppressive laws of the foreign leaders. The masses have power. However, to be effective in a non-violent struggle, it must of absolute necessity, be properly organised, harnessed and directed at the enemy. Timing is also essential. In this case, the manner in which this is organised and when each kind of action seen to be suitable, are determined by local circumstance.

The 1st of October was declared Independence Day of British Southern Cameroons by the UN 4th Committee in 1961, was commemorated in 2001 by Southern Cameroonians under the SCNC. Ceasing to be an ordinary day for Southern Cameroonians, it becomes a bone in the neck of the Yaoundé annexationist regime then. The troops are put on red alert and some sent into Southern Cameroons to reinforce the occupation crack down force permanently stationed in the annexed territory. Arrests start in mid-September. 1st October has come to stand as a constant reminder to both la République du Cameroun and Southern Cameroonians, even the apologists of the Yaoundé regime that the Southern Cameroonian issue, is a balloon forced under water which must float, and the sooner the better for the two nations concerned. As unfortunate as this is, it alerts the UN and international community of the long-standing, unfinished decolonisation process in British Southern Cameroons, which facilitated annexation and colonial occupation by the expansionist la République du Cameroun.

Even the most ruthless despot or tyrant knows that for the exercise political power, the loyalty, support and cooperation of the subjects are needed. Once the oppressed understand they have something the tyrant badly needs, they can withdraw support, declare the regime illegitimate, deny cooperation and resist all imposed laws. The dictator will find it difficult to continue enjoying and wielding great power and influence. The temptation that often seems right to dictators will be to inflict punishment to induce obedience and submission. Here, non-violence, a result of the political consciousness of the people, explains that punishment has a limit, especially when the people persist and bear it as the price for the positive change they stand for. Punishment is costly to both sides, and ends up exposing the dictator while winning sympathy and support for the oppressed, defending their rights and rightful place in the history of the world in which each people, under the law, freely shape their destiny, assert themselves and make legitimate contribution towards a better humanity.

The task of national liberation and reconstruction, and nation-building is enormous. Non-violence does not mean passivism. It imbues citizens with the spirit of patriotism, courage, self-discipline, sensitivity, consciousness of their role in society and responsibility, and remaining proactive and creative. It means building internal bridges for unity and peace since global peace starts with the small community and spreads to the nation and the world. Non-violence integrates people fighting for justice into the wider world, and makes them see their struggle as a legitimate contribution for global democracy, peace and justice for a better humanity. It requires the building of team and community spirit, synergy, being one another's keeper and vigilance, for victory comes with effective defence of gains acquire, which create conditions for future victories. Unity against the common enemy is vital not only for immediate victory; it is the engine of enduring peace and sustainable development.

Non-violence helps in preserving the little that the impoverished society has. What is available is saved from the ravages of war, which is carried out by the enemy using weapons of destruction to erase from history what they cannot loot. Such massive destruction, imposition of hunger and blockage of external source of supply are always used to cripple resistance, thus unduly prolonging the struggle for freedom. Consequently, mass suffering eats deep into the heart of the occupied and colonised. When this goes on for too long and mass suffering becomes unbearable, the freedom fighter and redeemer sometimes becomes an enemy in the eyes of cowardly nationals, making it easy for the enemy to break the ranks of the liberation movement through bribery, corruption, patronage and treachery. Non-violence builds a wall around its people and reduces the devastating effect of this happening, killing the struggle for justice. It protects individual weaknesses from being exposed and exploited by the enemy of the people.

In the promotion of national consensus for a noble cause, the force argument or non-violence seeks to reconcile the fragmented and fragile society. Southern Cameroonians are living witnesses to the enemies' diabolic tactics of poisoning the minds of the people of the coastal region – Southern zone – against the people of the grassland – Northern zone – and vice versa. With the policy of divide and rule, each is blackmailed against the other. The enemy pretends to prefer people of the coast to those of the grassland, for example, giving them jobs in the colonial administration. In reality, these are inferior positions and people of the southern zone grassland are more exploited than those of the northern zone. The policy of divide and rule and the pinning of one people against the other build hatred, distrust and hostility. Tribalism, segregation, regionalism, nepotism and corruption in high places have become national culture and a trademark of Biya's Government which he skilfully uses in pinning one ethnic group against another to perpetuate rule and the entrenchment of the Beti ruling oligarchy.

We cannot forget the Divisional Officer of Donga Matung, Peter Oben Ashu of Manyu in the Southern zone, who used brute force to suppress the supporters of freedom and democracy in Ndu, earning him his appointment as Governor of South West. When Governor in Buea, he campaigned against the Northern zone (North West Province) with his slogan, 'Come - no go', reducing people of that zone to becoming unwanted refugees in the Southern zone who had overstayed their welcome. This phenomenon was unknown in the good old days of Southern Cameroons. Thus, Dr Endeley's (a Bakweri of Buea) strong political base was Nkambe Division (Donga Mantung County) in the Northern zone, while J. N. Foncha easily won seats in parts of Victoria Division (Fako County) and Mamfe (Manyu) in the Southern zone. It must be noted that in operating parliamentary democracy, none of the three Premiers in British Southern Cameroons, Endeley, Foncha and Jua, formed the type of government based on tribalism and nepotism like Biya did.

While Endeley's last Government of 1958 composed two ministers from the grassland and three (including him) from the coastal region, counting four Britons, and was fairly balanced, J. N. Foncha's Government of 1959 was comprised of four ministers (including himself) from the grassland and seven ministers from the coastal region. On the other hand, the Government of A.N. Jua (1965 to 1968) comprised seven ministers (including himself) from the grassland and nine from the coastal region. Giving priority to national reconstruction and nation-building from the ruins caused by colonial rule, Foncha and Jua relied heavily on the political elite and meritocracy to achieve the goal of nation-building and economic development. Meritocracy was the base for appointment into positions of responsibility to serve the nation. If, at the material time, people from the coastal region dominated the government and the civil service, it was not tribalism or regionalism; it was an issue of getting the right person to do the job. What has been the basis of constant accusation of domination of the grassland over the coastal region, fanned by lackeys who prefer la République du Cameroun's annexation and colonial rule to restore Southern Cameroons' sovereign statehood?

Nation-building demands that merit, competence and patriotism are the basis for appointment to serve the nation, and constant effort made at maintaining a balance between the different Regions of the nation. Respect for unity in diversity should be the focal point, and all Regions must feel the sense of belonging. While meritocracy is encouraged as a national policy to build the spirit of hard work, devotion to national duty, selfless service and socio-economic development should be based on equitability without any region receiving undue advantage at the detriment of another other. Colonial rule gave some Regions an earlier start while others were badly disadvantaged. National duty makes it compelling for the new Southern Cameroons Government, committed to justice and balanced development, to pay special attention to disadvantaged Regions, for colonial act and discriminatory policy was no fault of the of the affected people and region.

The old tactics of pinning one against the other serves the interest of the colonial regime. As provocative as institutionalised colonial violence is, care must be taken, for disoriented and poorly organised effort to counter violence can only lead to the creation of an endemic culture of hatred and extremism. The Yaoundé regime has polarised the Southern Cameroonian society: the people to hate one another, blackmail one another, blame each other for wrongs or failures, and by doing this, divert attention from the fundamental problem of annexation and colonial occupation by la République du Cameroun. This will keep the people fragmented, weak, and polarised while the enemy becomes invulnerable and safe, and is even seen as a redeemer and protector for self-seeking politicians, and the co-opted educated elite and traditional rulers. Because of the imposed colonial or slave mentality, a Southern Cameroonian is not fit or qualified to hold certain posts; he is not fit to be a decision-maker. Worshipping the Yaoundé 'goddess', some Southern Cameroonians are, for crumbs, quick at mocking their fellow compatriots who venture to condemn la République du Cameroun for atrocities or raise a finger at the injustices perpetrated against the people of Southern Cameroons. With such a divided and weakened house, Yaoundé, with impunity, represses the people the more the plunder of their land and natural resources is intensified and goes on unchallenged.

To repay the damage caused or reverse the fragmentation and fragility of the Southern Cameroonian society, non-violence offers the opportunity for primacy to be placed on effective organisation of the people from the grassroots in the rural districts and urban centres, and not on the basis of tribes but, as citizens of a country with a common destiny. The SCNC has structures from the grassroots, namely, precincts, local government area and county, hierarchically structured for the national council within which matters of common national interest are discussed, debated and resolved democratically. While at the grassroots, for example, the precinct, local government area or county local issues are influenced by national programmes and policies, plans of action and policies which are an articulation and aggregation of what has come from below are implemented throughout the national territory and in the diaspora, wherever SCNC structures exist. The existence of these structures, led by democratically elected leaders of SCNC from different parts of the Southern Cameroonian nation, is detribalising the citizens and inculcating national consciousness. Plans of action adopted by the National Council have a national appeal. This is the solid foundation for national consensus and solidarity in nation-building.

The existence of structures, open to Southern Cameroonians, has made participation to all, irrespective of gender, religion, tribe or age in the liberation of their country, the right and bounding duty of all Southern Cameroonians, hence building a democratic culture, since the notion of freedom of assembly, speech, thought and opinion is a fundamental right to everyone. While in violent liberation struggle, the masses are excluded by circumstances of seeking shelter and refuge even outside their territory, in non-violence, in which primacy is given to popular political action such as resistance, non-cooperation, demonstrations, sit downs, sit ins and strikes, the masses, irrespective of gender, age, social status and religion are part and parcel of the decision-making process and its implementation. Success depends on effective sensitisation, education, proper coordination and planning, timing and proper identification of things that matter much to the masses. Here, we see primacy placed on the defence and promotion of the legitimate aspiration of the greater number of people.

This is not to say that non-violence faces no challenges. With bribery, corruption, patronage and spy-network, la République du Cameroun has made life very difficult for effective implementation of SCNC programmes and plans of action. Through non-violence, cultural bias, stigma and antagonism are broken, since wrong notions and beliefs about other people and ethnic groups are shattered as people from different ethnic groups interact in the building of a national culture and national consciousness. As unity grows stronger, each comes to see his well-being intrinsically linked with collective survival in dignity. Leadership that emerges from such cross-fertilisation of indigenous core values with the democratic principles and practices enjoys greater legitimacy than has been experienced in societies that underwent violent liberation struggles. Angola, for example, after several years of anti-colonialist war against imperial Portugal, was victim of a protracted bloody civil war between the MPLA and UNITA. Southern Cameroons must avoid such a costly, sad history.

The promotion of national consciousness and solidarity through non-violence is to turn things inside out, and removing the scales from the people's eyes, enable them to see the enemy's true colours. With effective political education to arm the people for national rebirth, the hate dynamic seeds that the enemy has used to keep the colonised society weak and subservient, is reversed and refocused against the enemy. The force of argument or non-violence creates no internal and external enemies. Properly organised and structured, it frustrates the enemy terribly. The message of non-violence, based on truth, is universally appealing. The SCNC's consistent and systematic use of historical facts, legal instruments, the UN Charter and Resolutions, the African Charter on Human and Peoples' Rights, and the AU Constitutive Act incontrovertibly project la République du Cameroun as the aggressor, coloniser and violator of international law, UN, AU and Commonwealth charters and conventions of which it is a signatory. While la République du Cameroun cannot prove by what instrument of international law it exercises sovereignty over Southern Cameroons or justifies its atrocities and human rights violations against the people, SCNC leaders find no difficulty in explaining this. Asking for help from the international community to dismantle neo-apartheid or black colonialism in West Africa, the SCNC's message is flawless in the defence of international instruments and universal values. By violating international law, la République du Cameroun's colonial occupation of Southern Cameroons is a monumental crime against the international system as well as humanity.

The force of argument taps from the inherent good qualities of Man to build bridges between ethnic communities, implore creative powers in reconciling peoples, engaged in confidence building, empowering the people and giving them hope in the new Southern Cameroons with opportunities for all Southern Cameroonians who, under la République, were deprived of the capacity to prosper, self-fulfilment, happiness and decency. On the contrary, la République du Cameroun, which has been using coercive instruments of violence to suppress and exploit Southern Cameroons, is promising its citizens nothing new. What it succeeds in doing best is nurturing the culture of violence, oppression, hatred, corruption, graft and patronage among its own citizens. Once Southern Cameroons becomes free and la République du Cameroun has no common enemy to oppress and exploit it, the endemic culture of violence hitherto used against British Southern Cameroons it will be turned inwards against themselves.

What has brought about fundamental change in human history is not war. Wars create and leave painful scars in the conscience of

Man and the world community. It constitutes the negative and dark side of human history and the nature of Man. It does not bring genuine peace but, dialogue builds peace which ends war. War, not being a norm in human life, should not be made to become a condition or logical means for solving conflicts between peoples and nations. Evidence points to the fact that it is always the greedy who are determined to satisfy self-interest who stockpiles weapons which are used against others. He who is in the right never provokes a war but, he who is in the wrong believes that might is right. Violence, which unfortunately has come to be seen as a shortcut to resolving a conflict put on the agenda of the international system, is used as a cover for the negative spirit and attitude built against others. Dialogue and preventive diplomacy must be given primacy in finding solutions to conflicts. For the building of a better world and greater humanity, let dialogue, not violence, be put on the fast track.

The SCNC, in adopting the force of argument or Gandhian non-violence, is taking la République du Cameroun to the court of international law and global conscience for its crimes of annexing the Southern Cameroons, and for impeding the inherent and inalienable right of self-determination of the Southern Cameroonians. By declaring that the conflict between Southern Cameroons and la République du Cameroun is the violation of the territorial integrity of the former, an issue of international politics and law is not an act of arrogance. It is not an act of despising the courts of la République du Cameroun either. On the contrary, it is an act of recognising the sovereignty of la République du Cameroun within its territorial boundaries inherited at independence on January 1, 1960 but in conformity with international law as foreign power. Although a neighbour, it has no rights under international law to extend and impose its sovereignty over Southern Cameroons. The question of right to self-determination of a people and territorial integrity under international law hinges on the equal right to sovereignty of any people and territory irrespective of size, economic potential and military might. Southern Cameroonians are only respecting and upholding international law, and defending good conscience, the basis for international cooperation as well as the building of global democracy, the rule of law and world peace.

Southern Cameroons is not asking the international system to grant it the right to secede from la République du Cameroun. It will be a violation of international law, the principle of international jurisprudence of *uti possidetis juris* and the critical date, and Article 4(b) of the AU Constitutive Act. As a defender of international system fully committed to working for global democracy and peace based on justice, Southern Cameroons subscribes to respect the UN Charter and international instruments, and the equality of all nations regardless of their size. As a principle, world democracy, peace, justice and human dignity will remain lip service until self-determination and democracy are the two sides of the same coin, cherished, respected and defended by all.

Self-preservation, it must be understood is a dynamic two-way process. You only preserve what is yours by respecting what belongs to the other person. This is why it is said that your right stops where the other person's starts. Endangering the right to the national self-existence of another nation endangers yours also. What is evident in the two Cameroons situation is that, as Biya has intensified the colonial occupation of Southern Cameroons, maintained by brute use of coercive force, destruction of the economy, bribery and corruption, which gnaw at the body politics of la République du Cameroun. They have become endemic and incurable. While Southern Cameroonians see these as a venom of the annexationist la République du Cameroun, a social malaise which will be cured with sovereign independence and the building of checks and balances, the rule of law and good governance in la République du Cameroun these will remain the trademark of despotism and national culture.

Conscious of the fact that Southern Cameroonian right to freedom and justice is intrinsically linked to world freedom and humanity's craving for enduring peace, the SCNC comes to the court of international law and global conscience for justice. And, cognisant of the fact that he who seeks justice must come to equity with clean hands, the SCNC has adopted non-violence, and the respect for international adjudication and mediation. For a permanent solution that will guarantee enduring peace, international pressure should absolutely be mounted on la République du Cameroun to respect its inherited boundaries, withdraw its proconsuls and colonial occupation forces from Southern Cameroons, and recognise Southern Cameroons' inherent right to self-determination and independence.

There can be no world peace without justice for all, and there can be no freedom without equality, safety without security, development without equity and fair sharing of God's gifts to humanity. The Southern Cameroonian problem resulting from a botched or imperfect decolonisation process is an international problem requiring global attention, action and solution as prescribed by the UN Charter, Resolutions and international instruments. The UN system started the decolonisation process of British Southern Cameroons but stopped mid-stream, and defenceless Southern Cameroons, was annexed by la République Cameroun which nursed this evil ambition. With support from the EU, Commonwealth, AU and supporters of human freedom, democracy and right to self-determination for SCNC's non-violent struggle, the UN should step in and accomplish its mission of effective decolonisation in conformity with the UN Charter and UNGA Resolution 1514 of 1960.

There can be no democracy without the inherent and inalienable right of self-determination. Those who rule must rule by the consent of the governed. Foreign rule or colonial rule is never predicated on laws and the consent of the governed. It is always illegal. It is imposed and sustained by brute force, and the colonial courts that are corrupt defend its establishment. Rebelling against annexation and foreign rule is not a crime since such act violates no law, local or international law. Such an act defends universal principles, and offends no law except the interest and greed of the imperial master.

Democracy and self-determination are two sides of the same coin. Democracy and self-determination are premised on the understanding that the best interest of each people can only be fulfilled by the people themselves, and those who rule must democratically be elected by the people, not appointed by decree by a foreign sovereign. The historical and cultural experiences of each people, and their environment shape the rhythm of their life, their core values and world view, and determine their needs and wants as well as condition their lifestyle. Historical and cultural forces make each people unique. By natural law, the legitimate aspirations and interests of another people can never best be understood, defended and served by foreign domination and alien rule.

Foreign aggression and alien rule destroy the fibres of internal cohesion, and halt the historical development of each people and shatters the hope of the people. For instance, Southern Cameroons has been set backwards through the systematic and deliberate destruction of established political, economic, financial and socio-cultural institutions.

To push the international community to positive action, Southern Cameroonians must accept the onus of achieving freedom, justice and the right to self-determination, and dignity lies on their shoulders. No one mourns your beloved mother better than you do. We must look inward and effectively mobilise and organise, build synergy, adopt strategies, identify priorities, specify set goals with timelines and be ready to learn from others. Above all, the citizens must be ready and willing to sacrifice and pay a price for their freedom. We must banish the finger-pointing, blame syndrome, and rise to the challenge of the moment. We must learn from the mistakes of yesterday and try to be pragmatic and positively different. Taking no action in the restoration of the Southern Cameroonian statehood is the same as sitting and dreaming it will be handed to you on a golden plate, in the same way the head of John the Baptist was handed to Herod's daughter. Non-violence aims to minimise the cost that must be paid. The world is moving forward. However, Southern Cameroonians are in the tragic pit of annexation and colonial occupation.

The destiny of Southern Cameroonians is in their hands. In order to rise and stand on their feet, and become masters of their destiny, they must refuse to be the donkeys for la République du Cameroun which uses them to ride on their backs. You have to wake up and be counted amongst the heroes of tomorrow. Southern Cameroonians of this age must, as an act of patriotic duty and absolute necessity, resolve to be the architects of their destiny, write their history themselves, and never to have it written and sung into their ears by others, worse still by their oppressors. It is the historic task and challenge of the moment for this generation.

The history, culture and beliefs of people set them apart. We must be proud of who we are, and by dint of our efforts and sacrifices, change our circumstances. We cannot pretend to be who we are not. We cannot stand outside our past history and culture and redeem ourselves from annexation and colonial occupation. The engine of progressive change for the oppressed starts with the rejection of the status quo imposed onto them, and with determination, goes for what ordinarily is described as impossible.

Southern Cameroonians of today must declare and hold onto their equality with the citizens of la République du Cameroun, Nigeria and any other nation in the world. They must be assertive and declare their inherent right to be their own masters, rulers and judges. The unyielding spirit will lead them to break free the shackles of neo-apartheid under la République du Cameroun. South Africans, Namibians or East Timorese did the same and triumphed. Why would Southern Cameroonians not undertake such an action? The future of Southern Cameroons will promise happiness, greatness and prosperity if the current chains of annexation and colonial occupation are broken through the positive use of people power.

We must believe in possibilities. The more you think of impossibilities, the more you impose fear on your own self, generating impossible conditions around you, and for others. Negative ideas are contagious, and like the HIV virus that destroys human immune system, it destroys the inherent potentialities and strength of human beings.

Confidence strengthens the belief possibilities, makes one optimistic and builds a positive attitude towards life, makes one believe in human equality and strife for justice, and opens the inherent mine of talents which consequent upon annexation, have been lying dormant. These positive attitudes, which will strengthen unity among the oppressed, will transform the people into achievers, and make everyone leader for their community and people. Believing in self and others creates the necessary conditions for success. There is no human problem without a solution. Before mountaineers ascend and conquer the Everest, it must first be conquered by believing in self.

While this concluding chapter is concentrated on proving the potent power of the force of argument or Gandhian non-violence, emphasis in this book is placed on the collective unity of purpose and rational use of political and people power for national rebirth. The winning spirit discussed above, which generates courage and makes the people so passionate about their historic mission, is fired and sustained by the vision of a better future. With visionary leadership, mass and resource mobilisation remain key to goal attainment. With this in mind, whatever setbacks or challenges the people may suffer, they are never deterred. Believing in the fairness of their mission, they never give up, surrender or retreat. Fired by vision and the winning spirit serving as an engine, their faith is permanently anchored on victory. Setbacks and obstacles are seen and treated as stepping stones towards expected victory.

As a truism and in the legitimate struggle to end neo-apartheid, we must accept that the welfare of each is dependent on collective well-being as a condition for victory. We are bound to hold that we have no other space on this planet to bequeath to our children but Southern Cameroons. Giving it to la République du Cameroun is to treacherously bequeath servitude to our descendants. Our survival as a people and nation in dignity is predicated upon patriotism, sincere and selfless effort, hard work and conscientious contribution of each in the liberation of the Fatherland from annexation and colonial occupation. This is the guarantor of freedom and the right to equality of Southern Cameroonians to free citizens of the world.

Humans need a new sense of awareness and consciousness

which will bring a moral and spiritual rebirth for humanity. This can only come from the inside; not by military might. The moral and spiritual strength of man will reshape the world for greater humanity; not military might and materialism. The storehouse of this is the force of argument or non-violence. Non-violence is in defence of true humanity, spirituality, morality and rationality at peace with nature and men. It works for a better world, indeed a community of nations, respecting, sharing and cooperating to build global democracy and peace based on justice for all humanity. The SCNC is determined not only to lead Southern Cameroons to freedom and independence; they are determined to place Southern Cameroons, and why not Africa, on the world stage as part of this new consciousness. The new force for better humanity must overshadow militarism and impunity, fundamentalism and extremism for global peace, the rule of law, justice and democracy.

For too long humankind has listened to peace being preached without it materialising. This is because it was peace as prescribed by the powerful. It was peace without justice for all. It was not peace based on the laws of nature and fervent belief in common humanity.

For too long democracy was preached at rooftops, even by the most brazen dictator and tyrant. However, it was democracy without the right to self-determination for the very peoples they brutally oppressed. They hid behind the cloak of national sovereignty and non-interference in internal affairs of a sovereign nation while exercising colonial occupation over some peoples against their sovereign will.

As from 1960, all the colonies and Trust Territories under British rule in Africa became independent nations within their colonial boundaries, except Eritrea and British Southern Cameroons. While Eritrea was annexed by imperial Ethiopia, British Southern Cameroons was annexed and subjected to colonial occupation by la République du Cameroun. It is sad to note that it was the failure of the international system to respect the UN Charter that facilitated the annexation of these Trust Territories under the UK administration with the Administering Authority looking the other way. To regain independence, Eritrea, because of the culture of silence of the UN and later the OAU, was forced into a liberation war against Ethiopia. The consequences have been enormous and long lasting, and contributed in no less measure to overthrow of Emperor Haile Selassie and the protracted civil wars that followed.

As stated above, non-violence should not be mistaken as the philosophy of the weak or the poor. On the contrary, the SCNC has adopted non-violence as the evidence of its faith in the changing world, the UN and international instruments, the growing emphasis on human freedom, democracy, and self-determination as the sustaining foundation of global peace and human progress. All these should diligently be respected and applied, not only for the good of Southern Cameroons, but for the good of all humanity. Southern Cameroons' problem and solution is well situated within the ambit of international instruments such as the UN Charter and the UNGA and Security Council Resolutions, the African Union Constitutive Act and the African Charter on Human and Peoples' Rights and international laws and Covenants in general. As the UN Trust Territory of French Cameroun became independent in 1960 under French administration and international instruments, Southern Cameroons, under United Kingdom administration, lays equal claim to the attainment of this same legal status to lead its people to attain self-fulfilment. Modern African nation states, ex-colonies and Trust Territories of yesteryear, attained international legal status under international instruments and global good conscience. Southern Cameroons is making no other claim but to the same consecrated principles that should shape and govern relationships between all peoples and nations for free enterprise, international cooperation, democracy, global peace and better humanity. For Southern Cameroons to compromise on this is to betray humanity.

It is evident that the most bloody and disastrous wars in recorded history have been provoked by aggression of the powerful states and the national self-defence of the weak states to preserve and promote its inalienable right to national self-existence. Through non-violence is sought the right to freedom, peace and justice, which must not lead to fundamentalism, impunity and extremism and cannot be without the will of the people to national self-determination being attained on mass graves, and atrocities against humanity.

Article 1 of the International Covenant on Cultural and Political Rights (ICCPR), which forms the bedrock of international humanitarian law states:

"All peoples have the right of self-determination. By virtue of that right, they freely determine their political status and freely pursue their economic, social and cultural development."

To reinforce the above provision, and ensure the collective will of humanity in guaranteeing that all nations respect and abide by it for the good of all humanity, Article 4 of the ICCPR states:

" with the provisions of the Charter of the UN."

This obligation must be respected by the UN system and all member nations.

The UN owes it to humanity to defend the wisdom that informed its founding and mission by supporting non-violence through effective application of preventive diplomacy in the Southern Cameroons, and where the oppressed cry for freedom, legality and justice. Humanity's quest for peace will be attained through the promotion of dialogue, democracy, the rule of law and national self-determination. The resolve of the UN, in making preventive diplomacy a priority instrument of taming, and avoiding conflicts from exploding into bloody wars, should be seen as a logical roadmap for global peace. The culture of silence by the UN and international community, leading to inaction and unbearable human suffering, have inevitably put violence on a fast track. By enforcing respect of the UN Charter and international instruments, the UN will be fulfilling its defined mission of avoiding wars and human calamities, and building world peace and international cooperation. Non-interference in internal affairs of a UN Member Nation should not be applied and respected by the UN and other democratic nations when foreign aggression, violation of territorial integrity of a neighbouring state and annexation is established. There is no better way of doing this other than by listening to victims, and examining treaties in force and boundaries inherited at independence by the perpetrator state, which will kill the spirit of might is right and expansionism, and condition a momentous weakening of the behaviour of aggressive governments with regard to the frequent use of force to suppress dissent and peaceful legitimate protests, even by college students and unarmed women, creating opportunities for tolerance and dialogue in a place of excessive use of force to silence the weak. Such positive action will open new possibilities in the promotion of democracy, and building of global peace based on justice for a better world and greater humanity.

Annextures

ANNEX (I): Boundary Treaty Between The British Southern Cameroons And French Cameroun.

Extracted from:
Declaration Made By The Governor Of The Colony And Protectorate Of Nigeria And The Governor Of The French Cameroun Defining The Boundary Between British And French Cameroun

The undersigned:
Sir Graeme Thomson, G.C.M.G., K.C.B., Governor of the Colony and Protectorate of Nigeria.
Dated 9 January 1931
(Treaty Series No. 34 (1931) [Cmd. 3936])
Exchange of Notes between His Majesty's Government in The United Kingdom and the French Government respecting the Boundary between British and French Cameroun
NOTE: 1-75 defines French Cameroun/British Northern Cameroons boundary.

(76) Thence a line parallel to the Koubokam-Koutopi path on its northern side until the stream Moinum (Banso) or Ketchouperin (Bamun) is reached, thus leaving the Koubokam-Koutopi path wholly in French territory.

(77) Thence the stream Ketchouperin or Moinun until its junction with the River Moinun (Banso and Bamun) or Upper Nun.

(78) Thence the Moinun to its junction with the River Nun.

(79) Thence the River Nun to its junction with the River Ngwanonsiaor Chawnga or Chawga.

(80) Thence the River Ngwanonsia upstream to the point where it is crossed by the Nkwefu-Bambalang Road.

(81) Thence a line westwards through the swamp to the northern extremity of the Island of Nkwefu (an elder of the Bagam village of Fombefu).

(82) Thence a line westwards through the swamp to the point where the Fombefu-Nkwefu path cuts the River Ta or Tantam.

(83) Thence the River Tantam upstream to its confluence with the River Sefu or Mekango.

(84) Thence the River Sefu upstream to its source.

(85) Thence a line south-westwards to the apex of the large isolated rock called Ngoma Fominyam.

(86) Thence a line southwards to the source of the River Webinga near point 1300 in Moisel's map and to the east of it.

(87) Thence the River Webinga to its confluence with the Mbonso (Bali-Bagam) or Momogo (Bagam).

(88) Thence the River Mbonso to its confluence with the River Mifi.

(89) Thence the River Mifi upstream to its confluence with the River Mogo or Dochi.

(90) Thence the River Mogo upstream to its confluence with the stream Dugum (Bali-Bagam) or Mousete-Fontchili (Bagam), which is slightly above where the Bagam-Bali-Bagam road crosses the River Mogo.

(91) Thence the stream Dugum to its source which is marked by a cairn of stones on the eastern side of Mount Ngenkoa (Bali-Bagam) or Koungo (Bagam).

(92) Thence a line to a cairn of stones at the top of the defile between Mount Ngenkoa in the south and Mount Tabira (Bali-Bagam) or Koumenou (Bagam) in the north.

(93) Thence a line to the bend in the River Bingwa (Bali-Bagam) or Seporo (Bagam), about 60 yards from the above-mentioned cairn.

(94) Thence the River Bingwa to its confluence with the River Mifi.

(95) Thence the River Mifi upstream to its confluence with the River Kongwong.

(96) Thence the River Kongwong upstream to its junction with the River Tooloo or Ntoulou.

(97) Thence the River Tooloo to a cairn at the top of the waterfall about 1 kilometre above the confluence of the Rivers

Tooloo and Kongwong.

(98) Thence a straight line on a magnetic bearing of 130° to the summit of a circular peak immediately to the north of the defile Zemembi, through which passes the Babadju-Bapinyi path.

(99) Thence the line of heights overlooking to the east of the valley of Babdju and to the west the valley of the Meso to the peak Asimi, where this line of heights ends.

(100) Thence a straight line to the centre of the marsh shown on Moisel's map as Mbetscho and called Kifi by the natives of Babinyi, and Tchinbintcho by those of Babadju.

(101) Thence the crest of the watershed between the Cross River on the west and the River Noun on the east to a beacon in the centre of a small area of forest named Mepong about 400 Metres south-east of Mount Lekonkwe or Etchemtankou on the crest of the watershed.

(102) Thence the stream Tantchempong, which has its source about 25 metres south-west of the above-mentioned beacon, to its confluence with the stream Mintchemecharlee.

(103) Thence the stream Mintchemecharlee upstream to the point where it most nearly reaches two small rocks named Tolezet which mark the boundary between the villages of Fossong Elelen and Fongo Tongo on the road between those villages.

(104) Thence a line passing through the two rocks named Tolezet to the source of the stream Monchenjemaw or Montchi Zemo.

(105) Thence this stream to its confluence with the stream Munchisemor or Montchi Zemoua, which has its source about 50 metres west of the largest of the three rocks called Melogomalee or Melegomele.

(106) Thence the stream Munchisemor to its source.

(107) Thence a line passing through the centre of the largest of the three rocks called Melogomalee to the source of the stream Monchita or Montchi Monie, about 100 metres south-south-east of the above-named rock.

(108) Thence the stream Monchita to its confluence with the River Bamig.

(109) Thence the River Bamig upstream to its source on a forest-covered hill called Nkenchop (the point where the River Bamig crosses the Dschang-Fontem Road is marked by a beacon).

(110) Thence a line through the crest of the hill Nkenchop to the crest of a forest-covered hill called Siambi

(111) Thence a straight line to a beacon placed on the watershed at a point known as Ntchoumgomo.

(112) Thence a line following the crest of the watershed between the Cross River on the west and the River Nkam on the east through the summits of Mounts Ngome and Jomen to the summit of Mount Wenmen.

(113) Thence a straight line running south-south-west to join the River Ngwe.

(114) Thence the River Ngwe for a distance of 3 kilometres to its affluent, the stream Liplo.

(115) Thence the stream Liplo to a point 500 metres west of the Moangekam-Lo track.

(116) Thence a line running parallel with this track and 500 metres west of it, until this line reaches the crest of Mount Njimba.

(117) Thence a line along the crest of Mount Njimba to its summit, which lies to the west of the French village of Moangekam.

(118) Thence a line through the summit of Mount Ngokela to the plain of Elung, leaving the Muanya compound of Nyan in British territory.

(119) Thence a track cut across the plain and marked with posts so as to leave the village of Nyan in British territory and the village of Po-Wassum in French territory, until this track reaches the stream Edidio.

(120) Thence this stream until it is crossed by the Poala-Muangel track.

(121) Thence a line running south-south-west along the summit of Mount Manenguba to the ridge surrounding the basin of the lakes.

(122) Thence a curved line along the eastward side of the ridge until the point where the Muandon-Poala track crosses the ridge.

(123) Thence the Muandon-Poala track in a westerly direction down the slopes of Mount Hahin and Mount Ebouye until it reaches the River Mbe.

(124) Thence the River Mbe, which runs parallel with Mount Mueba, until a line of cairns and posts, is reached.

(125) Thence this line of cairns and posts, which marks the boundary between the French villages of Muaminam (Grand Chef Nsasso) and the English villages of the Bakossi tribe (District Head Ntoko) and the Ninong tribe (district Head Makege), to the point where an unnamed tributary from the North joins the River Eko.

(126) Thence a line touching the two westernmost points of the boundary of the former German plantation of Ngoll to the crest of Mount Elesiang.

(127) Thence along the crest of Mount Elesiang to the northern-most point of the tobacco plantation of Nkolankote.

(128) Thence a line running south-south-west along Mount Endon, so as to leave the plantation of Nkolankote in French territory and the plantation of Essosung in British territory, to the summit of Mount Coupe.

(129) Thence a straight line running south-south-west to a cairn of stones on the Lum-Ngab Road at a point 6,930 metres along this road from the railway track.

(130) Thence a straight line in a south-westerly direction to the source of the River Bubu.

(131) Thence the River Bubu to a point 1,200 metres downstream from a place called Muanjong Farm.

(132) Thence in a straight line in a westerly direction to the source of the River Ediminjo.

(133) Thence the River Ediminjo to its confluence with the River Mungo.

(134) Thence the River Mungo to the point in its mouth where it meets the parallel 4° 2' 3" north.

(135) Thence this parallel of latitude westwards so as to reach the coast south of Tauben Island.

(136) Thence a line following the coast, passing south of Reiher Island to Mokola Creek, thus leaving the whole of the Moewe See

in British territory.

(137) Thence a line following the eastern banks of the Mokola, Mbakwele, Njubanan-Jau, and Matumal creeks, and cutting the mouths of the Mbossa-Bombe, Mikanje, Tende, Victoria and other unnamed creeks to the junction of Matumal and Victoria creeks.

(138) Thence a line running 35° west of true south to the Atlantic Ocean.

Signed:

GRAEME THOMSON, Governor of the Colony and Protectorate of Nigeria.

MARCHAND Gouverneur, Commissaire de la République française au Cameroun.

ANNEX (II): U.N. General Assembly 4th Committee Vote On Independence Of Southern Cameroons.

United Nation fourth committee,
1152nd Meeting
General Assembly
Wednesday, 19 April 1961,
　At 9 p.m.
Fifteenth session
Official Records
New York

Contents
Agenda item 13
Report of the Trusteeship Council (continued)
The future of the Cameroons under United Kingdom Administration (continued) ....

Chairman: Mr. Adnan M. Pachachi (Iraq)

Agenda item 13
Report of the Trusteeship Council (A/4404) (continued)

1. Miss Brooks (Liberia) said that Liberia, an African State imbued with democratic traditions, would be proud to join with the Commonwealth countries… would accept, as a co-sponsor of the draft resolution on the accession of Tanganyika to independence (A/C4/L686).

2. The Chairman suggested that Member States wishing to become co-sponsors of the draft resolution on the accession of to independence should contact the sponsors directly before the item came before the Committee for discussion.

The future of the Cameroons under United Kingdom administration (A/4695, A/4699, A/4726, A/4727, A/C.4/448,

479, 481,482, 486, 487, 490, 493, 494; A/C.4/L.684/Rev.2, L.685 and Add. I)

(continued)

3. The Chairman informed the Committee that a statement had been received from Mr. Mayi Matip, a petitioner and Chairman of the Parliamentary Group of the Union des populations du Cameroun. He proposed that the statement should be circulated to the members of the Committee.

It was so decided.

4. Mr. EDMONDS (New Zealand) explained the reasons which had led him to co-sponsor draft resolution A/C./4/L.685 and Add 1, and also his position on draft resolution A/C.4/L.684/Rev. 2. His delegation had been glad to hear the French representative state at the 1150th meeting that his primary concern was to preserve the prestige of the United Nations. The New Zealand delegation, while moved by the same concern, had arrived at different conclusions.

5. The question at issue was not a quarrel between two States, and even less a quarrel between two African States but, a question of appraising the report (A/4727) of the United Nations Plebiscite commissioner, an official in whose competence, both the General Assembly and his delegation, had full confidence. It would therefore be out of place and unjust to intimate, as some had done, that the Commissioner could not judge the conduct and results of the plebiscite. The problem facing the Committee was whether the Commissioner's conclusions concerning the freely and secretly expressed wishes of the people were sound, and whether the results of the plebiscite were valid. Attempts had been made in the Committee to show that the plebiscite in the Northern Cameroons was invalid, and that the results distorted by reason of the relationship between that part of the Territory and Nigeria. In answer to a question from the New Zealand delegation, the Commissioner had said at the 1145th meeting that, in carrying out his mission, he had borne in mind the condition and degree of separation between the Northern Cameroons and Nigeria, and had nevertheless concluded that the results of the plebiscite should not be declared invalid. His delegation considered Mr. Abdoh the best

qualified person to make such a judgment, especially when he had been paid unanimous tribute for the conduct of his mission in the Southern Cameroons.

100. Mr. YOMEKPE (Ghana) pointed out at the 1151st meeting that he had suggested the 1st of November should be submitted for the date 1st October. If the Guinean delegation pressed for a vote on the 1st June, he would submit a formal amendment.

101. Sir Andrew COHEN (United Kingdom) said he was sorry he had not known that a formal amendment had been submitted. Had he been aware of the fact, he would have stated his own views on the subject, and would have requested the Premier of the Southern Cameroons to do the same.

102. Miss BROOKS (Liberia) withdrew her amendment.

103. Mr. RAKOTOMALALA (Madagascar) reintroduced the Liberian delegation's amendment.

104. The Chairman said that the rules of procedure precluded the submission of an amendment after the voting had already begun. Any delegation, which had felt that the 1st of October 1961 required changing, should have submitted a proposal to that effect in the days following the submission of the draft resolution.

105. Mr. TRAORE (Mali) regretted the fact that the Liberian delegation had withdrawn its amendment. If the Committee voted against the date of 1st of October 1961, the Assembly would be placed in an extremely difficult position, as it would have before it a proposal requesting the independence for Southern Cameroons but, not specifying any date.

106. Mr. OKALA (Cameroun) thought that separate dates could not be established for the accession to independence of the two parts of the Cameroons without amending the Trusteeship Agreement. As there was only one Trusteeship Agreement, there could not be separate votes.

107. The Chairman put to the vote the words "I October 1961" in operative paragraph 4 (b) of the draft resolution.

108. Mr. OKALA (Cameroun) protested against a vote which he regarded as unconstitutional. He deplored the fact that the United Nations seemed to be disregarding its mission and showing

a servile deference to the directives of certain great Powers, and particularly the United Kingdom and the United States. The delegation of Cameroun would not participate in the vote, and would withdraw from the committee room.

The words "1 October 1961" were approved by 50 votes to 2, with 12 abstentions.

109. Mr. KORN (Austria) and Mr. KANE (Senegal) stated that their delegations had not participated in the vote.

110. The Chairman put to the vote the words "1 October 1961" in operative paragraphs 5 of the draft resolution.

Those words were approved by 50 votes to 2, with 12 abstentions.

111. The Chairman put to the vote the phrase "into a Federal United Cameroun Republic" in operative paragraph 5 of the draft resolution.

A vote was taken by roll-call.

Austria, having been drawn by lot by the Chairman, was called upon to vote first.

In favour: Burma, Costa Rica, Cube, Cyprus, Denmark, Dominican Republic, Ethiopia, Federation of Malaya, Finland, Honduras, India, Indonesia, Iran, Ireland, Libya, Mexico, Nepal, New Zealand, Nigeria, Norway, Pakistan, Philippines, Saudi Arabia, Sweden, Thailand, Turkey, Union of South Africa, the United Kingdom of Great Britain and Northern Ireland, Australia.

Against: Brazil, Ghana, Guinea, Italy, Mali, Argentina.

Abstaining: Bolivia, Bulgaria, Byelorussian Soviet Socialist Republic, Cambodia, Ceylon, Chile, Czechoslovakia, Greece, Haiti, Hungary, Iraq, Japan, Jordan, Lebanon, Liberia, Luxembourg, Poland, Portugal, Romania, Spain, Sudan, Togo, Tunisia, Ukrainian Soviet Socialist Republic, Union of Soviet Socialist Republics, United Arab Republic, United States of America, Venezuela, Yemen, Yugoslavia, Afghanistan, Albania.

Present and not voting: Austria, China

The phrase was approved by 29 votes to 6, with 33 abstentions.

112. The Chairman put to the vote operative paragraph 5 as a whole.

Operative paragraph 5 was approved by 61 to none, with 14 abstentions.

113. The Chairman announced that the sponsors of the draft resolution had accepted the amendment to paragraph 6 proposed by the representative of Guinea whereby the words "at the request of the parties concerned" should be inserted after the words "to assist." He then put operative paragraph 6 as thus revised to the vote.

Operative paragraph 6 as revised was approved by 48 votes to none, with 17 abstentions.

114. The Chairman put to the vote draft resolution A/C.4/L.685 and Add.1 as a whole, as revised.

A vote was taken by roll-call.

Liberia, having been drawn by lot by the Chairman, was called upon to vote first.

In favour: Liberia, Libya, Mali, Mexico, Nepal, New Zealand, Nigeria, Norway, Pakistan, Philippines, Poland, Romania, Saudi Arabia, Sudan, Sweden, Thailand, Tunisia, Turkey, Ukrainian Soviet Socialist Republic, Union of South Africa, Union of Soviet Socialist Republics, United Arab Republic, United Kingdom of Great Britain and Northern Ireland, United States of America, Venezuela, Yemen, Yugoslavia, Afghanistan, Albania, Australia, Austria, Bolivia, Bulgaria, Burma, Byelorussian Soviet Socialist Republic, Canada, Ceylon, Chile, Costa Rica, Cuba, Cyprus, Czechoslovakia, Denmark, Dominican Republic, Ethiopia, Federation of Malaya, Fatherland, Ghana, Guinea, Honduras, Hungary, India, Indonesia, Iran, Iraq, Ireland, Japan, Jordan, Lebanon.

Against: Luxembourg, Paraguay.

Abstaining: Portugal, Spain, Togo, Argentina, Brazil, Cambodia, Greece, Haiti, and Italy.

Present and not voting: China.

Draft resolution A/C.4/L.685 and Add.1 as and as revised was approved by 59 votes to 2, with abstentions.

The meeting rose on Thursday, 20 April, at 3:15 a.m.

ANNEX (III): U.N. General Assembly Vote on Resolution 1608 Of April 21, 1961.

COUNTRY	For	Against	Abstain	Absent	COUNTRY	For	Against	Abstain	Absent
Afghanistan	x				Japan	x			
Albania	x				Jordan	x			
Argentina					Laos	x			
Australia	x				Lebanon	x			
Austria	x				Liberia	x			
Belgium					Libya	x			
Bolivia	x				Luxembourg		x		
Brazil					Madagascar		x		
Bulgaria	x				Mali	x			
Burma	x				Mauritania		x		
Byeloruselan S.S.R	x				Mexico	x			
Cambodia					Mongolia	x			

Country				
Cameroon				
Canada	x			
Central African Republic				
Ceylon	x			
Chad				
Chile	x			
China				
Colombia				
Congo (Brazzaville)				
Congo (Leopoldville)				
Costa Rica	x			
Cuba	x			
Cyprus	x			
Czechoslovakia	x			
Dahomey				
Denmark	x			
Dominican	x			

Country				
Morocco				
Nepal				
Netherlands				
New Zealand				
Nicaragua				
Niger				
Nigeria				
Norway				
Pakistan				
Panama				
Paraguay				
Peru				
Philippines				
Poland				
Portugal				
Romania				
Saudi Arabia				
Senegal				

Country	Mark	Country	Mark
Republic		Sierra Leone	
Ecuador	x	Somalia	
Elsalvadol		South Africa	x
Ethiopia	x	Spain	
Federation of Malayaq	x	Sudan	x
Finland	x	Sweden	x
France		Syria	
Gabon	x	Tanganyika	x
Greece		Thailand	
Guatemala		Togo	x
Guinea	x	Tunisia	x
Haiti		Turkey	x
Hondurae	x	Ukraisian S.S.R	x
Hungary	x	U.S.S.R	x
Iceland	x	United Arab Republic	x
India	x	United Kingdom	x
Indonesia	x	U.S.A	x
Iran	x		
Iraq	x		

Ireland			x	
Israel		x		
Italy				x
Ivory Coast				

Upper Volta				
Uruguay				
Venezuela			x	
Yemen			x	
Yugoslavia			x	

TOTAL: FOR=64, AGAINST=23, ABSTAINED=10, ABSENT=2

Bibliography

Abdullahi Mahadi, George Kwanashie and Alhaji Mahmood Yakubu (Eds) Nigeria: The State of the Nation and The Way Forward, Arewa House, Kaduna, 1994 P. 61

Adebayo Adedeji, Towards a Dynamic African Economy; Selected Speeches and Lectures, 1975 – 1986, Franck Cass, 1989, p.97-8

Amartya Sen, Development as Freedom, Oxford University Press, Oxford, 1999

Asiwaju, Anthony I. The Bakassi Peninsula Crisis: An Alternative to War and Litigation, in Boundaries and Energy Problems and Prospects

Charles Kindleberger & Bruce Herrick (1977) quoted in Emmanuel A. Aka, The British Southern Cameroons 1922-1916: A study in colonialism and underdevelopment, Platteville, Madison, 2002

Colins Leys, Underdevelopment in Kenya: The Political Economy of neo-colonialism, University of California Press, Berkeley and Los Angeles, 1975

Eyongetah R. Brain, A History of the Cameroon, Longman Group Limited, London, 1974

Frantz Fanon, *Wretched of the Earth* (1959) publ. Pelican, 1959

Ian Brownlie, Principles of Public International Law, Claredon Press, Oxford, 4th edition, 1990

Immanuel Wallenstein, Africa: The Politics of Independence, Vintage Books, New York, 1961

Mbile, N. N, Cameroon Political Story: Memories of an Authentic Eye Witness, Limbe, Presbyterian Printing Press, 1999

Mukong, Albert W. (ed.) The Case for the Southern Cameroons, CAMFECO, USA, 1990

Ndi, Anthony, The Golden Age of Southern (West) Cameroon, 1946-1972: Impact of Christianity. Bamenda, 2005

Ndi Anthony, Southern/West Cameroon Revisited, 1950-1972: Unveiling Inescapable Traps, Volume One, Paul's Press, Bamenda, 2013

Ndongko, W. A. Planning for Economic Development in a Federal State: The Case of Cameroon, 1960-1971, Weltforum Verlag, Munchen, 1975

Nfor, N. Nfor, Southern Cameroons and La République du Cameroun union: The Hidden Agenda, Unique Printers, Bamenda, April, 1994

Nfor, N. Nfor. The Southern Cameroons: The Truth of the Matter, Quality Printers, Bamenda, 2002

Nfor N. Nfor; Cameroon Reunification: Costs and Problems of National Integration, (MSs Thesis, ABU Zaria, 1980, unpublished)

Nja'ah, Peter Toh, (Rev.) The Anglophone Problem: The Prospects for Non-Violent Transformation, Bamenda, 2001

Patrick F. Wilmot; In Search of Nationhood: The Theory and Practice of Nationalism in Africa, Lantern Books, Ibadan, 1979

Quincy Wright; Sovereignty of the Mandates in the American Journal of International Law, Vol. XVII, October 1923

Richard Joseph, (editor) Gaullist Africa: Cameroun under Ahmadou Ahidjo, Fourth Dimension Publishers, Enugu, 1978

Samuel P. Huntington, The Clash of Civilizations and The Making of World Order, Simon and Schuster, London, 1997

Shirley V. Scott, (editor) International Law & Politics, Lynne Rienner Publishers, Inc., London, 2006

Tunyi Olagunju, Adele Jinadu & Sam Oyovbaire, Transition to Democracy in Nigeria, 1985 – 1993, Ibadan, 1993

Walter Rodney; How Europe Underdeveloped Africa, 141 Coldershaw Road London W13, 1986

Wm Roger Louis, Great Britain and the African Peace Settlement of 1919 in American
Historical Review, Vol.61, 1966

UN, Government Official Documents and News Papers

UN Charter

UN General Assembly 4th Committee Vote on Independence of

Southern Cameroons. Fourth Committee, 1152nd Meeting, Wednesday, 19 April 1961
UN Document, The Two Alternatives, Buea, 1961

UN General Assembly Vote on Resolution 1608 of April 21, 1961
AU Constitutive Act & OAU Charter
African Charter on Human and Peoples' Rights
Anglo-French Boundary Treaty between British Southern Cameroons and French Cameroun, 1939
ICJ Ruling of 22nd December 1986, Boundary Dispute case, Rec.1986, p.566
Constitution of the Federal Republic of Cameroon, September 1, 1961, Yaoundé
Fourth-Five Year Development Plan 1976-1981, Yaoundé
Memoriam: Submission of la République du Cameroun to the ICJ on Land Dispute with the Federal Republic of Nigeria, 1994, par. 2, 143
Report of the International Conference of Experts on the Implementation of the Right to Self Determination as A contribution to Conflict Prevention, Held in Barcelona, from 21-27 November 1998
Cameroon Life, April/May 1994
The News, 21 March 1994.

www.ingramcontent.com/pod-product-compliance
Lightning Source LLC
Chambersburg PA
CBHW020612300426
44113CB00007B/607